Aspects of the

DRAMA

A *Handbook*

The "De Witt Drawing," actually Arend van Buchel's copy of the drawing Johannes de Witt made when he visited the Swan Theater in London, c. 1596. De Witt's original is not extant.

ASPECTS

OF

THE

DRAMA

A HANDBOOK

SYLVAN BARNET
Tufts University

MORTON BERMAN
Boston University

WILLIAM BURTO
Lowell State College

Boston　　　　　　*Toronto*
LITTLE, BROWN AND COMPANY

ACKNOWLEDGMENTS

Grateful acknowledgment is made to the following for permission
to quote from the works listed:

W. H. AUDEN for "A Public Art." Reprinted by permission of the
author and *Opera*, London. © W. H. Auden, 1961.

ERIC BENTLEY for his translation of "A New Technique of Acting"
by Bertolt Brecht, which is reprinted from *Theatre Arts*, Vol.
XXXIII (January 1949). Copyright 1949 by Eric Bentley.

BASIL BLACKWELL, PUBLISHER, for "The Tragic Form" by Richard
Sewall, from *Essays in Criticism* (October 1954).

CURTIS BROWN, LTD. for "A Public Art" by W. H. Auden. Reprinted by permission of the author and *Opera*, London. © W. H.
Auden, 1961.

CAMBRIDGE UNIVERSITY PRESS for *Aristotle on the Art of Fiction*
(a translation of Aristotle's *Poetics*) by L. J. Potts. Copyright 1953,
1959.

CORNELL UNIVERSITY PRESS for permission to reproduce pp. 110-
128 from *Tragedy: A View of Life* by Henry Alonzo Myers. Copyright 1956 by Cornell University.

FARRAR, STRAUS AND CUDAHY, INC. for "The American Realist Playwrights" from *On The Contrary* by Mary McCarthy. Copyright 1961 by Mary McCarthy. Reprinted by permission of Farrar, Straus and Cudahy, Inc.

BERNARD KNOX for his essay, "Sophocles' Oedipus" from *Tragic Themes in Western Literature*, ed. Cleanth Brooks. Copyright 1955, by Yale University Press.

MCA MANAGEMENT for "Tragedy and the Common Man" by Arthur Miller. Copyright *The New York Times*, 1949.

METHUEN AND COMPANY, LTD. for a selection from *Greek Tragedy* by H. D. F. Kitto. Copyright 1939, 1950.

THE NEW YORK TIMES for "Tragedy and the Common Man" by Arthur Miller. Copyright *The New York Times*, 1949.

OXFORD UNIVERSITY PRESS for "The Theatrical Story" from *Theory of Film* by Siegfried Kracauer. © 1960 by Oxford University Press, Inc. and reprinted by permission.

PRINCETON UNIVERSITY PRESS for "The Structure of Comedy" from *Anatomy of Criticism* by Northrop Frye. Copyright 1957 by Princeton University Press; for "Some Thoughts on Playwriting" by Thornton Wilder from *The Intent of the Artist*, ed. Augusto Centeno. Copyright 1941 by Princeton University Press.

THE PUBLIC TRUSTEE and THE SOCIETY OF AUTHORS for "Rules for Directors" by George Bernard Shaw, which is reprinted from *Theatre Arts*, Vol. XXXIII (August 1949).

LEAH SALISBURY, INC. for "Comedy" by Christopher Fry. Copyright © December 26, 1950 by Christopher Fry. Reprinted by permission of the author.

SUHRKAMP VERLAG for "A New Technique of Acting" by Bertolt Brecht. Original title: "Neue Technik de Schauspielkunst" from *Schriften zum Theater* by Bertolt Brecht. © Copyright 1957 by Suhrkamp Verlag, Frankfurt am Main. All rights reserved.

THEATRE ARTS BOOKS for a selection from *My Life in Art* by Konstantin Stanislavsky. Reprinted with the permission of Theatre Arts Books. Copyright 1924 by Little, Brown and Company. Copyright 1948 by Elizabeth Reynolds Hapgood.

PREFACE

We shall proceed "into't roundly, without hawking or spitting, or saying we are hoarse, which are the only prologues to a bad voice." The Introduction sets forth the nature of the book; here we mean only to thank the authors and publishers who have let us use copyrighted material; to thank the library staffs of Tufts University, Boston University, and Lowell State College, who were helpful and patient; to thank Dr. Theodore Schultz, who provided information about acoustics; to thank Professors Kalman Burnim, Albert Gilman, and George R. Kernodle, who made valuable comments on much of the manuscript; and to thank Messrs. Donald R. Hammonds and Ronald Q. Lewton, who kept pushing us.

S. B.

M. B.

W. B.

CONTENTS

INTRODUCTION

ASPECTS OF THE DRAMA is a handbook consisting of two sections: first, a collection of essays that examine basic issues, and second, a Dictionary (with bibliography) of dramatic terms.

The oldest essay in the book is Aristotle's *Poetics*; the newest essays are those by W. H. Auden and Mary McCarthy. The essays are not arranged chronologically but by subject; Aristotle and Miss McCarthy (along with several others), for example, are together in a grouping headed "Tragedy, Comedy, and Realism." We think the essays in *Aspects of the Drama* will enrich a student's understanding of drama — not by giving him answers but by stimulating him to think about important matters. A student who reads Lamb on "Stage Illusion" will probably not accept all that Lamb says, but he will be moved to think closely about the problems, and his experience as a play-goer will be enriched. Each essay was chosen because it is provocative, but only two further illustrations need be given. Arthur Miller's "Tragedy and the Common Man" is concerned with a problem that Aristotle glanced at; the student who has read a tragedy, whether *Oedipus the King* or *Death of a Salesman*, can hardly fail to be stimulated by Miller's essay. He may be moved to refute it; or he may be moved to argue whether, by Miller's standard, *Death of a Salesman* is a success or a failure, but he will be aware of a problem that deserves his attention. Similarly, Siegfried Kracauer's belief that good plays make bad films will force a student to become a more critical spectator.

The Dictionary is intended to provide students not only with the meanings of hundreds of words used in dramatic criticism but also with suggestions for further reading in both primary and secondary material. For example, the entry on "surrealism" briefly sketches the surrealist movement, mentions four playwrights and some of the plays, and concludes by citing a book about surrealism. Because the Dictionary aims at usefulness rather than completeness, we have devoted considerable space to many of the entries and have omitted some words that need no definition. Thus, we have not included definitions of "aisle," "program," etc., but have used the space gained thereby to give fuller definitions of more elusive words (*e.g.*, "comedy," "symbolism") and definitions of words not usually found in college dictionaries (*e.g.*, "Grand Guignol," "presentational staging"). In addition to omitting some words so common and unambiguous that no one would conceivably look them up, we have, of course, omitted — with very few exceptions — entries for actors, playwrights, plays, theaters, etc. But such terms as "Senecan tragedy" and "Stanislavsky System" are here.

The two divisions of the book are closely interrelated; the essays use the language of the Dictionary, and the Dictionary includes cross references to the essays. The student who looks up "epic theater" in the Dictionary will find not only a discussion and a suggestion for further reading, but also a reference to Brecht's essay on acting, printed in the first part of the book. A student who looks up "box set" will similarly find a discussion of the term, a suggestion for further reading, and a reference to Miss McCarthy's essay.

Both the essays and the Dictionary are intended to be of continual use to college students from their first course in drama onward. We hope that *Aspects of the Drama* will prove valuable — especially to students writing papers — by suggesting some approaches to drama and by providing them with the language of dramatic criticism. A critical approach will, hopefully, lead a student to enjoy works (in T. S. Eliot's phrase) for "the right reasons."

THE NATURE OF DRAMA

EVERYTHING is what it is and not another thing." Bishop Joseph Butler's statement, made in the early eighteenth century, should be borne in mind by every student of drama.

THORNTON WILDER (1897-   ) in the following essay tries to make clear the basic characteristics of the drama that set it apart from other kinds of art. He is well qualified; he is not only a distinguished scholar and novelist but also a playwright who has won Pulitzer Prizes for two plays, *Our Town* (1938) and *The Skin of Our Teeth* (1942).

Some Thoughts on Playwriting

THORNTON WILDER

FOUR FUNDAMENTAL conditions of the drama separate it from the other arts. Each of these conditions has its advantages and disadvantages, each requires a particular aptitude from the dramatist, and from each there are a number of instructive consequences to be derived. These conditions are:

1. The theater is an art which reposes upon the work of many collaborators;

2. It is addressed to the group-mind;

3. It is based upon a pretense and its very nature calls out a multiplication of pretenses;

4. Its action takes place in a perpetual present time.

We have been accustomed to think that a work of art is by definition the product of one governing selecting will.

A landscape by Cézanne consists of thousands of brushstrokes each commanded by one mind. *Paradise Lost* and *Pride and Prejudice*, even in cheap frayed copies, bear the immediate and exclusive message of one intelligence.

It is true that in musical performance we meet with intervening executants, but the element of intervention is slight compared to that which takes place in drama. Illustrations:

1. One of the finest productions of *The Merchant of Venice* in our time showed Sir Henry Irving as Shylock, a noble, wronged, and indignant being, of such stature that the Merchants of Venice dwindled before him into irresponsible schoolboys. He was confronted in court by a gracious, even queenly, Portia, Miss Ellen Terry. At the Odéon in Paris, however, Gémier played Shylock as a vengeful and hysterical buffoon, confronted in court by a Portia who was a *gamine* from the Paris streets with a lawyer's quill three feet long over her ear; at the close of the trial scene Shylock was driven screaming about the auditorium, behind the spectators' back and onto the stage again, in a wild Elizabethan revel. Yet for all their divergences both were admirable productions of the play.

2. If there were ever a play in which fidelity to the author's requirements were essential in the representation of the principal role, it would seem to be Ibsen's *Hedda Gabler*, for the play is primarily an exposition of her character. Ibsen's directions read: "Enter from the left Hedda Gabler. She is a woman of twenty-nine. Her face and figure show great refinement and distinction. Her complexion is pale and opaque. Her steel-gray eyes express an unruffled calm. Her hair is of an attractive medium brown, but is not particularly abundant; and she is dressed in a flowing loose-fitting morning gown." I once saw Eleonora Duse in this role. She was a woman of sixty and made no effort to conceal it. Her complexion was pale and transparent. Her hair was white, and she was dressed in a gown that suggested

some medieval empress in mourning. And the performance was
very fine.

One may well ask: why write for the theater at all? Why not
work in the novel where such deviations from one's intentions
cannot take place?

There are two answers:

1. The theater presents certain vitalities of its own so inviting
and stimulating that the writer is willing to receive them in
compensation for this inevitable variation from an exact image.

2. The dramatist through working in the theater gradually
learns not merely to take account of the presence of the collaborators, but to derive advantage from them; and he learns,
above all, to organize the play in such a way that its strength
lies not in appearances beyond his control, but in the succession of events and in the unfolding of an idea, in narration.

The gathered audience sits in a darkened room, one end of
which is lighted. The nature of the transaction at which it is
gazing is a succession of events illustrating a general idea — the
stirring of the idea; the gradual feeding out of information; the
shock and countershock of circumstances; the flow of action;
the interruption of action; the moments of allusion to earlier
events; the preparation of surprise, dread, or delight — all that
is the author's and his alone.

For reasons to be discussed later — the expectancy of the
group-mind, the problem of time on the stage, the absence of
the narrator, the element of pretense — the theater carries the
art of narration to a higher power than the novel or the epic
poem. The theater is unfolding action and in the disposition of
events the authors may exercise a governance so complete that
the distortions effected by the physical appearance of actors,
by the fancies of scene painters and the misunderstandings of
directors, fall into relative insignificance. It is just because the
theater is an art of many collaborators, with the constant danger
of grave misinterpretation, that the dramatist learns to turn his
attention to the laws of narration, its logic and its deep necessity of presenting a unifying idea stronger than its mere collection of happenings. The dramatist must be by instinct a storyteller.

There is something mysterious about the endowment of the storyteller. Some very great writers possessed very little of it, and some others, lightly esteemed, possessed it in so large a measure that their books survive down the ages, to the confusion of severer critics. Alexandre Dumas had it to an extraordinary degree; while Melville, for all his splendid quality, had it barely sufficiently to raise his work from the realm of non-fiction. It springs, not, as some have said, from an aversion to general ideas, but from an instinctive coupling of idea and illustration; the idea, for a born storyteller, can only be expressed imbedded in its circumstantial illustration. The myth, the parable, the fable are the fountainhead of all fiction and in them is seen most clearly the didactic, moralizing employment of a story. Modern taste shrinks from emphasizing the central idea that hides behind the fiction, but it exists there nevertheless, supplying the unity to fantasizing, and offering a justification to what otherwise we would repudiate as mere arbitrary contrivance, pretentious lying, or individualistic emotional association spinning. For all their magnificent intellectual endowment, George Meredith and George Eliot were not born storytellers; they chose fiction as the vehicle for their reflections, and the passing of time is revealing their error in that choice. Jane Austen was pure storyteller and her works are outlasting those of apparently more formidable rivals. The theater is more exacting than the novel in regard to this faculty, and its presence constitutes a force which compensates the dramatist for the deviations which are introduced into his work by the presence of his collaborators.

The chief of these collaborators are the actors.

The actor's gift is a combination of three separate faculties or endowments. Their presence to a high degree in any one person is extremely rare, although the ambition to possess them is common. Those who rise to the height of the profession represent a selection and a struggle for survival in one of the most difficult and cruel of the artistic activities. The three endowments that compose the gift are observation, imagination, and physical co-ordination.

1. An observant and analyzing eye for all modes of behavior

about us, for dress and manner, and for the signs of thought and
emotion in one's self and in others.

2. The strength of imagination and memory whereby the
actor may, at the indication in the author's text, explore his
store of observations and represent the details of appearance
and the intensity of the emotions — joy, fear, surprise, grief,
love, and hatred, and through imagination extend them to in-
tenser degrees and to differing characterizations.

3. A physical co-ordination whereby the force of these inner
realizatons may be communicated to voice, face, and body.

An actor must *know* the appearances and the mental states;
he must *apply* his knowledge to the role; and he must physically
express his knowledge. Moreover, his concentration must be so
great that he can effect this representation under conditions of
peculiar difficulty — in abrupt transition from the non-imagina-
tive conditions behind the stage; and in the presence of fellow-
actors who may be momentarily destroying the reality of the
action.

A dramatist prepares the characterization of his personages in
such a way that it will take advantage of the actor's gift.

Characterization in a novel is presented by the author's dogmatic assertion that the personage was such, and by an analysis
of the personage with generally an account of his or her past.
Since, in the drama, this is replaced by the actual presence of
the personage before us and since there is no occasion for the
intervening all-knowing author to instruct us as to his or her
inner nature, a far greater share is given in a play to (1) highly
characteristic utterances and (2) concrete occasions in which
the character defines itself under action and (3) a conscious
preparation of the text whereby the actor may build upon
the suggestions in the role according to his own abilities.

Characterization in a play is like a blank check which the
dramatist accords to the actor for him to fill in — not entirely
blank, for a number of indications of individuality are already
there, but to a far less definite and absolute degree than in the
novel.

The dramatist's principal interest being the movement of the
story, he is willing to resign the more detailed aspects of char-

acterization to the actor and is often rewarded beyond his expectation.

The sleepwalking scene from *Macbeth* is a highly compressed selection of words whereby despair and remorse rise to the surface of indirect confession. It is to be assumed that had Shakespeare lived to see what the genius of Sarah Siddons could pour into the scene from that combination of observation, self-knowledge, imagination, and representational skill, even he might have exclaimed, "I never knew I wrote so well!"

II. THE THEATER IS AN ART ADDRESSED TO A GROUP-MIND

Painting, sculpture, and the literature of the book are certainly solitary experiences; and it is likely that most people would agree that the audience seated shoulder to shoulder in a concert hall is not an essential element in musical enjoyment.

But a play presupposes a crowd. The reasons for this go deeper than (1) the economic necessity for support of the play and (2) the fact that the temperament of actors is proverbially dependent on group attention.

It rests on the fact that (1) the pretense, the fiction, on the stage would fall to pieces and absurdity without the support accorded to it by a crowd, and (2) the excitement induced by pretending a fragment of life is such that it partakes of ritual and festival, and requires a throng.

Similarly the fiction that royal personages are of a mysteriously different nature from other people requires audiences, levees, and processions for its maintenance. Since the beginnings of society, satirists have occupied themselves with the descriptions of kings and queens in their intimacy and delighted in showing how the prerogatives of royalty become absurd when the crowd is not present to extend to them the enhancement of an imaginative awe.

The theater partakes of the nature of festival. Life imitated is life raised to a higher power. In the case of comedy, the vitality of these pretended surprises, deceptions, and *contretemps* becomes so lively that before a spectator, solitary or regarding himself as solitary, the structure of so much event would inevitably expose the artificiality of the attempt and ring hol-

low and unjustified; and in the case of tragedy, the accumula-
tion of woe and apprehension would soon fall short of conviction. All actors know the disturbing sensation of playing before
a handful of spectators at a dress rehearsal or performance
where only their interest in pure craftsmanship can barely sustain them. During the last rehearsals the phrase is often heard:
"This play is hungry for an audience."

Since the theater is directed to a group-mind, a number of
consequences follow:

1. A group-mind presupposes, if not a lowering of standards,
a broadening of the fields of interest. The other arts may pre-
suppose an audience of connoisseurs trained in leisure and capable of being interested in certain rarefied aspects of life. The
dramatist may be prevented from exhibiting, for example, detailed representations of certain moments in history that require
specialized knowledge in the audience, or psychological states
in the personages which are of insufficient general interest to
evoke self-identification in the majority. In the Second Part of
Goethe's *Faust* there are long passages dealing with the theory
of paper money. The exposition of the nature of misanthropy
(so much more drastic than Molière's) in Shakespeare's *Timon
of Athens* has never been a success. The dramatist accepts this
limitation in subject matter and realizes that the group-mind
imposes upon him the necessity of treating material under-
standable by the larger number.

2. It is the presence of the group-mind that brings another
requirement to the theater — forward movement.

Maeterlinck said that there was more drama in the spectacle
of an old man seated by a table than in the majority of plays
offered to the public. He was juggling with the various meanings
in the word "drama." In the sense whereby drama means the
intensified concentration of life's diversity and significance he
may well have been right; if he meant drama as a theatrical
representation before an audience he was wrong. Drama on the
stage is inseparable from forward movement, from action.

Many attempts have been made to present Plato's dialogues,
Gobineau's fine series of dialogues, *La Renaissance*, and the
Imaginary Conversations of Landor; but without success.

Through some ingredient in the group-mind, and through the sheer weight of anticipation involved in the dressing up and the assumption of fictional roles, an action is required, and an action that is more than a mere progress in argumentation and debate.

III. THE THEATER IS A WORLD OF PRETENSE

It lives by conventions: a convention is an agreed-upon falsehood, a permitted lie.

Illustrations: Consider at the first performance of the *Medea,* the passage where Medea meditates the murder of her children. An anecdote from antiquity tells us that the audience was so moved by this passage that considerable disturbance took place.

The following conventions were involved:

1. Medea was played by a man.

2. He wore a large mask on his face. In the lip of the mask was an acoustical device for projecting the voice. On his feet he wore shoes with soles and heels half a foot high.

3. His costume was so designed that it conveyed to the audience, by convention: woman of royal birth and Oriental origin.

4. The passage was in metric speech. All poetry is an "agreed-upon falsehood" in regard to speech.

5. The lines were sung in a kind of recitative. All opera involves this "permitted lie" in regard to speech.

Modern taste would say that the passage would convey much greater pathos if a woman "like Medea" had delivered it — with an uncovered face that exhibited all the emotions she was undergoing. For the Greeks, however, there was no pretense that Medea was on the stage. The mask, the costume, the mode of declamation, were a series of signs which the spectator interpreted and reassembled in his own mind. Medea was being re-created within the imagination of each of the spectators.

The history of the theater shows us that in its greatest ages the stage employed the greatest number of conventions. The stage is fundamental pretense and it thrives on the acceptance of that fact and in the multiplication of additional pretenses. When it tries to assert that the personages in the action "really are," really inhabit such and such rooms, really suffer such and such emotions, it loses rather than gains credibility. The modern world is inclined to laugh condescendingly at the fact that in the plays of Racine and Corneille the gods and heroes of antiquity were dressed like the courtiers under Louis XIV; that in the Elizabethan age scenery was replaced by placards notifying the audience of the location; and that a whip in the hand and a jogging motion of the body indicated that a man was on horseback in the Chinese theater; these devices did not spring from naïveté, however, but from the vitality of the public imagination in those days and from an instinctive feeling as to where the essential and where the inessential lay in drama.

The convention has two functions:

1. It provokes the collaborative activity of the spectator's imagination; and

2. It raises the action from the specific to the general.

This second aspect is of even greater importance than the first.

If Juliet is represented as a girl "very like Juliet" — it was not merely a deference to contemporary prejudices that assigned this role to a boy in the Elizabethan age — moving about in a "real" house with marble staircases, rugs, lamps, and furniture, the impression is irresistibly conveyed that these events happened to this one girl, in one place, at one moment in time. When the play is staged as Shakespeare intended it, the bareness of the stage releases the events from the particular and the experience of Juliet partakes of that of all girls in love, in every time, place and language.

The stage continually strains to tell this generalized truth and it is the element of pretense that reinforces it. Out of the lie, the pretense, of the theater proceeds a truth more compelling than the novel can attain, for the novel by its own laws is constrained to tell of an action that "once happened" — "once upon a time."

IV. THE ACTION ON THE STAGE TAKES PLACE IN A PERPETUAL PRESENT TIME

Novels are written in the past tense. The characters in them, it is true, are represented as living moment by moment their present time, but the constant running commentary of the novelist ("Tess slowly descended into the valley"; "Anna Karenina laughed") inevitably conveys to the reader the fact that these events are long since past and over.

The novel is a past reported in the present. On the stage it is always now. This confers upon the action an increased vitality which the novelist longs in vain to incorporate into his work.

This condition in the theater brings with it another important element:

In the theater we are not aware of the intervening storyteller. The speeches arise from the characters in an apparently pure spontaneity.

A play is what takes place.

A novel is what one person tells us took place.

A play visibly represents pure existing. A novel is what one mind, claiming to omniscience, asserts to have existed.

Many dramatists have regretted this absence of the narrator from the stage, with his point of view, his powers of analyzing the behavior of the characters, his ability to interfere and supply further facts about the past, about simultaneous actions not visible on the stage, and above *all* his function of pointing the moral and emphasizing the significance of the action. In some periods of the theater he has been present as chorus, or prologue and epilogue or as *raisonneur*. But surely this absence constitutes an additional force to the form, as well as an additional tax upon the writer's skill. It is the task of the dramatist so to co-ordinate his play, through the selection of episodes and speeches, that, though he is himself not visible, his point of view and his governing intention will impose themselves on the spectator's attention, not as dogmatic assertion or motto, but as self-evident truth and inevitable deduction.

Imaginative narration — the invention of souls and destinies — is to a philosopher an all but indefensible activity.

Its justification lies in the fact that the communication of ideas from one mind to another inevitably reaches the point where exposition passes into illustration, into parable, metaphor, allegory, and myth.

It is no accident that when Plato arrived at the height of his argument and attempted to convey a theory of knowledge and a theory of the structure of man's nature he passed over into story telling, into the myths of the Cave and the Charioteer; and that the great religious teachers have constantly had recourse to the parable as a means of imparting their deepest intuitions.

The theater offers to imaginative narration its highest possibilities. It has many pitfalls and its very vitality betrays it into service as mere diversion and the enhancement of insignificant matter; but it is well to remember that it was the theater that rose to the highest place during those epochs that aftertime has chosen to call "great ages" and that the Athens of Pericles and the reigns of Elizabeth, Philip II, and Louis XIV were also the ages that gave to the world the greatest dramas it has known.

TRAGEDY, COMEDY, AND REALISM

U<small>NTIL</small> late in the nineteenth century, almost all great plays could be classified as either tragedies or comedies. Tragedies (to make generalizations even briefer and more sweeping than those in our Dictionary) are serious plays that depict man's suffering and nobility, or, to use Edith Hamilton's words, depict "the suffering of a soul that can suffer greatly"; comedies are amusing plays that usually depict man's follies, especially those follies that pester one's neighbors but that do no real harm. Realistic drama, instead of depicting men with a special capacity for suffering or with a special capacity for folly or delight, depicts ordinary men whose lives are neither heroic nor amusing but wretched.

A<small>RISTOTLE</small> (384 B.C.-322 B.C.), in a fragmentary treatise usually entitled the *Poetics* — perhaps what survives are the remains of a student's notes — raises almost all of the issues on drama that have been argued in the ensuing years. Among other things, he defines drama, touches on its origin, discusses the nature of the tragic and comic figures and the pleasure of tragedy. Though he chiefly describes rather than legislates, his authority has been immense; no other treatise has been so influential or has seemed so continuously contemporary.

H<small>ENRY</small> A<small>LONZO</small> M<small>YERS</small> (1906-1955), late Professor of English at Cornell University, suggests that tragedy and comedy differ largely according to the degree to which each emphasizes emotion and intellect, insight and detachment, and he attempts to support these propositions by calling attention to details in a tragedy and a comedy by Shakespeare, the only dramatist who has achieved greatness in both genres.

R<small>ICHARD</small> B. S<small>EWALL</small> (1908-   ) is professor of English at Yale.

The essay printed here, first published in *Essays in Criticism* (October 1954), considers, among other things, the nature of the tragic cosmos and several of the qualities in the tragic hero that distinguish him from the rebel, the saint, and the romantic hero. In *The Vision of Tragedy* (1959), Mr. Sewall returns to some of the problems he treats here, applying his concepts to novels as well as plays.

ARTHUR MILLER (1916-   ) is best known for *Death of a Salesman* (1949), a play that revived the question of whether tragedy can be made out of bourgeois life. Mr. Miller suggests that if a tragedy shakes us by arousing our "underlying fear of being displaced," the common man today is the best subject for tragedy. Yet bourgeois heroes often fail to command the respect that earlier tragic heroes command; plays with bourgeois heroes are usually pathetic rather than tragic. (Contrast Miller with W. H. Auden, who holds [p. 128] that "Drama is necessarily a public art. To be of public interest a human being must be heroic.") In *Death of a Salesman,* one of Willy's sons says that Willy "never knew who he was"; tragic heroes usually arrive at such knowledge.

CHRISTOPHER FRY (1907-   ) has been hailed as England's most promising contemporary writer of verse drama. He is best known for his comedies, especially *The Lady's Not for Burning* (1948); a religious play, *A Sleep of Prisoners* (1951), found less favor in the United States than in England. In "Comedy," the essay printed here, he gives his reasons for believing that comedy is no less important than tragedy.

NORTHROP FRYE (1912-   ), of the University of Toronto, analyzes not only the humor inherent in what he calls unincremental repetition, but also the basic movement of comedy and its basic characters. The essay printed here comes from his *Anatomy of Criticism,* a provocative work concerned with fiction and poetry as well as with drama.

MARY MCCARTHY (1912-   ), novelist and critic, examines the kind of play that has attracted many of the best dramatists since the middle of the nineteenth century. Usually the realistic play is neither tragic nor comic. The playwright's microscopic eye endeavors to catch the whole of ordinary life; it sees what books are in a bookcase on the stage, but it sees in life neither nobility (hence the plays are not tragic) nor mirth (hence the plays are not comic). Miss McCarthy examines the giants, Ibsen and O'Neill, and some of their descendants, Miller, Williams, Inge, and Chayefsky.

On the Art of Fiction[1]

ARISTOTLE

CHAPTER 1. Let us talk of the art of poetry as a whole, *Title* and its different species with the particular force of each of them; how the fables must be put together if the poetry is to be well formed; also what are its elements and their different qualities; and all other matters pertaining to the subject.

To begin in the proper order, at the beginning. The making of epics and of tragedies, and also comedy, and *First premise* the art of the dithyramb, and most flute and lyre art, all have this in common, that they are imitations. But they differ from one another in three respects: the different kinds of medium in which they imitate, the different objects they imitate, and the different manner in which they imitate (when it does differ).

Just as some people imitate many things in color *Medium* and outline, depicting them either by a deliberate technique or by trial and error, and others imitate by the voice, so the arts I have mentioned all do their imitating in one or more of the following media — rhythm, language, and music. The arts of the flute and lyre use only music and rhythm, and so does any other art that has a similar force, for example the art of the pipes. Ballet imitates by sheer rhythm, without music; for dancers too imitate characters and experiences and doings by the rhythm of their postures. . . .

---

[1] Though Aristotle's treatise is customarily called the *Poetics*, Mr. Potts entitles his translation *On the Art of Fiction* because, as he says in a note, "it is a treatise on fiction, rather than on what the word 'poetry' has stood for to the common reader for the last hundred and fifty years." He also explains his editorial devices: "Substantial additions — words or phrases that involve more than a difference between Greek and English idiom — I have marked by enclosing . . . in ⟨pointed brackets⟩. . . . I have marked the most important places where the Greek text is corrupt or doubtful with asterisks at the *beginning and end* of the passage. . . . The marginal headings are an addition of my own; I found that they helped me to follow the development of Aristotle's analysis, and although they have no authority I have inserted them to give a similar help to the reader."

CHAPTER 2.   When the imitators imitate the doings of   *Object*
people, the people in the imitation must be either high
or low; the characters almost always follow this line exclusively,
for all men differ in character according to their degree of goodness or badness. They must therefore be either above our norm,
or below it, or normal. . . . This is the difference that marks
tragedy out from comedy; comedy is inclined to imitate persons
below the level of our world, tragedy persons above it.

CHAPTER 3.   Again, a third difference between these   *Manner*
arts is the manner in which each of these objects can
be imitated. For given the same medium and the same object,
one can imitate partly by narration and partly by dramatic dialogue (as Homer does); or one can speak invariably in one's
own person; or one can use actors to imitate the whole thing as
though they were living it themselves.

   The imitation, then, differs in these three respects,   *Summary*
as we said at the beginning: in medium, in object,   *of classi-*
and in manner. Thus Sophocles would be in one re-   *fications*
spect in the same class of imitators as Homer, for both imitate
high people; but in another respect in the same class as Aristophanes, for they both imitate by means of actors in a performance.

   (Some say this is the origin of the term *drama*, from   *Etymo-*
the verb DRĀN (to perform). Hence the Dorians claim   *logical*
both tragedy and comedy. (The Megarians lay claim to   *digres-*
comedy: those in the mother country on the assump-   *sion*
tion that it belonged to the date when their city became a
democracy, and the Megarian colonists in Sicily because the
poet Epicharmus, who was a countryman of theirs, was much
earlier than Chionïdes and Magnes. Some of the Dorians in the
Peloponnese also lay claim to tragedy.) Their argument is ety-
mological. They say their name for a satellite village is KŌMĒ,
whereas the Athenian name is DEMOS; for they derive the word
comedy not from KŌMOS (revel), but from KOME, because the
comedians left the city, where they were looked down on, and
toured the villages. And their word for "act" is DRAN, whereas
the Athenian word is PRATTEIN.)

CHAPTER 4. There seem to be two causes that gave rise to poetry in general, and they are natural. The impulse to imitate is inherent in man from his childhood; he is distinguished among the animals by being the most imitative of them, and he takes the first steps of his education by imitating. Every one's enjoyment of imitation is also inborn. What happens with works of art demonstrates this: though a thing itself is disagreeable to look at, we enjoy contemplating the most accurate representations of it — for instance, figures of the most despicable animals, or of human corpses. The reason for this lies in another fact: learning is a great pleasure, not only to philosophers but likewise to every one else, however limited his gift for it may be. He enjoys looking at these representations, because in the act of studying them he is learning — identifying the object by an inference (for instance, recognizing who is the original of a portrait); since, if he happens not to have already seen the object depicted, it will not be the imitation as such that is giving him pleasure, but the finish of the workmanship, or the coloring, or some such other cause.

Origins of poetry: (a) Imitation

And just as imitation is natural to us, so also are music and rhythm (meters, clearly, are constituent parts of rhythms). Thus, from spontaneous beginnings, mankind developed poetry by a series of mostly minute changes out of these improvisations. . . . As soon as tragedy and comedy had become available, those whose natural temperaments impelled them towards one or the other kind of poetry wrote comedies instead of lampoons, and tragedies instead of epics, because comedy and tragedy were grander and esteemed more highly. . . .

(b) Music and rhythm

Going back to the improvisations in which [tragedy] at first consisted (and so did comedy — tragedy began with the leaders of the dithyramb, and comedy with the leaders of the phallic performances which still survive as customary practices in many of our cities), it grew up little by little as its character became clear and its form was developed. So after many transformations, tragedy settled down when its nature was formed. Aeschylus first increased the number of actors from one to two, reduced the chorus part, and put the chief weight on the speeches; Sophocles introduced three actors and scene-painting. As to its amplitude: it acquired its serious character at a late stage, when it outgrew slight fables and grotesque language in the process of transformation from satyr-drama; and at the same time the meter changed from trochaic tetrameters to iambics. At first they used the tetrameter, because their poetry was satyr-poetry and more akin to the dance; but when it began to be spoken, the very nature of the thing found its right meter, for the iambic is the best adapted of all meters to speech. For a demonstration of this: we use iambics most often in conversation with one another, but hexameters seldom, and by way of a departure from normal intonation. — (Also, division of the play into acts.) Lastly, we may pass over all the superficial graces of tragedy; for it would no doubt be a long business to go through their whole history in detail.

CHAPTER 5. Comedy is, as I have said, an imita-   *Defini-*
tion of lower types; though it does not include the   *tions:*
full range of badness, nevertheless to be ridiculous   1. *Comedy*
is a kind of deformity. The causes of laughter are errors and disgraces not accompanied by pain or injury; the comic mask, for instance, is deformed and distorted, but not painfully so. We know something of the stages through which tragedy passed and the men to whom they were due, but there are no early records of comedy, because it was not highly valued. It was a long time before comic dramas were licensed by the magistrate; the earlier comedies were produced by amateurs. Comedy had already acquired certain outlines by the time of the earliest comic poets whose names are known. Who added masks or prologues or extra actors, and other such matters, we have no means of knowing. The fable-structure first came from Sicily (Epicharmus and Phormis); at Athens, Crătes was the first to drop the lampoon form and make unified stories, that is to say fables.

Epic poetry coincides with tragedy *in so far as it is   2. *Epic*
an imitation, in metrical speech,* of high people; but
they differ in that the epic has the same meter throughout and is in narrative form. They also differ in length, because tragedy

tends as far as possible to keep within a single day and night or thereabouts, whereas the epic has no time-limit; though at first tragic poets followed the epic in this respect. As for their elements, some are the same and some are peculiar to tragedy. Accordingly, any one who can tell a tragedy of high value from a poor one can do the same for an epic; for tragedy has everything that the epic has, but the epic has not everything that there is in tragedy.

CHAPTER 6.   Of the art that imitates in hexameters, and of comedy, we will speak later; let us now dis- *3. Tragedy* cuss tragedy, having first picked up from what has been said the definition of its essence that has so far emerged. Tragedy, then, is an imitation of an action of high importance, complete and of some amplitude; in language enhanced by distinct and varying beauties; acted not narrated; by means of pity and fear effecting its purgation of these emotions. By the beauties enhancing the language I mean rhythm and melody; by "distinct and varying" I mean that some are produced by meter alone, and others at another time by melody.

Now since the imitating is done by actors, it would follow of necessity that one element in a tragedy must *Elements* be the *Mise en scène*. Others are Melody and Language, for these are the media in which the imitating is done. By Language I mean the component parts of the verse, whereas Melody has an entirely sensuous effect. Again, since the object imitated is an action, and doings are done by persons, whose individuality will be determined by their Character and their Thought (for these are the factors we have in mind when we define the quality of their doings), it follows that there are two natural causes of these doings, Thought and Character; and these causes determine the good or ill fortune of every one. But the Fable is the imitation of the action; and by the Fable I mean the whole structure of the incidents. By Character I mean the factor that enables us to define the particular quality of the people involved in the doings; and Thought is shown in everything they say when they are demonstrating a fact or disclosing an opinion. There are therefore necessarily six elements in every tragedy, which give it its quality; and they are the Fable, Character, Language, Thought, the *Mise en scène,* and Melody. Two of these are the media in which the imitating is done, one is the manner of imitation, and three are its objects; there is no other element besides these. Numerous poets have turned these essential components to account; all of them are always present — the *Mise en scène,* Character, the Fable, Language, Melody, and Thought.

The chief of these is the plotting of the incidents; for tragedy is an imitation not of men but of doings, life, happiness; unhappiness is located in doings, and our end is a certain kind of doing, not a personal quality; it is their characters that give men their quality, but their doings that make them happy or the opposite. So it is not the purpose of the actors to imitate character, but they include character as a factor in the doings. Thus it is the incidents (that is to say the Fable) that are the end for which tragedy exists; and the end is more important than anything else. Also, without an action there could not be a tragedy, but without Character there could. (In fact, the tragedies of most of the moderns are non-moral, and there are many non-moral poets of all periods. . . .) Again, if any one strings together moral speeches with the language and thought well worked out, he will be doing what is the business of tragedy; but it will be done much better by a tragedy that handles these elements more weakly, but has a fable with the incidents connected by a plot. Further, the chief means by which tragedy moves us, Irony of events and Disclosure, are elements in the Fable. A pointer in the same direction is that beginners in the art of poetry are able to get the language and characterization right before they can plot their incidents, and so were almost all the earliest poets.

So the source and as it were soul of tragedy is the Fable; and Character comes next. For, to instance a parallel from the art of painting, the most beautiful colors splashed on anyhow would not be as pleasing as a recognizable picture in black and white. Tragedy is an imitation of an action, and it is chiefly for this reason that it imitates the persons involved.

Third comes Thought: that is, the ability to say what circumstances allow and what is appropriate to them. It is the part played by social morality and rhetoric in making the dialogue: the old poets made their characters talk like men of the world, whereas our contemporaries make them talk like public speakers. Character is what shows a man's disposition — the kind of things he chooses or rejects when his choice is not obvious. Accordingly those speeches where the speaker shows no preferences or aversions whatever are non-moral. Thought, on the other hand, is shown in demonstrating a matter of fact or disclosing a significant opinion.

Fourth comes the Language [*of the speeches*]. By Language I mean, as has already been said, the expressive use of words. It has the same force in verse as in prose.

Of the remaining elements, Melody is the chief of the enhancing beauties. The *Mise en scène* can excite emotion, but it is the crudest element and least akin to the art of poetry; for the force of tragedy exists even without stage and actors; besides, the fitting out of a *Mise en scène* belongs more to the wardrobe-master's art than to the poet's.

CHAPTER 7.   So much for analysis. Now let us discuss in what sort of way the incidents should be plotted, since *Fable* that is the first and chief consideration in tragedy. Our data are that tragedy is an imitation of a whole and complete action of some amplitude (a thing can be whole and yet quite lacking in amplitude). Now a whole is that which has a beginning, a middle, and an end. A beginning is that which does not itself necessarily follow anything else, but which leads naturally to another event or development; an end is the opposite, that which itself naturally (either of necessity or most commonly) follows something else, but nothing else comes after it; and a middle is that which itself follows something else and is followed by another thing. So, well plotted fables must not begin or end casually, but must follow the pattern here described.

But, besides this, a picture, or any other composite object, if it is to be beautiful, must not only have its *Ampli* parts properly arranged, but be of an appropriate size; *tude* for beauty depends on size and structure. Accordingly, a minute picture cannot be beautiful (for when our vision has almost lost its sense of time it becomes confused); nor can an immense one (for we cannot take it all in together, and so our vision loses its unity and wholeness) — imagine a picture a thousand miles long! So, just as there is a proper size for bodies and pictures (a size that can be kept in view), there is also a proper amplitude for fables (what can be kept well in one's mind). The length of the performance on the stage has nothing to do with art; if a hundred tragedies had to be produced, the length of the production would be settled by the clock, as the story goes that another kind of performance once was. But as to amplitude, the invariable rule dictated by the nature of the action is the fuller the more beautiful so long as the outline remains clear; and for a simple rule of size, the number of happenings that will make a chain of probability (or necessity) to change a given situation from misfortune to good fortune or from good fortune to misfortune is the minimum.

CHAPTER 8.   Unity in a fable does not mean, as some   *Unity*
think, that it has one man for its subject. To any one
man many things happen — an infinite number — and some of them do not make any sort of unity; and in the same way one man has many doings which cannot be made into a unit of action. It seems, therefore, that all the poets who have composed *Heracleïds*, *Theseïds*, and suchlike, made a mistake; people think that because Hēracles was one man it follows that his fable has unity. Homer, as always, is an exception; he seems to have seen this admirably well, either by art or by nature. In writing his *Odyssey* he did not include everything that happened to Odysseus (for instance, his wound on Parnassus, or his pretense of madness at the mobilization, since there was no necessity or probability that either of these events should have led to the other); but he confined the plot of the *Odyssey* to an action that has the kind of unity I mean, and he did the same with the *Iliad*. Accordingly, just as in the other imitative arts the object of each imitation is a unit, so, since the fable is an imitation of an action, that action must be a complete unit, and the events of which it is made up must be so plotted that if any of these

elements is moved or removed the whole is altered and upset. For when a thing can be included or not included without making any noticeable difference, that thing is no part of the whole.

CHAPTER 9.   From what has been said it is also clear that it is not the poet's business to tell what has happened, but the kind of things that would happen — *Probability* what is possible according to probability or necessity. The difference between the historian and the poet is not the difference between writing in verse or prose; the work of Herodotus could be put into verse, and it would be just as much a history in verse as it is in prose. The difference is that the one tells what has happened, and the other the kind of things that would happen. It follows therefore that poetry is more philosophical and of higher value than history; for poetry universalizes more, whereas history particularizes. The universal occurs when a man says or does what is characteristic of his temperament, probably or necessarily, in the circumstances (this is the point of the descriptive proper names in poetry); what Alcibiades did or what happened to him is an aggregation of particulars. In comedy this has now become clear. They first plot the fable on a base of probabilities, and then find imaginary names for the people — unlike the lampooners, whose work was an aggregation of personalities. But in tragedy they keep to real people. This is because possibility depends on conviction; if a thing has not happened we are not yet convinced that it is possible, but if it has happened it is clearly possible, for it would not have happened if it were impossible. Even tragedies, however, sometimes have all their persons fictitious except for one or two known names; and sometimes they have not a single known name, as in the *Anthos* of Agathon, in which both the events and the names are equally fictitious, without in the least reducing the delight it gives. It is not, therefore, requisite at all costs to keep to the traditional fables from which our tragedies draw their subject-matter. It would be absurd to insist on that, since even the known legends are known only to a few, and yet the delight is shared by every one.

From all this, then, it is clear that the poet must be a maker of fables rather than of verses, in that he is a poet by virtue of his imitation and what he imitates is doings. And even if he happens to make a poem out of real events, he will not *ipso facto* cease to be a poet; for there is nothing to prevent some things that have happened from being in accordance with probability as well as possibility, in virtue of his poetic handling of them.

Of simple fables, those whose action is episodic are the worst. By an episodic fable I mean one in which scene follows scene without probability or necessity.   *Simple fables*
Such tragedies are written by bad poets of their own accord, and by good ones because of the actors — they write for theatrical effect and expand the fable more than it can bear, so that they are often forced to dislocate the sequence of events. True, the action imitated must contain incidents that evoke fear and pity, besides being a complete action; but this effect is accentuated when these incidents occur logically as well as unexpectedly, which will be more sensational than if they happen arbitrarily, by chance. Even when events are accidental the sensation is greater if they appear to have a purpose, as when the statue of Mitys at Argos killed the man who had caused his death, by falling on him at a public entertainment. Such things appear not to have happened blindly. Inevitably, therefore, plots of this sort are finer.

CHAPTER 10.   Some fables are simple, others complex: for the obvious reason that the original actions imitated by the fables are the one or the other. By a simple action I mean one that leads to the catastrophe in the way we have laid down, directly and singly, without Irony of events or Disclosure.

An action is complex when the catastrophe involves Disclosure, or Irony, or both. But these complications should develop out of the very structure of the fable,   *Complex fables*
so that they fit what has gone before, either necessarily or probably. To happen after something is by no means the same as to happen because of it.

CHAPTER 11. Irony[1] is a reversal in the course of
events, of the kind specified, and, as I say, in accord-   *Irony of
ance with probability or necessity. Thus in the *Oedi-*   *events*
pus the arrival of the messenger, which was expected to cheer
Oedipus up by releasing him from his fear about his mother, did
the opposite by showing him who he was; and in the *Lynceus*
⟨Abas⟩, who was awaiting sentence of death, was acquitted,
whereas his prosecutor Dănaüs was killed, and all this arose out
of what had happened previously.

A Disclosure, as the term indicates, is a change from
ignorance to knowledge; if the people are marked out   *Dis-*
for good fortune it leads to affection, if for misfortune, *closure*
to enmity. Disclosure produces its finest effect when it is connected with Irony, as the disclosure in the *Oedipus* is. There are
indeed other sorts of Disclosure: the process I have described
can even apply to inanimate objects of no significance, and
mistakes about what a man has done or not done can be cleared
up. But the sort I have specified is more a part of the fable and
of the action than any other sort; for this coupling of Irony
and Disclosure will carry with it pity or fear, which we have assumed to be the nature of the doings tragedy imitates; and further, such doings will constitute good or ill fortune. Assuming
then that it is a disclosure of the identity of persons, it may be
of one person only, to the other, when the former knows who
the latter is; or sometimes both have to be disclosed — for instance, the sending of the letter led Orestes to the discovery of
Iphigeneia, and there had to be another disclosure to make him
known to her.

This then is the subject-matter of two elements in the Fable,
Irony and Disclosure. A third element is the Crisis of
feeling. Irony and Disclosure have been defined; the   *Crisis of*
Crisis of feeling is a harmful or painful experience,   *feeling*
such as deaths in public, violent pain, physical injuries, and
everything of that sort.

[1] The Greek word here is PERIPETEIA [translator's note]. See also p. 266.
In the next paragraph, the Greek word translated as "disclosure" is ANAG-
NORISIS [editors' note]. See pp. 266-267.

CHAPTER 12. We have mentioned previously the   *Sections*
generic elements that should be employed in writing   *of a Greek*
a tragedy. Now as to the separate sections into which   *tragedy*
it is divided: they are Prologue, Epeisŏdion, Exodos, and Chorus
(divided into Parŏdos and Stăsĭmon) — these are common to
all tragedies; Songs by actors, and Kommos — these are op-
tional. The Prologue is the whole section of a tragedy before
the choric Parodos; an Epeisodion is a complete section of a
tragedy between complete choric songs; the Exodos is the whole
section of a tragedy after which there is no song by the chorus.
In the choric part, the Parodos is the first passage of words by
the whole chorus; a Stasimon is a song of the chorus not in ana-
paests or trochees; a Kommos is a lamentation in which both
chorus and actors take part. We have mentioned previously the
elements that should be employed in writing a tragedy; the
separate sections into which it is divided have now been given.

CHAPTER 13. Following the proper order, the next   *The*
subject to discuss after this would be: What one should   *tragic*
aim at and beware of in plotting fables; that is to say,   *pattern*
What will produce the tragic effect. Since, then, tragedy, to be
at its finest, requires a complex, not a simple, structure, and its
structure should also imitate fearful and pitiful events (for that
is the peculiarity of this sort of imitation), it is clear: first, that
decent people must not be shown passing from good fortune
to misfortune (for that is not fearful or pitiful but disgusting);
again, vicious people must not be shown passing from misfortune to good fortune (for that is the most untragic situation
possible — it has none of the requisites, it is neither humane,
nor pitiful, nor fearful); nor again should an utterly evil man
fall from good fortune into misfortune (for though a plot of that
kind would be humane, it would not induce pity or fear — pity
is induced by undeserved misfortune, and fear by the misfortunes of normal people, so that this situation will be neither
pitiful nor fearful). So we are left with the man between these
extremes: that is to say, the kind of man who neither is distinguished for excellence and virtue, nor comes to grief on
account of baseness and vice, but on account of some error;

a man of great reputation and prosperity, like Oedipus and Thyestes and conspicuous people of such families as theirs. So, to be well formed, a fable must be single rather than (as some say) double — there must be no change from misfortune to good fortune, but only the opposite, from good fortune to misfortune; the cause must not be vice, but a great error; and the man must be either of the type specified or better, rather than worse. This is borne out by the practice of poets; at first they picked a fable at random and made an inventory of its contents, but now the finest tragedies are plotted, and concern a few families — for example, the tragedies about Alcmeon, Oedipus, Orestes, Mĕlĕāger, Thyestes, Tēlĕphus, and any others whose lives were attended by terrible experiences or doings.

This is the plot that will produce the technically finest tragedy. Those critics are therefore wrong who censure Euripides on this very ground — because he does this in his tragedies, and many of them end in misfortune; for it is, as I have said, the right thing to do. This is clearly demonstrated on the stage in the competitions, where such plays, if they succeed, are the most tragic, and Euripides, even if he is inefficient in every other respect, still shows himself the most tragic of our poets. The next best plot, which is said by some people to be the best, is the tragedy with a double plot, like the *Odyssey*, ending in one way for the better people and in the opposite way for the worse. But it is the weakness of theatrical performances that gives priority to this kind; when poets write what the audience would like to happen, they are in leading strings. This is not the pleasure proper to tragedy, but rather to comedy, where the greatest enemies in the fable, say Orestes and Aegisthus, make friends and go off at the end, and nobody is killed by anybody.

CHAPTER 14. The pity and fear can be brought about by the *Mise en scène*; but they can also come from the mere plotting of the incidents, which is preferable, and better poetry. For, without seeing anything, the fable ought to have been so plotted that if one heard the bare facts, the chain of circumstances would make one shudder and pity. That would happen to any one who heard the fable of the *Oedipus*. To produce this effect by the *Mise en scène* is less artistic and puts one at the mercy of the technician; and those who use it not to frighten but merely to startle have lost touch with tragedy altogether. We should not try to get all sorts of pleasure from tragedy, but the particular tragic pleasure. And clearly, since this pleasure coming from pity and fear has to be produced by imitation, it is by his handling of the incidents that the poet must create it.

Let us, then, take next the kind of circumstances that seem terrible or lamentable. Now, doings of that kind must be between friends, or enemies, or neither. If an enemy injures an enemy, there is no pity either beforehand or at the time, except on account of the *The tragic mode: Pity and fear* bare fact; nor is there if they are neutral; but when sufferings are engendered among the affections — for example, if murder is done or planned, or some similar outrage is committed, by brother on brother, or son on father, or mother on son, or son on mother — that is the thing to aim at.

Though it is not permissible to ruin the traditional fables — I mean, such as the killing of Clytemnestra by Orestes, or Eriphҳle by Alcmeon — the poet should use his own invention to refine on what has been handed down to him. Let me explain more clearly what I mean by "refine." The action may take place, as the old poets used to make it, with the knowledge and understanding of the participants; this was how Euripides made Medea kill her children. Or they may do it, but in ignorance of the horror of the deed, and then afterwards discover the tie of affection, like the Oedipus of Sophocles; his act was outside the play, but there are examples where it is inside the tragedy itself — Alcmeon in the play by Astydămas, or Tēlĕgŏnus in *The Wounded Odysseus*. Besides these, there is a third possibility: when a man is about to do some fatal act in ignorance, but is enlightened before he does it. These are the only possible alternatives. One must either act or not act, and either know or not know. Of these alternatives, to know, and to be about to act, and then not to act, is thoroughly bad — it is disgusting without being tragic, for there is no emotional crisis; accordingly poets only rarely create such situations, as in the *Antigone*, when Haemon fails to kill Creon. Next in order is to act; and if the deed is done in ignorance and its nature is disclosed afterwards, so much the better — there is no bad taste in it, and the revelation is overpowering. But the last is best; I mean, like Mĕrŏpe in the *Cresphontes*, intending to kill her son, but recognizing him and not killing him; and the brother and sister in the *Iphigeneia*; and in the *Helle*, the son recognizing his mother just as he was going to betray her. — This is the reason for what was mentioned earlier: that the subject-matter of our tragedies is drawn from a few families. In their search for matter they discovered this recipe in the fables, not by cunning but by luck. So they are driven to have recourse to those families where such emotional crises have occurred.

That is all that need be said about the plotting of the incidents, and what the fables should be like.

CHAPTER 15. In Character there are four things to aim at. First and foremost, that it should be good of *Character* its kind: a speech or action will be moral if (as I have said) it shows a preference, and the morality will be good if the preference is good of its kind. This is possible in every class. There are good women and good slaves; yet the former class is no doubt inferior, and the latter altogether low. — Secondly, that it should be appropriate: for instance, *any one can have a brave character, but there are kinds of courage, as well as kinds of sagacity, that may be inappropriate to a woman.* — Thirdly, that it should be lifelike; this is distinct from making the character good and appropriate as defined above. — And fourthly, that it should be consistent; even if the person who is the original of the imitation is inconsistent, and inconsistency is the basis of his character, it is none the less necessary to make him consistently inconsistent. An example of an unnecessarily low character is Menelaus in the *Orestes*; of the unseemly and inappropriate, the lament of Odysseus in the *Scylla*, and the speech of Mĕlănippe; of the inconsistent, Iphigeneia at Aulis — her character as a suppliant is quite unlike her later self.

And in the characterization, as in the plotting of the incidents, the aim should always be either necessity or probability:

so that they say or do such things as it is necessary or probable that they would, being what they are; and that for this to follow that is either necessary or probable. (Thus it is clear that the untying of the fable should follow on the circumstances of the fable itself, and not be done *ex machina*, as it is in the *Medea*, or in Book 2 of the *Iliad*. But the *deus ex machina* should be used for matters outside the drama — either things that happened before and that man could not know, or future events that need to be announced prophetically; for we allow the gods to see everything. As for extravagant incidents, there should be none in the story, or if there are they should be kept outside the tragedy, as is the one in the *Oedipus* of Sophocles.)

Since tragedy is an imitation of people above the normal, we must be like good portrait-painters, who follow the original model closely, but refine on it; in the same way the poet, in imitating people whose character is choleric or phlegmatic, and so forth, must keep them as they are and at the same time make them attractive. *So Homer made Achilles noble, as well as a pattern of obstinacy.*

Look out for these points; and also for aesthetic effects mixed up with though not relevant to poetry, for they too can often lead to failure. But enough has been said about them in the published works.

CHAPTER 16. What Disclosure is has been explained above; the different species of Disclosure are as follows. First, the most inartistic, and usually a makeshift, Disclosure by visible clues. *Kinds of disclosure*. They may be birth-marks, like "the spear-head that the Earth-born bear," or the stars in the *Thyestes* of Carcĭnus; or they may be acquired, either physical marks such as scars, or accessories like necklaces and the disclosure in the *Tyro* by the skiff. But even with these clues there are degrees of badness, according to the way they are used; for instance, Odysseus was disclosed by his scar in one way to the nurse and in another way to the herdsmen. Used deliberately as passports they are more inartistic — indeed this applies to any kind of disclosure used for that purpose — whereas those that come from an irony in the events (like the one in Book 19 of the *Odyssey*) are better.

Next come those that are made by the poet and are on that account inartistic. Thus in the *Iphigeneia*, Orestes himself disclosed who he was: Iphigeneia was disclosed by her letter, but the poet tells her (through the mouth of Orestes) what he wants her to know, instead of making the fable do it. This is nearly as faulty as the former kind, for Orestes might just as well have handed something to her. Or again, the "tale told by the loom" in the *Tēreūs* of Sophocles.

Thirdly, through a memory, by the awakening of a sense of something familiar: like the disclosure in the *Cyprians* of Dǐcaeogĕnes, when ⟨Teucer⟩ burst into tears at the sight of the picture; or in Book 8 of the *Odyssey*, when the memories revived by hearing the harper made ⟨Odysseus⟩ weep. So they disclosed who they were.

Fourthly, by logic; as in the *Chŏĕphŏri* ("A man like me has come; there is no man like me but Orestes; therefore he has come"). And the disclosure suggested by Polyīdus the sophist for the *Iphigeneia:* it is probable that Orestes would have drawn the parallel between the sacrificing of his sister and the accident that he himself was being sacrificed. And in the *Tȳdeūs* of Theodectes, the speech about coming to find his son and being lost himself. And the one in the *Phīnēidae:* when they saw the place they argued that it was their fate — they were fated to die at that place, because they had been exposed there in infancy. . . .

But of all disclosures the best are those that arise out of the story itself and cause astonishment by probable events; as in the *Oedipus* of Sophocles, and the *Iphigeneia* — it is probable that she would want to send a letter. These are the only ones without prefabricated clues, or necklaces. The next best are the logical kind.

CHAPTER 17. When you are putting together your fables and working out the composition in words, you should as far as possible set the play before your eyes; those who see in this way, as though they were present at the

Imagination

performance, will find the right thing in its most vivid form, and make the fewest unconscious blunders. This is borne out by the trouble Carcinus got into; if the spectator did not actually see Amphiǎraüs appearing out of the temple he would not notice it, but when it was staged the audience took it amiss and damned the play. You should even as far as possible act the parts as you compose the speeches; for the best way of making a man's emotions convincing is to take his very nature to yourself — the manifestations of stormy or angry feelings are most lifelike in a man who is himself in a storm or rage. Poetry therefore goes with genius or madness; for the former is responsive, and the latter subject to delusions.

Whether the story is an old one or whether you are yourself making it up, you should first reduce it to a significant and unified outline, and afterwards expand and interpolate your scheme. By viewing a story in unified outline, I mean this kind of thing (from the *Iphigeneia*). A girl was sacrificed; vanished from the sight of her sacrificers; was deposited in another country, where there was a custom of sacrificing strangers to the goddess; became the priestess of the goddess; some time afterwards the brother of the priestess turned up there (that he was sent there by an oracle for a reason, and his purpose in going, are no part of the fable); having arrived he was arrested; was about to be sacrificed; revealed himself — either as Euripides made it happen, or, in the probable way Polyidus worked out, by saying that not only his sister but he too had to be sacrificed; hence their escape. This done, you should now interpolate, with the individuality of the people as your foundation; and take care that your interpolations are correctly particularized — for example, by making the capture of Orestes depend on his madness, and using the purification to bring about their escape. . . .

Reduction and interpolation

CHAPTER 18.   Every tragedy consists in the tying and untying of a knot. What is outside the play, and usually also some of the incidents inside it, are the tying; and the rest is the untying. By the tying, I mean from the beginning up to the point immediately before the change to good fortune

Tying and untying

or misfortune; and by the untying, from the beginning of the change to the end. Thus in the *Lynceus* of Theodectes, the tying is what happened before the play, together with the arrest of the boy; *and ⟨the untying⟩ of these events again is from the capital indictment to the end.*

There are four kinds of tragedy, for that is the num- *The* ber of elements we specified: Complex tragedy, which *kinds of* consists entirely of an ironical plot with Disclosure; *tragedy* Emotional tragedy, like the *Ajax* and *Ixīon* plays; Moral tragedy, like the *Women of Phthia* and the *Pēleūs*; and fourthly *Spectacular* tragedy, like the *Phorcīdes* and the *Prometheus* and all the stories located in Hades. But try to develop all the elements of tragedy if you can, or at least as many as possible of the most important, especially considering the unfair fault-finding poets suffer from nowadays; as there have already been poets who have done well with each of the elements separately, every one is expected to outdo all their specialties single-handed. Yet to discriminate justly between tragedies one should concentrate on the fable: that is, the tangling and untying of the knot. Many writers tangle it well and then untie it badly; but it is necessary always to master both.

And you should remember what has been said many *Miscel-* times, and not try to make an epic compilation into a *laneous* tragedy — by epic I here mean multifabular. For exam- *injunc-* ple, suppose one were to try and work the whole fable *tions* of the *Iliad* into a tragedy. In the epic, because of its length, the parts can be properly developed, but to do so in a play often turns out to be an error of judgment. For instance, all the poets who have written whole *Falls of Troy* instead of taking parts of the story as Euripides did, or whole *Niŏbes* instead of following the example of Aeschylus, either fail completely or do badly on the stage. Indeed, even Agathon had a play damned for this alone. But both in the use of Irony, and in simple stories, *he is* remarkably successful in what they aim at, which is to be tragic and satisfy human feeling; as when he shows us a clever but wicked man (like Sīsўphus) outwitted, or a brave unscrupulous man put down. That kind of situation is also probable; as Agathon says, we must expect the unexpected often to happen.

Treat the chorus as though it were one of the actors; it should be an organic part of the play and reinforce it, not as it is in Euripides, but as in Sophocles. In their successors the songs belong *⟨no⟩* more to the fable than to that of any other tragedy. This has led to the insertion of borrowed lyrics, an innovation for which Agathon was responsible. Yet what difference is there between inserting a borrowed lyric and sticking in a speech or a whole act from another play?

CHAPTER 19. So much for the other elements; it remains to discuss Language and Thought. As for Thought, I have nothing to add to what is said about it in my *Rhetoric*, since it is more germane to that subject. Thought controls all the effects that have to be produced by language: including proof — refutation — the manipulation of feelings such as pity, fear, anger, and so forth — as well as aggrandizement and depreciation. Clearly also you require Thought on the same lines for the incidents, whenever you need to make them pathetic or terrible, or larger than life or probable; with this much difference, that you have to make the point clear without stating it, whereas in the language the effects are produced by a speaker in so many words. Indeed, what would be the use of the dialogue *if the pleasure were obvious* without words? . . .

Thought

CHAPTER 25. . . . First, criticisms touching the essentials of the art. "Impossibilities have been put into the poem." That is a fault. But it is all right provided the art attains its end, which I have specified — provided, that is, they enable it to make the incident, or another incident, more impressive. . . .

Practical criticism

Next, if the criticism is "That is not true." Perhaps the answer is "No, but it ought to be"; as Sophocles said "I depict man as he ought to be, whereas Euripides depicts him as he is." If that will not do, there is tradition: as in the stories about gods, which are no doubt what Xĕnŏphănes says they are, neither better than the truth, nor true; still, they pass for true. And in some instances perhaps the answer is not "It is better than the truth," but "It used to be true": as in the statement in *Iliad* 10. 152-3 "their spears were planted upright on the butt-end"; that was then the custom, as it is to this day among the Illyrians. . . .

CHAPTER 26. . . . Since Tragedy has everything the Epic has (she can even use the epic meter), and in addition the considerable elements of Music and the *Mise en scène*, by which our pleasures are set in most *Superiority of tragedy* vivid motion; again, she is vivid enough in the mere reading, and has the added vividness of stage performance; again, she achieves the end of the imitation in a shorter length, and what is more compact gives greater pleasure than what is spun out for a long time, as you will realize if you imagine the *Oedipus* of Sophocles re-written in as many lines as there are in the *Iliad*; again, the imitation by epic poets has less unity (by way of evidence, any one such imitation goes to make several tragedies; if they write one with a single fable, it either is told rapidly and seems abrupt, or has to be watered down in order to reach the proper length; but I mean one combining several actions, like the *Iliad* and the *Odyssey*, which contain many such sections, each of some amplitude; and yet the Homeric poems are plotted as well as they could be, and the action they imitate is as unified as possible) —

If, then, tragedy is superior in all these ways, and also in fulfilling her artistic function (for the mere giving of pleasure is not enough, they must give the kind of pleasure I have specified), it would seem clear that she is better than epic poetry, because she achieves her end better. . . .

Romeo and Juliet and
A Midsummer Night's Dream:
Tragedy and Comedy

HENRY ALONZO MYERS

AT THE END of Plato's *Symposium* we find an amusing picture of a great philosopher putting Agathon, the tragic poet, and

Aristophanes, the greatest comic poet of Athens, to sleep with his discourse on the nature of tragedy and comedy. As Plato tells the story, it happened in the early hours of the morning, after a night spent in feasting and singing the praises of love:

> There remained [of the company] only Socrates, Aristophanes, and Agathon, who were drinking out of a large goblet which they passed round, and Socrates was discoursing to them. Aristodemus was only half awake, and he did not hear the beginning of the discourse; the chief thing which he remembered was Socrates compelling the other two to acknowledge that the genius of comedy was the same with that of tragedy, and that the true artist in tragedy was an artist in comedy also. To this they were constrained to assent, being drowsy, and not quite following the argument. And first of all Aristophanes dropped off, then, when the day was already dawning, Agathon. Socrates, having laid them to sleep, rose to depart. [Jowett translation]

Like all good comedy, this scene is entertaining as well as instructive. It is entertaining because it presents the opposite of the order we naturally expect: a tragic poet and a comic poet, whom we expect to be interested in a discourse on the nature of tragedy and comedy, fall asleep; it is instructive because it makes the point, evident elsewhere in literary history, that tragic and comic poets do not need explicitly formulated theories of tragedy and comedy, that they are often indifferent to such abstract speculations.

The distinctive form and significance of tragedies and comedies indicate, however, that the successful poets have had an adequate sense of the tragic and the comic. Apparently the appreciative reader or spectator also possesses this mysterious but adequate sense of the nature of tragedy and comedy, for as the artist can create without an explicitly formulated theory, so the reader can appreciate and enjoy the specific work of art without the benefit of definitions and generalizations. But although speculation about the nature of tragedy and comedy is not indispensable to either creation or appreciation, it is, nevertheless, a natural and, indeed, inevitable result of our curiosity as rational beings. If it did not begin before, dramatic theory began as the first spectators were leaving the first performance in the first theater. When we have had an intensely interesting experience, we are eager to know its nature and its causes. Why do we enjoy the spectacle of a man who falls from prosperity to adversity? Why do we laugh at fools? As long as we are interested in drama and in its sources in life, we shall be asking these questions and trying to answer them.

The assertion that the genius of tragedy is the same as that of comedy and that the true artist in tragedy is an artist in comedy also is the kind of provocative conundrum or apparent paradox which Socrates loved to discuss. It was a bold speculative assertion rather than a description of known facts, for the Greek dramatic poets, as we know them, kept tragedy and comedy apart and excelled in one or the other, not in both. Plato, who recorded the assertion, supported it in practice by displaying a sharp comic sense in the *Symposium* and a deep tragic sense in the dialogues which describe the trial and death of Socrates. But its support in drama did not come until the 1590's, when Shakespeare wrote *Romeo and Juliet* and *A Midsummer Night's Dream*, displaying genius in both tragedy and comedy.

What did Socrates have in mind? If the genius of tragedy is the same as that of comedy, what is the difference between the two? Certainly, he rejected the popular choice of the distinction between an unhappy and a happy ending as the difference between tragedy and comedy: in Plato's *Philebus* he maintains that we view both forms of drama with mingled pleasure and pain, smiling through our tears at tragedy and responding to the ridiculous in others with laughter, which is pleasant, tinged with envy, which is unpleasant. But this view, although it supports the assertion that tragedy and comedy are similar, leaves us, if both have the same effect, with no way of distinguishing one from the other. It can hardly be all that Socrates had in mind.

After years of wondering what he had in mind when his audience at the symposium failed him, I do not know the answer, but I have reached the point where I know what I should have said if I had been Socrates and if I had been more fortunate then he in holding my audience.

Man, I should have said, is a rational animal: he is always looking for meaning in his experience. He looks for meaning and order everywhere, but since the desire to find some significant pattern in his joys and sorrows, some just relation between good and evil, is closest to his heart, surpassing even his desire to grasp the order of the physical world, he looks most intently for meaning in the realm of values. That is why tragedy, which is an artistic demonstration that justice governs our joys and sorrows, has always seemed to most critics to be the highest form of art.

Since man has only a finite intelligence, he cannot always find the order he craves, either in the inner world of values or in the outer world of science and external description. In his search for order he is everywhere confronted by disorder, absurdity, nonsense, and incongruity. Fortunately, however, he finds in laughter, at least in his relaxed moments, an enjoyable emotional reaction to these disappointments to his reason. We rightly honor the comic poet, who by presenting nonsense in contrast to sense points up the difference between the two and who through laughter reconciles us to those experiences which frustrate the effort of reason to find meaningful patterns in all experience.

Order and disorder, the congruous and the incongruous, sense and nonsense, profundity and absurdity are pairs of opposites; each member of each pair throws light on the other so that whoever has a keen sense of order, congruity, sense, and profundity must also have a keen sense of disorder, incongruity, nonsense, and absurdity. Clearly, then, if the discovery of order in the realm of good and evil is the glory of tragedy, which finds intelligibility and justice in our seemingly chance joys and sorrows, and if the glory of comedy lies in its transformation of the frustrations of reason into soothing laughter, the artist in tragedy may also be an artist in comedy, and vice versa; and it may also be said that the genius of tragedy is similar to that of comedy.

Socrates, who was a rationalist, might well have expounded his apparent paradox in this fashion; very probably, however, the rivalry between philosophers and poets in his time would have made it difficult for him to recognize the tragic poets as the discoverers of justice in our joys and sorrows and the comic poets as the teachers of the difference between sense and nonsense. Since we can never know what Socrates had in mind, the final episode of the *Symposium* must remain, as Plato intended, a frustration of reason made pleasant by laughter at the absurdity of the ideal audience falling asleep in the presence of the right speaker on the right subject. This pleasant frustration does not prevent us, however, from determining for ourselves whether the great teacher's provocative conundrum will serve as a key to the meaning of tragedy and comedy.

The hypothesis which I have offered as a substitute for the slumber-stifled discussion needs amplification and verification by specific examples. What better test can be found than the first test afforded by the history of dramatic literature — the appearance of *Romeo and Juliet* and *A Midsummer Night's Dream* as the works of one author? These plays prove that Shakespeare, at least, was an artist in both tragedy and comedy. Do they indicate also that the genius of tragedy is similar to that of comedy? Do they indicate that the two are related as order is related to disorder — that the function of tragedy is to reveal a just order in our joys and sorrows and the function of comedy to turn disorder into soothing laughter?

II

The answers to two questions lead us directly to the heart of the tragic meaning of *Romeo and Juliet*. The first question is, What causes the downfall of the hero and of the heroine who shares his fate? The second question is, In what sense does the play have universality: does the fate of Romeo and Juliet represent the fate of all lovers?

Shakespeare himself could not have correctly answered the first question — What causes the downfall of the hero and heroine? — before he finished the play. *Romeo and Juliet* is Shakespeare's first true tragedy; as he wrote it, he was developing his own sense of the tragic. He started the play with a view which he found unsatisfactory as he went on writing and ended with a view which he upheld in all his later tragedies. He started with the view that something outside the hero is the cause of his downfall, that something outside man is the cause of the individual's particular fate.

His first view is stressed in the Prologue, which announces that "a pair of star-cross'd lovers take their life." This forecast points ahead to Romeo's exclamation, when he hears and believes the report of Juliet's death:

> Is it even so? then I defy you, stars!

From this point on, every step he takes leads to his downfall. He buys poison from the apothecary, goes to Juliet's tomb, drinks the poison, and dies — while Juliet still lives. The stars are triumphant. Romeo's defiance of his fate hastens its fulfillment.

The stars are symbolic of the elements of bad luck and chance in the action of the play, of the bad luck which involves Romeo in a renewal of the feud and of the chance delay of the messenger who would have told him that Juliet lived. But do the stars, do chance and bad luck, determine the particular fate of the individual? Bad luck and chance are facts of life, but is there a deeper fact than chance and bad luck, a truer cause of the individual's fate? Like Romeo, we all suffer at times from bad luck. Like Romeo, we all hear rumors and alarms and false warnings and reports of danger and disaster. We know from experience that our response to these chance and unlucky events is more important than the events themselves; and our responses depend upon our characters. Character is a deeper and more important influence in human affairs than luck or chance.

Some time ago a radio program presented, as a remarkable illustration of chance and bad luck, the story of a man from Pennsylvania who had been hit by a train three times at the same crossing. When we reflect upon his story, we are likely to conclude that it is a revelation of character rather than an illustration of chance. If we had been in his place, most of us, after the first accident, would have taken all possible precautionary measures to see that it did not happen again; and if by chance we were struck again by an unscheduled train on a day when the crossing signals were not working, it seems likely that we would never again cross the tracks at that point. It is difficult for us to avoid the conclusion that the man from Pennsylvania was the kind of man who gets hit by trains.

Examples of "chance" and "bad luck" are common in the news. The following is representative of many: "A year to the day after he broke his left leg in a fall caused by a loose plank in his doorstep, John Jones, 47, of . . . , broke his right leg when he tripped over the same plank." Obviously, this is another revelation of character: Jones is the kind of man who will risk another leg rather than fix the plank.

While writing his first tragedy, Shakespeare discovered that the individual's fate is determined from within, by character, and not from without, by chance or bad luck. Although the character of Romeo is not as clearly revealed as the characters of Lear, Hamlet, Macbeth, and Othello, it is nevertheless certain from a point early in the play that Romeo is the kind of person who is inclined to accept bad news at its face value and who is inclined, when he is confronted by apparent disaster, toward some despairing deed. In his despair when the feud broke out — at a time when he knew that Juliet lived — he would have killed himself if the Nurse and Friar Laurence had not prevented him from so doing. Since the Nurse and Friar Laurence could not always be present in his despairing moments and since the temptations to despair are all too common in life, it was with Romeo only a matter of time.

The stars remain in *Romeo and Juliet*, as well as the chance and bad luck of which they are symbols, but the play also offers a better explanation for the downfall of Romeo. It suggests that "a man's character is his fate," as Heraclitus said — a dictum which sums up one pattern of tragic meaning, one aspect of the tragic poet's vision of order in the universe.

In all his later plays, Shakespeare looked within to character, and not to the stars or to chance or luck, for the causes of individual fates:

> The fault, dear Brutus, is not in our stars,
> But in ourselves, that we are underlings.

We come now to the second question: How is the fate of Romeo and Juliet representative of the fate of all lovers: in what sense does the play have universality?

In looking for the answer to this question, we should first notice how neatly balanced are the feelings of the principals in the play. Taking love as a representative emotional experience, Shakespeare stresses both sides of the experience — the joy and exaltation of the lovers when they are united and their anxiety and unhappiness when they are separated. We see the lovers at both extremes of feeling. The balanced pyramidal form of the play, the five-act structure with the turn at the middle following the rise and fall of the fortunes of the principals, parallels the balance between joy and sorrow which Shakespeare's insight finds in human experience. The artistic structure of the play is an outward show of its inner meaning.

In *Romeo and Juliet* the ending is a dramatic summing up of the whole action: the death of the lovers is symbolical of their lives. Each realizes at the end the extremes of good and evil. In one sense they are united forever, as they wished to be; in another sense they are separated forever in death. Here we see not a happy ending, as in a fairy story, and not an unhappy ending, as in some grim naturalistic tale, in which the worm finally is stilled after wriggling on the hook, but a truly tragic ending, in which joy and sorrow are inevitably joined together — a victory in defeat, a victory of the human spirit accompanied by the inevitable defeat of finite human beings.

Shakespearean tragedy is an artistic vision and revelation of a kind of divine justice which regulates the lives of men and women. Through poetic insight, Shakespeare finds a pattern, an order, in the realm of values; through insight he measures the extremes of feeling, which cannot be measured in any other way. Whoever sees in Shakespearean tragedy only a spectacle of suffering, only an unhappy ending, is seeing only half the story, only one side of life. The artist has done his best to present the whole story and both sides of life. For in the relation between the poles of experience, good and evil, he finds order in the universe. First, he finds that the individual fate of the hero is determined by character, not by chance. Second, he finds that the universality of the hero rests on the fact that, like all of us, the hero is fated to experience the extremes of feeling; and, in accordance with his capacity for feeling, in something like balanced and equal measures, when we follow the rise and fall of the hero's fortunes, we feel ourselves joined to him and to all mankind in the justice of a common fate: this is the secret of the reconciliation to suffering which we find in tragedy.

III

At the time of writing *Romeo and Juliet* and *A Midsummer Night's Dream*, Shakespeare must have been deeply impressed by the thought that the same material — the theme of love, for example, or life itself — may be treated as either tragic or comic. At the beginning of *A Midsummer Night's Dream*, the Athenian lovers, Hermia and Lysander, are in a predicament as serious as the plight of Romeo and Juliet; well may Lysander say, "The course of true love never did run smooth." But the roughness in the course of their love turns out to be the laughable ups and down of comedy while the roughness in the course of Romeo's love turns into a profoundly tragic change of fortune. The story of Pyramus and Thisbe, the play within a play in *A Midsummer Night's Dream* is, in its main outlines, the same as the story of Romeo and Juliet, yet it becomes in production, as Hippolyta says, "the silliest stuff that ever I heard," while the story of Romeo and Juliet becomes in production a great demonstration that order and justice prevail.

What difference in treatment of the same material — what difference in point of view toward the same material — makes possible the difference between comedy and tragedy?

A Midsummer Night's Dream presents the theme of love on three levels: the level of common sense; the level of nonsense, incongruity, and absurdity; and the level of fantasy. The level of common sense is represented by the love and marriage of Theseus and Hippolyta, who provide the necessary contrast to nonsense. The level of nonsense is represented by the Athenian lovers, Lysander, Demetrius, Helena, and Hermia, and by the workmen, Quince, Snug, Bottom, Flute, Snout, and Starveling, who turn the tragic story of Pyramus and Thisbe into a comic revelation of their own inadequacies. The level of fantasy is represented by the loves of Titania and Oberon, and by the juice of the flower called love-in-idleness, which here serves Shakespeare as an explanation of the influence of chance, caprice, and propinquity on love between the sexes. Since two of these levels, sense and nonsense, are always represented in all comedies, they deserve a few words of comment and definition.

The world of sense is the world of orderly and meaningful patterns, both rational and conventional. Its first law is the law of identity, namely, A is A, which "simply expresses the fact that every term and idea which we use in our reasonings" and practical calculations "must remain what it is." Shakespeare, for example, can make "sense" of the world of human values and find a just order in it only if the law of identity holds true. A is A; and if Romeo is Romeo — that is, if we can be sure that Romeo's character does not change or will not change, then we can understand his fate or even in a general way predict it. Similarly, if for Romeo good is to-be-united-with-Juliet and evil is to-be-separated-from-her — if his values do not change — then we can see in the rise and fall of his fortunes a just balance between good and evil.

The world of nonsense is, in contrast, governed by a law which is the exact opposite of the law of identity. A is not always A; A is sometimes B, or C, or D; and for this reason the world of nonsense is a world of disorder and incongruities. The laughable absurdities and incongruities in A *Midsummer Night's Dream* are for the most part direct consequences of this law of change of identity. Every change of identity leads to incongruities or comic ups and downs. Lysander, for example, is first presented to us as the lover of Hermia; later, touched by the juice of the magic flower, he becomes the lover of Helena; still later through magic he becomes the lover of Hermia again: A becomes B, and then becomes A again. Helena, we are told, was once the object of Demetrius' love; she is first presented to us as an unloved maiden; later through magic she is the object of Lysander's love, later still the object of the love of both

Lysander and Demetrius; and finally the object of Demetrius' love only. A becomes B, and then becomes C, and then becomes D, and finally becomes A again. And so on with the Athenian lovers.

In contrast, Theseus and Hippolyta, who represent sense, remain what they are throughout the play.

Bottom, that king of the world of nonsense, undergoes a series of "translations." An ass in the eyes of the audience from the beginning, but a man of parts to his fellows, he later becomes through magic an ass in appearance, later the object of Titania's doting, later still the object of her loathing, and later still Bottom once more. Meanwhile, to complicate the scheme, he wishes to become Pyramus in the play, and also Thisbe, and also Lion. (I'll spare you the working out of his "translations" in ABC's.)

The most effective comedy in A *Midsummer Night's Dream* comes from the subtle use of change of identity in the production of the play within the play, "Pyramus and Thisbe." In the world of sense we accept the convention whereby the actor assumes the identity of the part he plays. In the theater Brian Aherne is Romeo, Katharine Cornell is Juliet. Not so in "Pyramus and Thisbe": Shakespeare reverses the convention and changes order into disorder and incongruity, so that the production excites in us uproarious laughter rather than tragic sympathy and insight. Following the convention of the theater, we would accept Lion and forget the actor, but Lion insists on telling us that he is not Lion but Snug the joiner. Similarly, by every device at his command, Shakespeare makes certain that we cannot see Pyramus, Thisbe, Wall, Moonshine, and Lion because we must see Snug, Bottom, Flute, Snout, and Starveling. By such devices, based on change of identity, first principle in the world of nonsense and incongruity, what might be seen as tragedy must be seen as comedy.

If tragedy reveals significant patterns in experience, demonstrating that character is fate and that men are united in the justice which apportions equal measures of joy and sorrow to each individual, and if comedy reconciles us through laughter to the disorder, the nonsense, the incongruities and absurdities which we meet everywhere in experience, how does the artist, working with the same material, with love or with life itself, make the choice between comedy and tragedy and determine whether we shall respond to his work of art with laughter or with tragic insight? Shakespeare must have thought of this question in some form while he was writing *Romeo and Juliet* and *A Midsummer Night's Dream;* and possibly his answer is to be found in the reply of Theseus to Hippolyta's verdict on the workers' production of "Pyramus and Thisbe": Hippolyta exclaimed, "This is the silliest stuff that ever I heard." And Theseus replied, "The best in this kind are but shadows, and the worst are no worse, if imagination amend them." If there exists anywhere a wiser comment on drama and the theater, I have not read or heard it.

Undoubtedly Shakespeare must have been thinking, as he wrote the reply of Theseus to Hippolyta, that the same imagination which willingly accepts actors as Romeo, or Hamlet, or Macbeth, or Lear, that accepts the past as the present, the stage as a series of faraway places, and fiction as life itself, could also accept, if it were permitted to do so, his "Pyramus and Thisbe." He knew that his "Pyramus and Thisbe," with the incongruities in the diction removed, and with competent actors losing themselves in their parts (including Lion, Moonshine, and Wall), could be successfully presented as tragedy. For he knew that the chief difference between "silly stuff" and profound art is caused by the artist's power to enlist the spectator's imagination. We can be sure that he knew this because in "Pyramus and Thisbe," as we see it, he has deliberately frustrated, for the sake of laughter, our imagination and prevented us at every point from amending the inherent limitations of drama.

Perhaps he was thinking also of the wider question of what difference in the artist's point of view determines whether we shall focus our attention on the underlying order in experience or on its superficial disorder and incongruities. Can the answer be found in imagination understood as sympathetic insight?

In "Pyramus and Thisbe" we are never permitted to see the story from the point of view of the lovers themselves; we see it only from the outside, as detached and unsympathetic observers.

Indeed, we are not permitted to see the lovers at all: we see only the incongruity of the workers presuming to play the parts of a highborn couple. Again, we see the Athenian lovers only from the outside. Hermia, Lysander, Demetrius, and Helena — each is identified for us only as the object of another's affection. They have no inwards for us, and since this is so, how can we possibly tell, from watching them, whether character is fate or whether each suffers and enjoys in equal measures?

Our experience in witnessing *Romeo and Juliet* is altogether different. Soon after the beginning, we follow the action with sympathetic insight from within, from the point of view of the lovers themselves. Inwardness — where character and values may be found and measured by insight — becomes for us the only reality. We live with Romeo and Juliet, seeing the world with their eyes, and as we rise and fall with their fortunes, we are carried finally beyond envy and pity and filled with a sense that all men share a common fate.

IV

Can we say, then, that life is comic if we view it chiefly from the outside, as detached observers whose attention is focused mainly on the disorder and incongruities of the surface? And can we say that life is tragic when we view it from within, from the point of view of an individual — our own point of view or that of someone with whom we identify ourselves by sympathetic insight, as we do with Romeo and Juliet?

Walpole's famous dictum that "the world is a comedy to those that think, a tragedy to those who feel" on first consideration may seem to sum up satisfactorily at this point, for the detached, outer view of man, which permits us to smile at nonsense and incongruity, is at least partially the kind of objectivity which we associate with thought. And sympathetic insight, indispensable in the appreciation of tragedy, obviously involves us in the world of feelings and values. But Walpole's equation of the difference between comedy and tragedy with the difference between thought and feeling does not take into account that, in the first place, laughter is itself an emotion and that, therefore, our response even to "pure" comedy is emotional. Secondly, the emotion of laughter mixes freely with other emotions, and this fact explains the existence of various kinds of comedy.

When the comic poet is amused by someone or something that he dislikes, the result is satire; when he is amused by someone or something that he likes, the result is humor. The spirit of *A Midsummer Night's Dream*, for example, is one of good humor rather than of satire. Shakespeare, we feel, likes human beings even while he laughs at them and is not motivated by a desire to change their ways. Their ways, especially the ways of lovers, are often absurd and nonsensical, but Shakespeare does not view these absurdities as a stern moralist or a cynic might.

A Midsummer Night's Dream is saved from cynicism by the third level of the comedy — the level of fantasy, the imaginative level which softens the sharp distinctions between the world of sense and the world of nonsense. If all the changes of identity on the part of the lovers were attributed to caprice and propinquity, the result would be cynicism, but most of them are attributed to magic in the world of fantasy, and the result is a softer, kindlier humor, which transforms our rational distress at chance and disorder into soothing laughter. There is insight in the background of *A Midsummer Night's Dream*, as in all great comedy. The magic juice of the flower called love-in-idleness seems to tell us that if only we knew the true causes of what seems to be mere chance and caprice in affairs of the heart, then even these apparent absurdities would make sense to us. The fact that it is a creature from fairyland, not a man, who exclaims: "Lord, what fools these mortals be!" takes the poison out of the comment.

Nor can tragedy be satisfactorily explained as the view of a man who is only a man of feeling — if such a man exists. Tragedy can best be explained by its appeal to our rational craving for order, for patterns of meaning; it satisfies this craving at the important point where our reason and our feelings unite. Tragedy offers a vision of order in the universe, which we grasp with sympathetic insight and respond to emotionally as we rise and fall, or fall and rise, with the hero's fortunes. Furthermore, tragedy requires artistic objectivity as well as in-

sight. Sympathetic insight alone might tempt Shakespeare —
who as artist enjoys the omnipotence of a creator — to save
Romeo from the fate which inevitably flows from his character,
but artistic objectivity will not permit him to do so. Even Zeus
must bow to necessity.

The spectator also views serious drama with a combination
of insight and artistic objectivity, and he applauds the tragic
artist who offers both as greater than the writer who is tempted
by sympathy to sacrifice objectivity and provide us with a happy
ending. We readily recognize such writings as one-sided, as un-
true to life, as appeals to our weakness.

Thought and feeling are involved in the creation and appreciation of both comedy and tragedy. In seeing each, we experience an intellectual awareness accompanied by appropriate emotional responses. The main difference is that in tragedy our
intelligence is directed toward order in the universe; in comedy,
toward disorder and incongruity. Without sympathetic insight,
we cannot behold the tragic vision of the fate common to all
men. Without detachment, we cannot realize the effect of
comedy, which transforms the frustrations of reason into laughter. But there is objectivity as well as insight in the tragic vision,
and there is always insight in the background of great comedy.
The difference between the point of view of tragedy and that
of comedy cannot, therefore, be equated simply with the difference between insight and detachment, but rather is to be
found in a subtler proportion whereby insight is stressed in
tragedy and detachment is stressed in comedy.

The Tragic Form

RICHARD B. SEWALL

A DISCUSSION of tragedy is confronted at the outset with the
strenuous objections of Croce, who would have no truck with the
genres. "Art is one," he wrote in his famous *Britannica* article,[1]
"and cannot be divided." For convenience, he would allow the

[1] Eleventh edition, article "Aesthetics."

division of Shakespeare's plays into tragedies, comedies, and histories, but he warned of the dogmatism that lay in any further refining of distinctions. He made a special point of tragedy, which as usual was the fighting issue. No artist, he said, will submit to the servitude of the traditional definition: that a tragedy must have a subject of a certain kind, characters of a certain kind, and a plot of a certain kind and length. Each work of art is a world in itself, "a creation, not a reflection, a monument, not a document." The concepts of aesthetics do not exist "in a transcendent region" but only in innumerable specific works. To ask of a given work "is it a tragedy?" or "does it obey the laws of tragedy?" is irrelevant and impertinent.

Although this may be substituting one dogmatism for another, there is sense in it. Nothing is more dreary than the textbook categories; and their tendency, if carried too far, would rationalize art out of existence. The dilemma is one of critical means, not ends: Croce would preserve tragedy by insuring the autonomy of the artist; the schoolmen would preserve it by insuring the autonomy of the form.

But the dilemma is not insurmountable, as Eliot and a number of others have pointed out. There is a life-giving relationship between tradition and the individual talent, a "wooing both ways" (in R. P. Blackmur's phrase) between the form which the artist inherits and the new content he brings to it. This wooing both ways has been especially true of the development of tragedy, where values have been incremental, where (for instance) each new tragic protagonist is in some degree a lesser Job and each new tragic work owes an indispensable element to the Greek idea of the chorus. So I should say that, provided we can get beyond the stereotypes Croce seems to have had in mind, we should continue to talk about tragedy, to make it grow in meaning, impel more artists, and attract a greater and more discerning audience.

But we must first get a suitable idea of form. Blackmur's article[2] from which I have just quoted provides, I think, a use-

[2] "The Loose and Baggy Monsters of Henry James: Notes on the Underlying Classic Form in the Novel," *Accent*, Summer, 1951; see also Eliseo Vivas, "Literature and Knowledge," *Sewanee Review*, Autumn, 1952.

ful suggestion. It is the concept of "theoretic form," which he distinguishes from technical or "executive" form. "Technical form," he writes, "is our means of getting at . . . and then making something of, what we feel the form of life itself is: the tensions, the stresses, the deep relations and the terrible dis-relations that inhabit them. . . . This is the form that underlies the forms we merely practice. . . ." This (and here Croce's full concept of form is more adequately represented) is "what Croce means by theoretic form for feeling, intuition, insight, what I mean by the theoretic form of life itself." Discussion of the "form" of tragedy in this sense need be neither prescriptive nor inhibiting, but it may define a little more precisely a vital area of thought and feeling.

Here is the kind of situation in which such a discussion might be helpful: Two years ago, in *Essays in Criticism* (October 1952), Miss K. M. Burton defended what she called the "political tragedies" of Ben Jonson and George Chapman as legitimate tragedies, although non-Aristotelian. *Sejanus* was perhaps the clearest case in point. Herford and Simpson, in their commentary, had set the play down as at best "the tragedy of a satirist," a "proximate" tragedy, with no tragic hero and with no cathartic effect. "Whatever effect (Jonson) aimed at," they wrote, "it was not the purifying pity excited by the fatal errors of a noble nature." Miss Burton's reply lay in her concept of political tragedy. She saw Jonson's tragic theme as "the manner in which evil penetrates the political structure." The "flaw" that concerned him lay "within the social order," and whatever purifying pity we feel would come from contemplating the ordeal of society, not the fatal errors of a noble nature. The play for her had "tragic intensity"; it was both "dramatic, and a tragedy."

Whether one agrees with her or not, the question, despite Croce, is out: "Is the play a tragedy?" And many others follow. Can there be a tragedy without a tragic hero? Can "the social order" play his traditional role? Is catharsis the first, or only, or even a reliable test? In a recent article, Professor Pottle wrote, "I shall be told Aristotle settled all that." And added, "I wish he had." The disagreement on *Sejanus* is symptomatic. F. L. Lucas once pointed out that (on much the same issues) Hegel thought only the Greeks wrote true tragedy; and I. A. Richards, only Shakespeare. Joseph Wood Krutch ruled out the moderns, like Hardy, Ibsen and O'Neill; and Mark Harris ruled them in.[3] The question arises about every new "serious" play or novel; we seem to care a great deal about whether it is, or is not, a tragedy.

I have little hope of settling all this, but I am persuaded that progress lies in the direction of theoretic form, as Blackmur uses the term. Is it not possible to bring the dominant feelings, intuitions, insights that we meet in so-called tragic writings into some coherent relationship to which the word "form" could be applied without too great violence? This is not to tell artists what to do, nor to set up strict *a priori* formulae, nor to legislate among the major genres. The problem of evaluating the total excellence of a given work involves much more than determining its status as a tragedy, or as a "proximate" tragedy, or as a non-tragedy. It involves, among other things, the verbal management within the work and the ordering of the parts. Furthermore, our discussion need not imply the superiority of tragedy over comedy (certainly not as Dante conceived of comedy) or over epic, although, if we look upon these major forms as presenting total interpretations of life, the less inclusive forms (lyric, satire) would seem to occupy inferior categories. But as we enter the world of any play or novel to which the term tragedy is at all applicable, we may well judge it by what we know about the possibilities of the form, without insisting that our judgment is absolute. If, set against the full dimensions of the tragic form, Jonson's *Sejanus* or Hemingway's *A Farewell to Arms* (for instance) reveal undeveloped possibilities or contrary elements, we can still respect their particular modes of expression.

In indicating these dimensions of tragedy, I shall be mindful of Unamuno's warning[4] that tragedy is not a matter, ultimately, to be systematized. He speaks truly, I think, about "the tragic sense of life." He describes it as a sub-philosophy, "more or less

[3] F. A. Pottle, "Catharsis," *Yale Review*, Summer, 1951; F. L. Lucas, *Tragedy in Relation to Aristotle's Poetics*, N.Y., 1928; Joseph Wood Krutch, *The Modern Temper*, N.Y., 1929; Mark Harris, *The Case for Tragedy*, N.Y., 1932.
[4] *The Tragic Sense of Life*, tr. J. E. C. Flitch, London, 1921, pp. 17-18.

formulated, more or less conscious," reaching deep down into temperament, not so much "flowing from ideas as determining them." It is the sense of ancient evil, of the mystery of human suffering, of the gulf between aspiration and achievement. It colors the tragic artist's vision of life (his theoretic form) and gives his works their peculiar shade and tone. It speaks, not the language of systematic thought, but through symbolic action, symbol and figure, diction and image, sound and rhythm. Such a recognition should precede any attempt to talk "systematically" about tragedy, while not denying the value of the attempt itself.

Two more comments remain to be made about method. The first is the problem of circular evidence,[5] the use of tragedies to define tragedy. I am assuming that we can talk meaningfully about a body of literature which reveals certain generic qualities and which can be distinguished from the body of literature called comedy, epic, satire, or the literature of pathos. My purpose is to isolate these qualities and to refer to the works themselves as illustrations rather than proof.

The second comment involves the problem of affectivism, which is the problem of catharsis: "This play is a tragedy because it makes me feel thus and so." As Max Scheler puts it, this method would bring us ultimately to the contemplation of our own ego. Thus, I would reverse the order of F. L. Lucas' discussion, which assumes that we must know what tragedy does before we can tell what it is: "We cannot fully discuss the means," Lucas wrote, "until we are clear about the ends." It is true that the usual or "scientific" way is to define natures by effects, which are observable. But rather than found a definition of tragedy on the infinite variables of an audience's reactions, I would consider first the works themselves as the "effects" and look in them for evidences of an efficient cause: a world-view, a form that "underlies the forms we merely practice." What are the generic qualities of these effects? Do they comprise a "form"? I think they do; and for convenience I shall use the

---

[5] Cf. Max Scheler, "On the Tragic," *Cross Currents*, Winter, 1954. This is a selection from Scheler's *Vom Umsturtz der Werte*, vol. I (1923), tr. Bernard Stambler.

term from the start as if I had already proved its legitimacy.

Basic to the tragic form is its recognition of the inevitability of paradox, of unresolved tensions and ambiguities, of opposites in precarious balance. Like the arch, tragedy never rests — or never comes to rest, with all losses restored and sorrows ended. Problems are put and pressed, but not solved. An occasional "happy ending," as in *The Oresteia* or *Crime and Punishment*, does not mean a full resolution. Though there may be intermittences, there is no ultimate discharge in the war. Although this suggests formlessness, as it must in contrast with certain types of religious orthodoxy or philosophical system, it would seem the essence of the tragic form. Surely it is more form than chaos. For out of all these tensions and paradoxes, these feelings, intuitions, insights, there emerges a fairly coherent attitude towards the universe and man. Tragedy makes certain distinguishable and characteristic affirmations, as well as denials, about (I) the cosmos and man's relation to it; (II) the nature of the individual and his relation to himself; (III) the individual in society.

(I) *The tragic cosmos.* In using the term cosmos to signify a theory of the universe and man's relation to it, I have, of course, made a statement about tragedy: that tragedy affirms a cosmos of which man is a meaningful part. To be sure, the characteristic locale of tragedy is not the empyrean. Tragedy is primarily humanistic. Its focus is an event in this world; it is uncommitted as to questions of ultimate destiny, and it is non-religious in its attitude toward revelation. But it speaks, however vaguely or variously, of an order that transcends time, space and matter.[6] It assumes man's connection with some supersensory or supernatural, or metaphysical being or principle, whether it be the Olympians, Job's Jehovah or the Christian God; Fate, Fortune's Wheel, the "elements" that Lear invoked, or Koestler's "oceanic sense," which comes in so tentatively (and pathetically) at the end of *Darkness at Noon*. The first thing that tragedy says about the cosmos is that, for good or ill, it is; and in this respect tragedy's theoretic opposite is naturalism or mechanism. Tragedy is

[6] Cf. Susan Taubes, "The Nature of Tragedy," *Review of Metaphysics*, December 1953.

witness (secondly) to the cosmic mystery, to the "wonderful" surrounding our lives; and in literature the opposite of tragedy is not only writing based upon naturalistic theory but also upon the four-square, "probable" [7] world of satire and rationalistic comedy. Finally, what distinguishes tragedy from other forms which bespeak this cosmic sense — for tragedy of course is not unique in this — is its peculiar and intense preoccupation with the evil in the universe, whatever it is in the stars that compels, harasses, and bears man down. Tragedy wrestles with the evil of the mystery — and the mystery of the evil. And the contest never ends.

But, paradoxically, its view of the cosmos is what sustains tragedy. Tragedy discerns a principle of goodness that coexists with the evil. This principle need be nothing so pat as The Moral Order, the "armies of unalterable law," and it is nothing so sure as the orthodox Christian God. It is nearer the folk sense that justice exists somewhere in the universe, or what Nietzsche describes as the orgiastic, mystical sense of oneness, of life as "indestructibly powerful and pleasurable." It may be a vision of some transcendent beauty and dignity against which the present evil may be seen as evil and the welter as welter. This is what keeps tragedy from giving up the whole human experiment, and in this respect its opposite is not comedy or satire but cynicism and nihilism, as in Schopenhauer's theory of resignation. The "problem of the good" plays as vital a part in tragedy as the "problem of evil." It provides the living tension without which tragedy ceases to exist.

Thus tragedy contemplates a universe in which man is not the measure of all things. It confronts a mystery. W. Macneile Dixon[8] pointed out that tragedy started as "an affair with the

[7] The "wonderful" and the "probable" are the basic categories in Albert Cook's distinction between tragedy and comedy. (*The Dark Voyage and the Golden Mean*, Cambridge, Mass., 1949, chap. I.)

[8] *Tragedy*, London, 1924. The extent of my indebtedness to this book, and to the other discussions of tragedy mentioned in this paper, is poorly indicated by such passing references as this. Since observations on tragedy and the theory of tragedy appear in innumerable discussions of particular authors, eras, and related critical problems, a complete list would be far too cumbersome. Among them would be, surely, the standard work of A. C. Bradley and Willard Farnham on Shakespearean tragedy; C. M. Bowra and

gods"; and the extent to which literature has become "secular-
ized and humanized," he wrote, is a sign of its departure from
(to use our present term) the tragic form. While agreeing with
him as to the tendency, one may question the wholesale verdict
which he implies. The affair with the gods has not, in the minds
of all our artists, been reduced to an affair with the social order,
or the environment, or the glands. But certainly where it becomes so, the muse of tragedy walks out; the universe loses its
mystery and (to invoke catharsis for a moment) its terror.

The terms "pessimism" and "optimism," in view of the universe as conceived in the tragic form, do not suggest adequate
categories, as Nietzsche first pointed out.[9] Tragedy contains
them both, goes beyond both, illuminates both, but comes to
no conclusion. Tragedy could, it is true, be called pessimistic in
its view of the evil in the universe as unremitting and irremedi-
able, the blight man was born for, the necessary condition of
existence. It is pessimistic, also, in its view of the overwhelming
proportion of evil to good and in its awareness of the mystery
of why this should be — the "unfathomable element" in which
Ahab foundered. But it is optimistic in what might be called its
vitalism, which is in some sense mystical, not earth-bound; in
its faith in a cosmic good; in its vision, however fleeting, of a
world in which all questions could be answered.

(II) *Tragic man.* If the tragic form asserts a cosmos, some
order behind the immediate disorder, what does it assert about
the nature of man, other than that he is a being capable of
cosmic affinities? What is tragic man as he lives and moves on
this earth? Can he be distinguished meaningfully from the man
of comedy, satire, epic, or lyric? How does he differ from "pa-

---

Cedric Whitman on Sophocles; W. L. Courtney (*The Idea of Tragedy*,
London, 1900); Maxwell Anderson, *The Essence of Tragedy*, Washington,
1939; Northrop Frye, "The Archetypes of Literature," *Kenyon Review*,
Winter, 1951; Moody Prior, *The Language of Tragedy*, N.Y., 1947; and
Herbert Weisinger, *Tragedy and the Paradox of the Fortunate Fall*, Michi-
gan State College Press, 1953, which makes rich use of the archaeological
and mythographic studies of the origin of tragedy (Cornford, Harrison, Mur-
ray). I am indebted, also, to my colleague Laurence Michel, for frequent
conversations and helpful criticism.
[9] See also Reinhold Niebuhr, *Beyond Tragedy*, London, 1938.

thetic man" or "religious man"? or from man as conceived by the materialistic psychologies? Tragic man shares some qualities, of course, with each of these. I shall stress differences in the appropriate contexts.

Like the cosmos which he views, tragic man is a paradox and a mystery. He is no child of God; yet he feels himself more than a child of earth. He is not the plaything of Fate, but he is not entirely free. He is "both creature and creator" (in Niebuhr's phrase) — "fatefully free and freely fated" (in George Schrader's). He recognizes "the fact of guilt" while cherishing the "dream of innocence" (Fiedler), and he never fully abandons either position. He is plagued by the ambiguity of his own nature and of the world he lives in. He is torn between the sense in common-sense (which is the norm of satire and rationalistic, or corrective, comedy) and his own uncommon sense. Aware of the just but irreconcilable claims within and without, he is conscious of the immorality of his own morality and suffers in the knowledge of his own recalcitrance.

The dynamic of this recalcitrance is pride. It sustains his belief, however humbled he may become by later experience, in his own freedom, in his innocence, and in his uncommon sense. Tragic man is man at his most prideful and independent, man glorying in his humantiy. Tragic pride, like everything else about tragedy, is ambiguous; it can be tainted with arrogance and have its petty side; but it is not to be equated with sin or weakness. The Greeks feared it when it threatened the gods or slipped into arrogance, but they honored it and even worshiped it in their heroes. It was the common folk, the chorus, who had no pride, or were "flawless." [10] The chorus invariably argue against pride, urging caution and moderation, because they know it leads to suffering; but tragedy as such does not prejudge it.

While many of these things, again, might be said of other than tragic man, it is in the peculiar nature of his suffering, and in his capacity for suffering, that his distinguishing quality lies. For instance (to ring changes on the Cartesian formula), tragic

[10] Cf. Arthur Miller, "Tragedy and the Common Man," *New York Times*, February 27th, 1949. [See p. 63.]

man would not define himself, like the man of corrective comedy or satire, "I think, therefore I am"; nor like the man of achievement (epic): "I act, or conquer, therefore I am": nor like the man of sensibility (lyric): "I feel, therefore I am": nor like the religious man: "I believe, therefore I am." Although he has all these qualities (of thought, achievement, sensibility, and belief) in various forms and degrees, the essence of his nature is brought out by suffering: "I suffer, I will to suffer, I learn by suffering; therefore I am." The classic statement, of course, is Aeschylus': "Wisdom comes alone through suffering" (Lattimore's translation); perhaps the most radical is Dostoevski's: "Suffering is the sole origin of consciousness." [11]

This is not to say that only tragic man suffers or that he who suffers is tragic. Saints and martyrs suffer and learn by suffering; Odysseus suffered and learned; Dante suffered and learned on his journey with Virgil. But tragic man, I think, is distinguishable from these others in the nature of his suffering as conditioned by its source and locus, in its characteristic course and consequences (that is, the ultimate disaster and the "knowledge" it leads to), and in his intense preoccupation with his own suffering.

But to consider these matters in turn and to illustrate them briefly:

I have already suggested the main sources and locus of tragic man's suffering. He suffers because he is more than usually sensitive to the "terrible disrelations" he sees about him and experiences in himself. He is more than usually aware of the mighty opposites in the universe and in man, of the gulf between desire and fulfilment, between what is and what should be. This kind of suffering is suffering on a high level, beyond the reach of the immature or brutish, and for ever closed to the extreme optimist, the extreme pessimist,[12] or the merely indifferent. It was Job on the ash-heap, the proto-type of tragic man, who was first struck by the incongruity between Jehovah's nature and His actions, between desert and reward in this life;

[11] *Notes from Underground*, tr. B. G. Guerney.
[12] Cf. William Van O'Connor, *Climates of Tragedy*, Baton Rouge, La., 1943.

and it was he who first asked, not so much for a release from physical suffering as a reasonable explanation of it. But above all, the source of tragic suffering is the sense, in the consciousness of tragic man, of simultaneous guilt and guiltlessness. Tillich called tragedy "a mixture of guilt and necessity." If tragic man could say, "I sinned, therefore I suffer" or "He (or They or God) sinned, therefore I suffer," his problem would be resolved, and the peculiar poignancy of his suffering would be removed. If he felt himself entirely free or entirely determined, he would cease to be tragic. But he is neither — he is, in short, a paradox and mystery, the "riddle of the world."

To draw further distinctions: The element of guilt in tragic suffering distinguishes it from the pathetic suffering of the guiltless and from the suffering of the sentimentalist's bleeding heart. On the other hand, tragic man's sense of fate, and of the mystery of fate, distinguishes his suffering from the suffering (which is little more than embarrassment) of the man of corrective comedy and satire. The suffering of the epic hero has little of the element of bafflement or enigma; it is not, characteristically, spiritual suffering. The Christian in his suffering can confess total guilt and look to the promise of redemption through grace.[13] The martyr seeks suffering, accepts it gladly, "glories in tribulation." Tragic man knows nothing of grace and never glories in his suffering. Although he may come to acquiesce in it partly and "learn" from it (a stage I shall discuss below), his characteristic mood is resentment and dogged endurance. He has not the stoic's patience, although this may be part of what he learns. Characteristically, he is restless, intense, probing and questioning the universe and his own soul (Job, Lear, Ahab). It is true that, from Greek tragedy to tragedy written in the Christian era (Shakespeare and beyond) emphasis shifts from the universe to the soul, from the cosmic to the psychological. But Prometheus had an inner life; Antigone, for all her composure, suffered an ultimate doubt; Oedipus suffered spiritually as he grew to understand the dark ambiguities in his own nature. And we should be mistaken if we tried to interpret

[13] Cf. Karl Jaspers, *Tragedy Is Not Enough,* tr. Reiche, Moore, Deutsch; Boston, 1952.

the divine powers in the plays of Shakespeare simply as "allegorical symbols for psychological realities." [14]

Tragic man, then, placed in a universe of irreconcilables, acting in a situation in which he is both innocent and guilty, and peculiarly sensitive to the "cursed spite" of his condition, suffers. What in the tragic view is the characteristic course of this suffering and what further aspects of tragic man are revealed by it? The tragic form develops, not only the partial outlines of a cosmology and psychology, but of an ethic.

(III) *Tragic man and society.* The tragic sufferer may now be viewed in his social and moral relationships. In the tragic world there are several alternatives. A man can default from the human condition — "Curse God and die" — and bring his suffering to an end: he can endure and be silent; he can turn cynic. Tragic man understands these alternatives, feels their attractions, but chooses a different way. Rising in his pride, he protests: he pits himself in some way against whatever, in the heavens above and in the earth beneath, seems to him to be wrong, oppressive, or personally thwarting. This is the hero's commitment, made early or late, but involving him necessarily in society and in action — with Prometheus and Antigone early, with Hamlet late. What to the orthodox mind would appear to be the wisdom or folly, the goodness or badness, of the commitment is not, in the beginning, the essence of the matter. In the first phase of his course of suffering, the hero's position may be anarchic, individual, romantic. Herein tragedy tests all norms — as, by contrast, satire,[15] comedy, or epic tend to confirm them. The commitment may even be expressed in what society knows as a crime, but, as with tragic pride (of which the commitment is in part the expression) tragedy does not prejudge it. Thus it is said that tragedy studies "the great offenders," and Dostoevski sought among criminals and outcasts for his greatest spiritual discoveries. But the commitment must grow in meaning to include the more-than-personal. Ultimately, and ideally, the tragic hero stands as universal man, speaking for all men. The tragic sufferer, emerging from his early stage of la-

[14] Susan Taubes, *op. cit.*, p. 196.
[15] Cf. Maynard Mack, "The Muse of Satire," *Yale Review*, Spring, 1952.

ment or rebellion (Job's opening speech; the first scenes of Prometheus; Lear's early bursts of temper), moves beyond the "intermittences" of his own heart and makes a "pact with the world that is unremitting and sealed." [16]

Since the commitment cannot lead in the direction of escape or compromise, it must involve head-on collision with the forces that would oppress or frustrate. Conscious of the ambiguities without and within, which are the source of his peculiar suffering, tragic man accepts the conflict. It is horrible to do it, he says, but it is more horrible to leave it undone. He is now in the main phase of his suffering — the "passion." [17]

In his passion he differs from the rebel, who would merely smash; or the romantic hero, who is not conscious of guilt; or the epic hero, who deals with emergencies rather than dilemmas. Odysseus and Aeneas, to be sure, face moral problems, but they proceed in a clear ethical light. Their social norms are secure. But the tragic hero sees a sudden, unexpected evil at the heart of things that infects all things. His secure and settled world has gone wrong, and he must oppose his own ambiguous nature against what he loves. Doing so involves total risk, as the chorus and his friends remind him. He may brood and pause, like Hamlet, or he may proceed with Ahab's fury; but proceed he must.

He proceeds, suffers, and in his suffering "learns." This is the phase of "perception." Although it often culminates in a single apocalyptic scene, a moment of "recognition," as in *Oedipus* and *Othello*, it need not be separate in time from the passion phase. Rather, perception is all that can be summed up in the spiritual and moral change that the hero undergoes from first to last and in the similar change wrought by his actions or by his example in those about him.

For the hero, perception may involve an all-but-complete

[16] Wallace Fowlie, "Swann and Hamlet: A Note on the Contemporary Hero," *Partisan Review*, 1942.
[17] Cf. Francis Fergusson, *The Idea of a Theater*, Princeton, N.J., 1949, chap. I, "The Tragic Rhythm of Action." Fergusson translates Kenneth Burke's formulation "Poiema, Pathema, Mathema" into "Purpose, Passion, Perception." (See *A Grammar of Motives*, pp. 38ff.) Cf. also Susan Taubes, *op. cit.*, p. 199.

transformation in character, as with Lear and Oedipus; or a gradual development in poise and self-mastery (Prometheus, Hamlet); or the softening and humanizing of the hard outlines of a character like Antigone's. It may appear in the hero's change from moody isolation and self-pity to a sense of his sharing in the general human condition, of his responsibility for it and to it. This was one stage in Lear's pilgrimage ("I have ta'en too little care of this") and as far as Dostoevski's Dmitri Karamazov ever got. In all the manifestations of this perception there is an element of Hamlet's "readiness," of an acceptance of destiny that is not merely resignation. At its most luminous it is Lear's and Oedipus' hard-won humility and new understanding of love. It may transform or merely inform, but a change there must be.

And it is more, of course, than merely a moral change, just as the hero's problem is always more than a moral one. His affair is still with the gods. In taking up arms against the ancient cosmic evil, he transcends the human situation, mediating between the human and the divine. It was Orestes' suffering that, in the end, made the heavens more just. In the defeat or death which is the usual lot of the tragic hero, he becomes a citizen of a larger city, still defiant but in a new mood, a "calm of mind," a partial acquiescence. Having at first resented his destiny, he has lived it out, found unexpected meanings in it, carried his case to a more-than-human tribunal. He sees his own destiny, and man's destiny, in its ultimate perspective.

But the perception which completes the tragic form is not dramatized solely through the hero's change, although his pilgrimage provides the traditional tragic structure.[18] The full

---

18 Indeed, it has been pointed out that, in an age when the symbol of the hero as the dominating center of the play seems to have lost its validity with artist and audience, the role is taken over by the artist himself, who is his own tragic hero. That is, "perception" is conveyed more generally, in the total movement of the piece and through all the parts. The "pact with the world" and the suffering are not objectified in a hero's ordeal but seem peculiarly the author's. This quality has been noted in Joyce's *Ulysses*; Berdiaev saw it in Dostoevski; Hardy, Conrad, Faulkner are examples that come to mind. At any rate, the distinction may be useful in determining matters of tone, although it is not clear cut, as distinctions in tone seldom are. But it is one way of pointing to the difference between the tragic tone and the

nature and extent of the new vision is measured also by what happens to the other figures in the total symbolic situation — to the hero's antagonists (King Creon, Claudius, Iago); to his opposites (the trimmers and hangers-on, the Osrics); to his approximates (Ismene, Horatio, Kent, the Chorus). Some he moves, some do not change at all. But his suffering must make a difference somewhere outside himself. After Antigone's death the community (even Creon) re-forms around her; the "new acquist" at the end of *Samson Agonistes* is the common note, also, at the end of the Shakespearean tragedies. For the lookers-on there is no sudden rending of the veil of clay, no triumphant assertion of The Moral Order. There has been suffering and disaster, ultimate and irredeemable loss, and there is promise of more to come. But all who are involved have been witness to new revelations about human existence, the evil of evil and the goodness of good. They are more "ready." The same old paradoxes and ambiguities remain, but for the moment they are transcended in the higher vision.

Tragedy and the Common Man

ARTHUR MILLER

IN THIS AGE few tragedies are written. It has often been held that the lack is due to a paucity of heroes among us, or else that modern man has had the blood drawn out of his organs of belief by the skepticism of science, and the heroic attack on life cannot feed on an attitude of reserve and circumspection. For one reason or another, we are often held to be below tragedy — or tragedy above us. The inevitable conclusion is, of course, that the tragic mode is archaic, fit only for the very highly placed, the

Olympian distance of Meredithian comedy, the harmony of the final phase of Dantesque comedy, or the ironic detachment of satire. Nietzsche spoke of the difference between the Dionysian (or tragic) artist and "the poet of the dramatized epos . . . the calm, unmoved embodiment of Contemplation, whose wide eyes see the picture before them" (*Birth of Tragedy* in *Works*, ed. O. Levy, Edinburgh and London, 1909, III, p. 96).

kings or the kingly, and where this admission is not made in so many words it is most often implied.

I believe that the common man is as apt a subject for tragedy in its highest sense as kings were. On the face of it this ought to be obvious in the light of modern psychiatry, which bases its analysis upon classific formulations, such as the Oedipus and Orestes complexes, for instance, which were enacted by royal beings, but which apply to everyone in similar emotional situations.

More simply, when the question of tragedy in art is not at issue, we never hesitate to attribute to the well-placed and the exalted the very same mental processes as the lowly. And finally, if the exaltation of tragic action were truly a property of the high-bred character alone, it is inconceivable that the mass of mankind should cherish tragedy above all other forms, let alone be capable of understanding it.

As a general rule, to which there may be exceptions unknown to me, I think the tragic feeling is evoked in us when we are in the presence of a character who is ready to lay down his life, if need be, to secure one thing — his sense of personal dignity. From Orestes to Hamlet, Medea to Macbeth, the underlying struggle is that of the individual attempting to gain his "rightful" position in his society.

Sometimes he is one who has been displaced from it, sometimes one who seeks to attain it for the first time, but the fateful wound from which the inevitable events spiral is the wound of indignity, and its dominant force is indignation. Tragedy, then, is the consequence of a man's total compulsion to evaluate himself justly.

In the sense of having been initiated by the hero himself, the tale always reveals what has been called his "tragic flaw," a failing that is not peculiar to grand or elevated characters. Nor is it necessarily a weakness. The flaw, or crack in the character, is really nothing — and need be nothing — but his inherent unwillingness to remain passive in the face of what he conceives to be a challenge to his dignity, his image of his rightful status. Only the passive, only those who accept their lot without active retaliation, are "flawless." Most of us are in that category.

But there are among us today, as there always have been, those who act against the scheme of things that degrades them, and in the process of action, everything we have accepted out of fear or insensitivity or ignorance is shaken before us and examined, and from this total onslaught by an individual against the seemingly stable cosmos surrounding us — from this total examination of the "unchangeable" environment — comes the terror and the fear that is classically associated with tragedy.

More important, from this total questioning of what has been previously unquestioned, we learn. And such a process is not beyond the common man. In revolutions around the world, these past thirty years, he has demonstrated again and again this inner dynamic of all tragedy.

Insistence upon the rank of the tragic hero, or the so-called nobility of his character, is really but a clinging to the outward forms of tragedy. If rank or nobility of character was indispensable, then it would follow that the problems of those with rank were the particular problems of tragedy. But surely the right of one monarch to capture the domain from another no longer raises our passions, nor are our concepts of justice what they were to the mind of an Elizabethan king.

The quality in such plays that does shake us, however, derives from the underlying fear of being displaced, the disaster inherent in being torn away from our chosen image of what and who we are in this world. Among us today this fear is as strong, and perhaps stronger, than it ever was. In fact, it is the common man who knows this fear best.

Now, if it is true that tragedy is the consequence of a man's total compulsion to evaluate himself justly, his destruction in the attempt posits a wrong or an evil in his environment. And this is precisely the morality of tragedy and its lesson. The discovery of the moral law, which is what the enlightenment of tragedy consists of, is not the discovery of some abstract or metaphysical quantity.

The tragic right is a condition of life, a condition in which the human personality is able to flower and realize itself. The wrong is the condition which suppresses man, perverts the flowing out of his love and creative instinct. Tragedy enlightens — and it must, in that it points the heroic finger at the enemy of man's freedom. The thrust for freedom is the quality in tragedy which exalts. The revolutionary questioning of the stable environment is what terrifies. In no way is the common man debarred from such thoughts or such actions.

Seen in this light, our lack of tragedy may be partially accounted for by the turn which modern literature has taken toward the purely psychiatric view of life, or the purely sociological. If all our miseries, our indignities, are born and bred within our minds, then all action, let alone the heroic action, is obviously impossible.

And if society alone is responsible for the cramping of our lives, then the protagonist must needs be so pure and faultless as to force us to deny his validity as a character. From neither of these views can tragedy derive, simply because neither represents a balanced concept of life. Above all else, tragedy requires the finest appreciation by the writer of cause and effect.

No tragedy can therefore come about when its author fears to question absolutely everything, when he regards any institution, habit or custom as being either everlasting, immutable or inevitable. In the tragic view the need of man to wholly realize himself is the only fixed star, and whatever it is that hedges his nature and lowers it is ripe for attack and examination. Which is not to say that tragedy must preach revolution.

The Greeks could probe the very heavenly origin of their ways and return to confirm the rightness of laws. And Job could face God in anger, demanding his right, and end in submission. But for a moment everything is in suspension, nothing is accepted, and in this stretching and tearing apart of the cosmos, in the very action of so doing, the character gains "size," the tragic stature which is spuriously attached to the royal or the high born in our minds. The commonest of men may take on that stature to the extent of his willingness to throw all he has into the contest, the battle to secure his rightful place in his world.

There is a misconception of tragedy with which I have been struck in review after review, and in many conversations with writers and readers alike. It is the idea that tragedy is of necessity allied to pessimism. Even the dictionary says nothing more about the word than that it means a story with a sad or unhappy ending. This impression is so firmly fixed that I almost hesitate to claim that in truth tragedy implies more optimism in its author than does comedy, and that its final result ought to be the reinforcement of the onlooker's brightest opinions of the human animal.

For, if it is true to say that in essence the tragic hero is intent upon claiming his whole due as a personality, and if this struggle must be total and without reservation, then it automatically demonstrates the indestructible will of man to achieve his humanity.

The possibility of victory must be there in tragedy. Where pathos rules, where pathos is finally derived, a character has fought a battle he could not possibly have won. The pathetic is achieved when the protagonist is, by virtue of his witlessness, his insensitivity, or the very air he gives off, incapable of grappling with a much superior force.

Pathos truly is the mode for the pessimist. But tragedy requires a nicer balance between what is possible and what is impossible. And it is curious, although edifying, that the plays we revere, century after century, are the tragedies. In them, and in them alone, lies the belief — optimistic, if you will — in the perfectibility of man.

It is time, I think, that we who are without kings, took up this bright thread of our history and followed it to the only place it can possibly lead in our time — the heart and spirit of the average man.

Comedy

CHRISTOPHER FRY

A FRIEND once told me that when he was under the influence of ether he dreamed he was turning over the pages of a great book, in which he knew he would find, on the last page, the meaning of life. The pages of the book were alternately tragic

and comic, and he turned page after page, his excitement
growing, not only because he was approaching the answer but
because he couldn't know, until he arrived, on which side of
the book the final page would be. At last it came: the universe
opened up to him in a hundred words: and they were uproar-
iously funny. He came back to consciousness crying with laughter, remembering everything. He opened his lips to speak. It
was then that the great and comic answer plunged back out of
his reach.

If I had to draw a picture of the person of Comedy it is so
I should like to draw it: the tears of laughter running down the
face, one hand still lying on the tragic page which so nearly
contained the answer, the lips about to frame the great revelation, only to find it had gone as disconcertingly as a chair
twitched away when we went to sit down. Comedy is an escape, not from truth but from despair: a narrow escape into
faith. It believes in a universal cause for delight, even though
knowledge of the cause is always twitched away from under us,
which leaves us to rest on our own buoyancy. In tragedy every
moment is eternity; in comedy eternity is a moment. In tragedy
we suffer pain; in comedy pain is a fool, suffered gladly.

Charles Williams once said to me — indeed it was the last
thing he said to me: he died not long after: and it was shouted
from the tailboard of a moving bus, over the heads of pedes-
trians and bicyclists outside the Midland Station, Oxford —
"When we're dead we shall have the sensation of having enjoyed life altogether, whatever has happened to us." The distance between us widened, and he leaned out into the space so
that his voice should reach me: "Even if we've been murdered,
what a pleasure to have been capable of it!"; and, having spoken
the words for comedy, away he went like the revelation which
almost came out of the ether.

He was not at all saying that everything is for the best in the
best of all possible worlds. He was saying — or so it seems to me
— that there is an angle of experience where the dark is dis-
tilled into light: either here or hereafter, in or out of time:
where our tragic fate finds itself with perfect pitch, and goes
straight to the key which creation was composed in. And

comedy senses and reaches out to this experience. It says, in effect, that, groaning as we may be, we move in the figure of a dance, and, so moving, we trace the outline of the mystery.

Laughter did not come by chance, but how or why it came is beyond comprehension, unless we think of it as a kind of perception. The human animal, beginning to feel his spiritual inches, broke in on to an unfamiliar tension of life, where laughter became inevitable. But how? Could he, in his first unlaughing condition, have contrived a comic view of life and then developed the strange rib-shaking response? Or is it not more likely that when he was able to grasp the tragic nature of time he was of a stature to sense its comic nature also; and, by the experience of tragedy and the intuition of comedy, to make his difficult way? The difference between tragedy and comedy is the difference between experience and intuition. In the experience we strive against every condition of our animal life: against death, against the frustration of ambition, against the instability of human love. In the intuition we trust the arduous eccentricities we're born to, and see the oddness of a creature who has never got acclimatized to being created. Laughter inclines me to know that man is essential spirit; his body, with its functions and accidents and frustrations, is endlessly quaint and remarkable to him; and though comedy accepts our position in time, it barely accepts our posture in space.

The bridge by which we cross from tragedy to comedy and back again is precarious and narrow. We find ourselves in one or the other by the turn of a thought; a turn such as we make when we turn from speaking to listening. I know that when I set about writing a comedy the idea presents itself to me first of all as tragedy. The characters press on to the theme with all their divisions and perplexities heavy about them; they are already entered for the race to doom, and good and evil are an infernal tangle skinning the fingers that try to unravel them. If the characters were not qualified for tragedy there would be no comedy, and to some extent I have to cross the one before I can light on the other. In a century less flayed and quivering we might reach it more directly; but not now, unless every word we write is going to mock us. A bridge has to be crossed, a thought has to be turned. Somehow the characters have to un-mortify themselves: to affirm life and assimilate death and persevere in joy. Their hearts must be as determined as the phoenix; what burns must also light and renew: not by a vulnerable optimism but by a hard-won maturity of delight, by the intuition of comedy, an active patience declaring the solvency of good. The Book of Job is the great reservoir of comedy. "But there is a spirit in man. . . . Fair weather cometh out of the north. . . . The blessing of him that was ready to perish came upon me: and I caused the widow's heart to sing for joy."

I have come, you may think, to the verge of saying that comedy is greater than tragedy. On the verge I stand and go no further. Tragedy's experience hammers against the mystery to make a breach which would admit the whole triumphant answer. Intuition has no such potential. But there are times in the state of man when comedy has a special worth, and the present is one of them: a time when the loudest faith has been faith in a trampling materialism, when literature has been thought un-realistic which did not mark and remark our poverty and doom. Joy (of a kind) has been all on the devil's side, and one of the necessities of our time is to redeem it. If not, we are in a poor sort to meet the circumstances, the circumstances being the contention of death with life, which is to say evil with good, which is to say desolation with delight. Laughter may seem to be only like an exhalation of air, but out of that air we came; in the beginning we inhaled it; it is a truth, not a fantasy, a truth voluble of good which comedy stoutly maintains.

The Structure of Comedy

NORTHROP FRYE

Dramatic comedy, from which fictional comedy is mainly de-scended, has been remarkably tenacious of its structural princi-ples and character types. Bernard Shaw remarked that a comic dramatist could get a reputation for daring originality by steal-ing his method from Molière and his characters from Dickens: if we were to read Menander and Aristophanes for Molière and Dickens the statement would be hardly less true, at least as a general principle. The earliest extant European comedy, Aristo-phanes' *The Acharnians*, contains the *miles gloriosus* or military braggart who is still going strong in Chaplin's *Great Dictator*; the Joxer Daly of O'Casey's *Juno and the Paycock* has the same character and dramatic function as the parasites of twenty-five hundred years ago, and the audiences of vaudeville, comic strips, and television programs still laugh at the jokes that were de-clared to be outworn at the opening of *The Frogs*.

The plot structure of Greek New Comedy, as transmitted by Plautus and Terence, in itself less a form than a formula, has become the basis for most comedy, especially in its more highly conventionalized dramatic form, down to our own day. It will be most convenient to work out the theory of comic construction from drama, using illustrations from fiction only incidentally. What normally happens is that a young man wants a young woman, that his desire is resisted by some opposition, usually paternal, and that near the end of the play some twist in the plot enables the hero to have his will. In this simple pattern there are several complex elements. In the first place, the move-ment of comedy is usually a movement from one kind of society to another. At the beginning of the play the obstructing charac-ters are in charge of the play's society, and the audience recog-nizes that they are usurpers. At the end of the play the device in the plot that brings hero and heroine together causes a new society to crystallize around the hero, and the moment when this crystallization occurs is the point of resolution in the action, the comic discovery, *anagnorisis* or *cognitio*.

The appearance of this new society is frequently signalized by some kind of party or festival ritual, which either appears at the end of the play or is assumed to take place immediately after-ward. Weddings are most common, and sometimes so many of them occur, as in the quadruple wedding at the end of *As You Like It*, that they suggest also the wholesale pairing off that takes place in a dance, which is another common conclusion, and the normal one for the masque. The banquet at the end of *The Taming of the Shrew* has an ancestry that goes back to Greek Middle Comedy; in Plautus the audience is sometimes jocosely invited to an imaginary banquet afterwards; Old Comedy, like the modern Christmas pantomime, was more generous, and occasionally threw bits of food to the audience. As the final society reached by comedy is the one that the audience has recognized all along to be the proper and desirable state of affairs, an act of communion with the audience is in order. Tragic actors expect to be applauded as well as comic ones, but nevertheless the word "plaudite" at the end of a Roman comedy, the invitation to the audience to form part of the comic society, would seem rather out of place at the end of a tragedy. The resolution of comedy comes, so to speak, from the audience's side of the stage; in a tragedy it comes from some mysterious world on the opposite side. In the movie, where darkness permits a more erotically oriented audience, the plot usually moves toward an act which, like death in Greek tragedy, takes place offstage, and is symbolized by a closing embrace.

The obstacles to the hero's desire, then, form the action of the comedy, and the overcoming of them the comic resolution. The obstacles are usually parental, hence comedy often turns on a clash between a son's and a father's will. Thus the comic dramatist as a rule writes for the younger men in his audience, and the older members of almost any society are apt to feel that comedy has something subversive about it. This is certainly one element in the social persecution of drama, which is not peculiar to Puritans or even Christians, as Terence in pagan Rome met much the same kind of social opposition that Ben Jonson did. There is one scene in Plautus where a son and father are making love to the same courtesan, and the son asks his father pointedly if he really does love mother. One has to see this scene against the background of Roman family life to understand its importance as psychological release. Even in Shakespeare there are startling outbreaks of baiting older men, and in contemporary movies the triumph of youth is so relentless that the moviemakers find some difficulty in getting anyone over the age of seventeen into their audiences.

The opponent to the hero's wishes, when not the father, is generally someone who partakes of the father's closer relation to established society: that is, a rival with less youth and more money. In Plautus and Terence he is usually either the pimp who owns the girl, or a wandering soldier with a supply of ready cash. The fury with which these characters are baited and exploded from the stage shows that they are father-surrogates, and even if they were not, they would still be usurpers, and their claim to possess the girl must be shown up as somehow fraudulent. They are, in short, imposters, and the extent to which they have real power implies some criticism of the society that allows them their power. In Plautus and Terence this criticism seldom goes beyond the immorality of brothels and professional harlots, but in Rennaissance dramatists, including Jonson, there is some sharp observation of the rising power of money and the sort of ruling class it is building up.

The tendency of comedy is to include as many people as possible in its final society: the blocking characters are more often reconciled or converted than simply repudiated. Comedy often includes a scapegoat ritual of expulsion which gets rid of some irreconcilable character, but exposure and disgrace make for pathos, or even tragedy. *The Merchant of Venice* seems almost an experiment in coming as close as possible to upsetting the comic balance. If the dramatic role of Shylock is ever so slightly exaggerated, as it generally is when the leading actor of the company takes the part, it is upset, and the play becomes the tragedy of the Jew of Venice with a comic epilogue. *Volpone* ends with a great bustle of sentences to penal servitude and the galleys, and one feels that the deliverance of society hardly needs so much hard labor; but then *Volpone* is exceptional in being a kind of comic imitation of a tragedy, with the point of Volpone's *hybris* carefully marked.

The principle of conversion becomes clearer with characters whose chief function is the amusing of the audience. The original *miles gloriosus* in Plautus is a son of Jove and Venus who has killed an elephant with his fist and seven thousand men in one day's fighting. In other words, he is trying to put on a good show: the exuberance of his boasting helps to put the play over.

The convention says that the braggart must be exposed, ridiculed, swindled, and beaten. But why should a professional dramatist, of all people, want so to harry a character who is putting on a good show — *his* show at that? When we find Falstaff invited to the final feast in *The Merry Wives*, Caliban reprieved, attempts made to mollify Malvolio, and Angelo and Parolles allowed to live down their disgrace, we are seeing a fundamental principle of comedy at work. The tendency of the comic society to include rather than exclude is the reason for the traditional importance of the parasite, who has no business to be at the final festival but is nevertheless there. The word "grace," with all its Renaissance overtones from the graceful courtier of Castiglione to the gracious God of Christianity, is a most important thematic word in Shakespearean comedy.

The action of comedy in moving from one social center to another is not unlike the action of a lawsuit, in which plaintiff and defendant construct different versions of the same situation, one finally being judged as real and the other as illusory. This resemblance of the rhetoric of comedy to the rhetoric of jurisprudence has been recognized from earliest times. A little pamphlet called the *Tractatus Coislinianus*, closely related to Aristotle's *Poetics*, which sets down all the essential facts about comedy in about a page and a half, divides the *dianoia* [theme, meaning] of comedy into two parts, opinion (*pistis*) and proof (*gnosis*). These correspond roughly to the usurping and the desirable societies respectively. Proofs (i.e., the means of bringing about the happier society) are subdivided into oaths, compacts, witnesses, ordeals (or tortures), and laws — in other words the five forms of material proof in law cases listed in the *Rhetoric*. We notice how often the action of a Shakespearean comedy begins with some absurd, cruel, or irrational law: the law of killing Syracusans in the *Comedy of Errors*, the law of compulsory marriage in *A Midsummer Night's Dream*, the law that confirms Shylock's bond, the attempts of Angelo to legislate people into righteousness, and the like, which the action of the comedy then evades or breaks. Compacts are as a rule the conspiracies formed by the hero's society; witnesses, such as overhearers of conversations or people with special knowledge (like the hero's old nurse with her retentive memory for birthmarks), are the commonest devices for bringing about the comic discovery. Ordeals (*basanoi*) are usually tests or touchstones of the hero's character: the Greek word also means touchstones, and seems to be echoed in Shakespeare's Bassanio whose ordeal it is to make a judgment on the worth of metals.

There are two ways of developing the form of comedy: one is to throw the main emphasis on the blocking characters; the other is to throw it forward on the scenes of discovery and reconciliation. One is the general tendency of comic irony, satire, realism, and studies of manners; the other is the tendency of Shakespearean and other types of romantic comedy. In the comedy of manners the main ethical interest falls as a rule on the blocking characters. The technical hero and heroine are not often very interesting people: the *adulescentes* of Plautus and Terence are all alike, as hard to tell apart in the dark as Demetrius and Lysander, who may be parodies of them. Generally the hero's character has the neutrality that enables him to represent a wish-fulfilment. It is very different with the miserly or ferocious parent, the boastful or foppish rival, or the other characters who stand in the way of the action. In Molière we have a simple but fully tested formula in which the ethical interest is focused on a single blocking character, a heavy father, a miser, a misanthrope, a hypocrite, or a hypochrondiac. These are the figures that we remember, and the plays are usually named after them, but we can seldom remember all the Valentins and Angeliques who wriggle out of their clutches. In *The Merry Wives* the technical hero, a man named Fenton, has only a bit part, and this play has picked up a hint or two from Plautus' *Casina*, where the hero and heroine are not even brought on the stage at all. Fictional comedy, especially Dickens, often follows the same practice of grouping its interesting characters around a somewhat dullish pair of technical leads. Even Tom Jones, though far more fully realized, is still deliberately associated, as his commonplace name indicates, with the conventional and typical.

Comedy usually moves toward a happy ending, and the

normal response of the audience to a happy ending is "this should be," which sounds like a moral judgment. So it is, except that it is not moral in the restricted sense, but social. Its opposite is not the villainous but the absurd, and comedy finds the virtues of Malvolio as absurd as the vices of Angelo. Molière's misanthrope, being committed to sincerity, which is a virtue, is morally in a strong position, but the audience soon realizes that his friend Philinte, who is ready to lie quite cheerfully in order to enable other people to preserve their self-respect, is the more genuinely sincere of the two. It is of course quite possible to have a moral comedy, but the result is often the kind of melodrama that we have described as comedy without humor, and which achieves its happy ending with a self-righteous tone that most comedy avoids. It is hardly possible to imagine a drama without conflict, and it is hardly possible to imagine a conflict without some kind of enmity. But just as love, including sexual love, is a very different thing from lust, so enmity is a very different thing from hatred. In tragedy, of course, enmity almost always includes hatred; comedy is different, and one feels that the social judgment against the absurd is closer to the comic norm than the moral judgment against the wicked.

The question then arises of what makes the blocking character absurd. Ben Jonson explained this by his theory of the "humor," the character dominated by what Pope calls a ruling passion. The humor's dramatic function is to express a state of what might be called ritual bondage. He is obsessed by his humor, and his function in the play is primarily to repeat his obsession. A sick man is not a humor, but a hypochrondiac is, because, *qua* hypochrondiac, he can never admit to good health, and can never do anything inconsistent with the role that he has prescribed for himself. A miser can do and say nothing that is not connected with the hiding of gold or saving of money. In *The Silent Woman*, Jonson's nearest approach to Molière's type of construction, the whole action recedes from the humor of Morose, whose determination to eliminate noise from his life produces so loquacious a comic action.

The principle of the humor is the principle that unincremental repetition, the literary imitation of ritual bondage, is funny. In a tragedy — *Oedipus Tyrannus* is the stock example — repetition leads logically to catastrophe. Repetition overdone or not going anywhere belongs to comedy, for laughter is partly a reflex, and like other reflexes it can be conditioned by a simple repeated pattern. In Synge's *Riders to the Sea* a mother, after losing her husband and five sons at sea, finally loses her last son, and the result is a very beautiful and moving play. But if it had been a full-length tragedy plodding glumly through the seven drownings one after another, the audience would have been helpless with unsympathetic laughter long before it was over. The principle of repetition as the basis of humor both in Jonson's sense and in ours is well known to the creators of comic strips, in which a character is established as a parasite, a glutton (often confined to one dish), or a shrew, and who begins to be funny after the point has been made every day for several months. Continuous comic radio programs, too, are much more amusing to habitués than to neophytes. The girth of Falstaff and the hallucinations of Quixote are based on much the same comic laws. Mr. E. M. Forster speaks with disdain of Dickens' Mrs. Micawber, who never says anything except that she will never desert Mr. Micawber: a strong contrast is marked here between the refined writer too finicky for popular formulas, and the major one who exploits them ruthlessly.

The humor in comedy is usually someone with a good deal of social prestige and power, who is able to force much of the play's society into line with his obsession. Thus the humor is intimately connected with the theme of the absurd or irrational law that the action of comedy moves toward breaking. It is significant that the central character of our earliest humor comedy, *The Wasps*, is obsessed by law cases: Shylock, too, unites a craving for the law with the humor of revenge. Often the absurd law appears as a whim of a bemused tyrant whose will is law, like Leontes or the humorous Duke Frederick in Shakespeare, who makes some arbitrary decision or rash promise: here law is replaced by "oath," also mentioned in the

Tractatus. Or it may take the form of a sham Utopia, a society of ritual bondage constructed by an act of humorous or pedantic will, like the academic retreat in *Love's Labor's Lost.* This theme is also as old as Aristophanes, whose parodies of Platonic social schemes in *The Birds* and *Ecclesiazusae* deal with it.

The society emerging at the conclusion of comedy represents, by contrast, a kind of moral norm, or pragmatically free society. Its ideals are seldom defined or formulated: definition and formulation belong to the humors, who want predictable activity. We are simply given to understand that the newly-married couple will live happily ever after, or that at any rate they will get along in a relatively unhumorous and clear-sighted manner. That is one reason why the character of the successful hero is so often left undeveloped: his real life begins at the end of the play, and we have to believe him to be potentially a more interesting character than he appears to be. In Terence's *Adelphoi,* Demea, a harsh father, is contrasted with his brother Micio, who is indulgent. Micio being more liberal, he leads the way to the comic resolution, and converts Demea, but then Demea points out the indolence inspiring a good deal of Micio's liberality, and releases him from a complementary humorous bondage.

Thus the movement from *pistis* to *gnosis,* from a society controlled by habit, ritual bondage, arbitrary law and the older characters to a society controlled by youth and pragmatic freedom is fundamentally, as the Greek words suggest, a movement from illusion to reality. Illusion is whatever is fixed or definable, and reality is best understood as its negation: whatever reality is, it's not *that.* Hence the importance of the theme of creating and dispelling illusion in comedy: the illusions caused by disguise, obsession, hypocrisy, or unknown parentage.

The comic ending is generally manipulated by a twist in the plot. In Roman comedy the heroine, who is usually a slave or courtesan, turns out to be the daughter of somebody respectable, so that the hero can marry her without loss of face. The *cognitio* in comedy, in which the characters find out who their relatives are, and who is left of the opposite sex not a relative, and hence available for marriage, is one of the features of comedy that have never changed much: *The Confidential Clerk* indicates that it still holds the attention of dramatists. There is a brilliant parody of a *cognitio* at the end of *Major Barbara* (the fact that the hero of this play is a professor of Greek perhaps indicates an unusual affinity to the conventions of Euripides and Menander), where Undershaft is enabled to break the rule that he cannot appoint his son-in-law as successor by the fact that the son-in-law's own father married his deceased wife's sister in Australia, so that the son-in-law is his own first cousin as well as himself. It sounds complicated, but the plots of comedy often are complicated because there is something inherently absurd about complications. As the main character interest in comedy is so often focused on the defeated characters, comedy regularly illustrates a victory of arbitrary plot over consistency of character. Thus, in striking contrast to tragedy, there can hardly be such a thing as inevitable comedy, as far as the action of the individual play is concerned. That is, we may know that the convention of comedy will make some kind of happy ending inevitable, but still for each play the dramatist must produce a distinctive "gimmick" or "weenie," to use two disrespectful Hollywood synonyms for *anagnorisis*. Happy endings do not impress us as true, but as desirable, and they are brought about by manipulation. The watcher of death and tragedy has nothing to do but sit and wait for the inevitable end; but something gets born at the end of comedy, and the watcher of birth is a member of a busy society.

The manipulation of plot does not always involve metamorphosis of character, but there is no violation of comic decorum when it does. Unlikely conversions, miraculous transformations, and providential assistance are inseparable from comedy. Further, whatever emerges is supposed to be there for good: if the curmudgeon becomes lovable, we understand that he will not immediately relapse again into his ritual habit. Civilizations which stress the desirable rather than the real, and the religious as opposed to the scientific perspective, think of drama almost entirely in terms of comedy. In the classical drama of India, we are told, the tragic ending was regarded as bad taste, much as the manipulated endings of comedy are regarded as bad taste by novelists interested in ironic realism.

The total *mythos* [narrative] of comedy, only a small part of which is ordinarily presented, has regularly what in music is called a ternary form: the hero's society rebels against the society of the *senex* [old man] and triumphs, but the hero's society is a Saturnalia, a reversal of social standards which recalls a golden age in the past before the main action of the play begins. Thus we have a stable and harmonious order disrupted by folly, obsession, forgetfulness, "pride and prejudice," or events not understood by the characters themselves, and then restored. Often there is a benevolent grandfather, so to speak, who overrules the action set up by the blocking humor and so links the first and third parts. An example is Mr. Burchell, the disguised uncle of the wicked squire, in *The Vicar of Wakefield*. A very long play, such as the Indian *Sakuntala*, may present all three phases; a very intricate one, such as many of Menander's evidently were, may indicate their outlines. But of course very often the first phase is not given at all: the audience simply understands an ideal state of affairs which it knows to be better than what is revealed in the play, and which it recognizes as like that to which the action leads. This ternary action is, ritually, like a contest of summer and winter in which winter occupies the middle action; psychologically, it is like the removal of a neurosis or blocking point and the restoring of an unbroken current of energy and memory.

The American Realist Playwrights

MARY McCARTHY

As soon as this title is announced for a lecture or an article, a question pops up: who are they? Is there, as is assumed

abroad, a school of realists in the American theater or is this
notion a critical figment? The question is legitimate and will
remain, I hope, in the air long after I have finished. Nevertheless, for purposes of discussion, I am going to take for granted
that there is such a group, if not a school, and name its members: Arthur Miller, Tennessee Williams, William Inge, Paddy
Chayefsky, the Elmer Rice of *Street Scene*. Behind them, casting them in the shadow, stands the great figure of O'Neill, and
opposite them, making them seem more homogeneous, are
writers like George Kelly, Wilder, Odets, Saroyan. Their coun-
terparts in the novel are Dreiser, Sherwood Anderson, James T.
Farrell, the early Thomas Wolfe — which illustrates, by the
way, the backwardness of the theater in comparison with the
novel. The theater seems to be chronically twenty years behind, regardless of realism, as the relation of Beckett to Joyce,
for example, shows. The theater feeds on the novel; never
vice versa: think of the hundreds of dramatizations of novels,
and then try to think of a book that was "novelized" from a
play. There is not even a word for it. The only actual case I
can call to mind is *The Other House* by Henry James — a
minor novel he salvaged from a play of his own that failed. To
return to the main subject, one characteristic of American
realism in the theater is that none of its practitioners currently
— except Chayefsky — wants to call himself a realist. Tennessee Williams is known to his admirers as a "poetic realist,"
while Arthur Miller declares that he is an exponent of the
"social play" and identifies himself with the Greek playwrights,
whom he describes as social playwrights also. This delusion was
dramatized, if that is the word, in A *View from the Bridge*.

The fact that hardly a one of these playwrights cares to be
regarded as a realist without some qualifying or mitigating ad-
jective's being attached to the term invites a definition of
realism. What does it mean in common parlance? I have looked
the word "realist" up in the Oxford English Dictionary. Here
is what they say: ". . . In reference to art and literature sometimes used as a term of commendation, when precision and
vividness of detail are regarded as a merit, and sometimes un-
favorably contrasted with idealized description or representa-

tion. In recent use it has often been used with the implication that the details are of an unpleasant or sordid character." This strikes me as a very fair account of the historical fate of the notion of realism, but I shall try to particularize a little, in the hope of finding out why and how this happened. And I shall not be condemning realism but only noting what people seem to think it is.

When we say that a novel or a play is realistic, we mean, certainly, that it gives a picture of ordinary life. Its characters will be drawn from the middle class, the lower middle class, occasionally the working class. You cannot write realistic drama about upper-class life; at least, no one ever has. Aristocracy does not lend itself to realistic treatment, but to one or another kind of stylization: romantic drama, romantic comedy, comedy of manners, satire, tragedy. This fact in itself is a realistic criticism of the aristocratic idea, which cannot afford, apparently, to live in the glass house of the realistic stage. Kings and noble men, said Aristotle, are the protagonists of tragedy — not women or slaves. The same is true of nobility of character or intellect. The exceptional man, whether he be Oedipus or King Lear or one of the romantic revolutionary heroes of Hugo or Musset, is fitted to be the protagonist of a tragedy, but just this tragic fitness disqualifies him from taking a leading role in a realist drama. Such figures as Othello or Hernani can never be the subject of realistic treatment, unless it is with the object of deflating them, showing how *ordinary* — petty or squalid — they are. But then the hero is no longer Othello but an impostor posing as Othello. Cut down to size, he is just like everybody else but worse, because he is a fraud into the bargain.

This abrupt foreshortening is why realistic treatment of upper-class life always takes the harsh plunge into satire. No man is a hero to his valet, and Beaumarchais' Figaro is the spokesman of social satire — not of realism; his personal and private realism turns his master into a clown. Realism deals with ordinary men and women or, in extreme forms, with subordinary men, men on the level of beasts or of blind conditioned reflexes (*La Bête Humaine, The Hairy Ape*). This tendency is

usually identified with naturalism, but I am regarding naturalism as simply a variety of realism.

Realism, historically, is associated with two relatively modern
inventions, *i.e.*, with journalism and with photography. "Photographic realism" is a pejorative term, and enemies of realistic
literature often dismissed it as "no more than journalism,"
implying that journalism was a sordid, seamy affair — a daily
photographic close-up, as it were, of the clogged pores of society. The author as sheer observer likened himself to a camera
(Dos Passos, Christopher Isherwood, Wright Morris), and in-
sofar as the realistic novel was vowed to be a reflector of ordinary life, the newspapers inevitably became a prime source
of material. Newspaper accounts impressed the nineteenth
century with their quality of "stark objectivity," and newspapers, which appeared every day, seemed to be the reposi-
tories of everydayness and to give a multiple image of the little
tragedies and vicissitudes of daily life. In America, in the early
part of this century, the realistic novel was a partner of what
was called "muckraking" journalism, and both were linked with
populism and crusades for political reform.

Hence, perhaps, in part, the unsavory associations in common
speech of the word "realistic," even when applied in nonliterary
contexts. Take the phrase "a realistic decision." If someone
tells you he is going to make "a realistic decision," you immediately understand that he has resolved to do something bad.
The same with "Realpolitik." A "realistic politics" is a euphe-
mism for a politics of harsh opportunism; if you hear someone
say that it is time for a government to follow a realistic line,
you can interpret this as meaning that it is time for principles to
be abandoned. A politician or a political thinker who calls himself a political realist is usually boasting that he sees politics,
so to speak, in the raw; he is generally a proclaimed cynic and
pessimist who makes it his business to look behind words and
fine speeches for the motive. This motive is always low.

Whatever the field, whenever you hear that a subject is to be
treated "realistically," you expect that its unpleasant aspects
are to be brought forward. So it is with the play and the novel.
A delicate play like Turgenev's *A Month in the Country*,

though perfectly truthful to life, seems deficient in realism in comparison with the stronger medicine of Gorki's *The Lower Depths*. This is true of Turgenev's novels as well and of such English writers as Mrs. Gaskell. And of the peaceful parts of *War and Peace*. Ordinary life treated in its uneventful aspects tends to turn into an idyl. We think of Turgenev and Mrs. Gaskell almost as pastoral writers, despite the fact that their faithful sketches have nothing in common with the artificial convention of the true pastoral. We suspect that there is something Arcadian here — something "unrealistic."

If realism deals with the ordinary man embedded in ordinary life, which for the most part is uneventful, what then is the criterion that makes us forget Turgenev or Mrs. Gaskell when we name off the realists? I think it is this: what we call realism, and particularly dramatic realism, tends to single out the ordinary man at the moment he might get into the newspaper. The criterion, in other words, is drawn from journalism. The ordinary man must become "news" before he qualifies to be the protagonist of a realistic play or novel. The exceptional man is news at all times, but how can the ordinary man get into the paper? By committing a crime. Or, more rarely, by getting involved in a spectacular accident. Since accidents, in general, are barred from the drama, this leaves crime — murder or suicide or embezzlement. And we find that the protagonists of realistic drama, by and large, are the protagonists of newspaper stories — "little men" who have shot their wives or killed themselves in the garage or gone to jail for fraud or embezzlement. Now drama has always had an affinity for crime; long before realism was known, Oedipus and Clytemnestra and Macbeth and Othello were famous for their deeds of blood. But the crimes of tragedy are the crimes of heroes, while the crimes of realistic drama are the crimes of the nondescript person, the crimes that are, in a sense, all alike. The individual in the realistic drama is regarded as a cog or a statistic; he commits the uniform crime that sociologically he might be expected to commit. That is, supposing that 1,031 bookkeepers in the state of New York are destined to tamper with the accounts, and 304 policemen are destined to shoot their wives, and 1,115 householders to do away with themselves in the garage, each individual book-keeper, cop, and householder has been holding a ticket in this statistical lottery, like the fourteen Athenian youths and maidens sent off yearly to the Minotaur's labyrinth, and he acquires interest for the realist theater only when his "number" comes up.

To put it as simply as possible, the cop in *Street Scene* commits his crime — wife murder — without having the moral freedom to choose to commit it, just as Willy Loman in *Death of a Salesman* commits suicide — under sociological pressure. The hero of tragedy, on the contrary, is a morally free being who identifies himself with his crime (*i.e.*, elects it), and this is true even where he is fated, like Oedipus, to commit it and can be said to have no personal choice in the matter. Oedipus both rejects and accepts his deeds, embraces them in free will at last as *his*. It is the same with Othello or Hamlet. The distinction will be clear if you ask yourself what tragedy of Shakespeare is closest to the realistic theater. The answer, surely, is *Macbeth*. And why? Because of Lady Macbeth. Macbeth really doesn't choose to murder the sleeping Duncan; Lady Macbeth chooses for him; he is like a middle-class husband, nagged on by his ambitious wife, the way the second vice president of a bank is nagged on by his Mrs. Macbeth, who wants him to become first vice president. The end of the tragedy, however, reverses all this; Macbeth becomes a hero only late in the drama, when he pushes Lady Macbeth aside and takes all his deeds on himself. Paradoxically, the conspicuous tragic hero is never free *not* to do his deed; he cannot escape it, as Hamlet found. But the mute hero or protagonist of a realistic play is always free, at least seemingly, not to emerge from obscurity and get his picture in the paper. There is always the chance that not he but some other nondescript bookkeeper or policeman will answer the statistical call.

The heroes of realistic plays are clerks, bookkeepers, police-men, housewives, salesmen, schoolteachers, small and middling businessmen. They commit crimes but they cannot be profes-sional criminals (unlike the heroes of Genêt or the characters in *The Beggar's Opera*), for professional criminals, like kings and noble men, are a race apart. The settings of realistic plays are offices, drab dining rooms or living rooms, or the backyard, which might be defined as a place where some grass has once been planted and failed to grow. The backyard is a favorite locus for American realist plays, but no realist play takes place in a garden. Nature is excluded from the realist play, as it has been from the realistic novel. The presence of Nature in Turgenev (and in Chekhov) denotes, as I have suggested, a pastoral intrusion. If a realist play does not take place in the backyard, where Nature has been eroded by clothes-poles, garbage cans, bottled-gas tanks, and so on, it takes place indoors, where the only plant, generally, is a rubber plant. Even with Ibsen, the action is confined to a room or pair of rooms until the late plays like *The Lady from the Sea, The Master Builder, John Gabriel Borkman,* when the realistic style has been abandoned for symbolism and the doors are swung open to the garden, mountains, the sea. Ibsen, however, is an exception to the general rule that the indoor scene must be unattractive; his middle-class Scandinavians own some handsome furniture; Nora's house, like any doll's house, must have been charmingly appointed. But Ibsen is an exception to another rule that seems to govern realistic drama (and the novel too, for that matter) — the rule that it must not be well written. (Thanks to William Archer's wooden translations, his work now falls into line in English.) This rule in America has the force, almost, of a law, one of those iron laws that work from within necessity itself, apparently, and without conscious human aid. Our American realists do not *try* to write badly. Many, like Arthur Miller, strive to write "well," *i.e.,* pretentiously, but like Dreiser in the novel they are cursed with inarticulateness. They "grope." They are, as O'Neill said of himself, "fogbound."

The heroes are petty or colorless; the settings are drab; the language is lame. Thus the ugliness of the form is complete. I am not saying this as a criticism, only observing that when a play or a novel fails to meet these norms, we cease to think of it as realistic. Flaubert, known to be a "stylist," ceases to count for us as a realist, and even in the last century, Matthew Arnold, hailing Tolstoy as a realist, was blinded by categorical thinking — with perhaps a little help from the translations — into calling his novels raw "slices of life," sprawling, formless, and so on. But it is these clichés, in the long run, that have won out. The realistic novel today is more like what Arnold thought Tolstoy was than it is like Tolstoy or any of the early realists. This question of the beauty of form also touches the actor. An actor formerly was supposed to be a good-looking man, with a handsome figure, beautiful movements, and a noble diction. These attributes are no longer necessary for a stage career; indeed, in America they are a positive handicap. A good-looking young man who moves well and speaks well is becoming almost unemployable in American "legit" theater; his best hope today is to look for work in musical comedy. Or posing for advertisements. On the English stage, where realism until recently never got a foothold, the good-looking actor still rules the roost, but the English actor cannot play American realist parts, while the American actor cannot play Shakespeare or Shaw. A pretty girl in America may still hope to be an actress, though even here there are signs of a change: the heroine of O'Neill's late play, *A Moon for the Misbegotten*, was a freckled giantess five feet eleven inches tall and weighing 180 pounds.

Eisenstein and the Italian neo-realists used people off the street for actors — a logical inference from premises which, being egalitarian and documentary, are essentially hostile to professional élites, including Cossacks, Swiss Guards, and actors. The professional actor in his grease paint is the antithesis of the pallid man on the street. But film and stage realism are not so democratic in their principles as may at first appear. To begin with, the director and a small corps of professionals — electricians and cameramen — assume absolute power over the masses, *i.e.*, over the untrained actors picked from the crowd; no resistance is encountered, as it would be with professional actors, in molding the human material to the director-dictator's will. And even with stars and all-professional casts, the same tendency is found in the modern realist or neo-realist director. Hence the whispered stories of stars deliberately broken by a director: James Dean and Brigitte Bardot. Similar stories of brainwashing are heard backstage. This is not surprising if realism, as we now know it, rejects as nonaverage whatever is noble, beautiful, or seemly, whatever is capable of "gesture," whatever in fact is free. Everything I have been saying up till now can be summed up in a sentence. Realism is a depreciation of the real. It is a gloomy puritan doctrine that has flourished chiefly in puritan countries — America, Ireland, Scandinavia, northern France, nonconformist England — chilly, chilblained countries, where the daily world is ugly and everything is done to keep it so, as if as a punishment for sin. The doctrine is spreading with industrialization, the growth of ugly cities, and the erosion of Nature. It came late to the English stage, long after it had appeared in the novel, because those puritan elements with which it is naturally allied have, up until now, considered the theater to be wicked.

At the same time, in defense of realism, it must be said that its great enemy has been just that puritan life whose gray color it has taken. The original realists — Ibsen in the theater, Flaubert in the novel — regarded themselves as "pagans," in opposition to their puritan contemporaries, and adhered to a religion of Beauty or Nature; they dreamed of freedom and hedonistic license (Flaubert) and exalted (Ibsen) the autonomy of the individual will. Much of this "paganism" is still found in O'Casey and in the early O'Neill, a curdled puritan of Irish-American stock. The original realists were half Dionysian aesthetes ("the vine-leaves in his hair") and their heroes and heroines were usually rebels, protesting the drabness and meanness of the common life. Ibsen's characters complain that they are "stifling"; in the airless hypocrisy of the puritan middle-class parlor, people were being poisoned by the dead gas of lies. Hypocrisy is the cardinal sin of the middle class, and the exposure of a lie is at the center of all Ibsen's plots. The strength and passion of realism is its resolve to tell the whole truth; this explains why the realist in his indictment of society avoids the old method of satire with its delighted exaggeration.

The realist drama at its highest is an implacable exposé. Ibsen rips off the curtain and shows his audiences to themselves, and there is something inescapable in the manner of the confrontation, like a case slowly being built. The pillars of society who sit in the best seats are, bit by bit, informed that they are rotten and that the commerce they live on is a commerce of "coffin ships." The action on the Ibsen stage is too close for comfort to the lives of the audience; only the invisible "fourth wall" divides them. "This is the way we live now!" Moral examination, self-examination are practiced as a duty, a Protestant stock-taking, in the realist mission hall.

For this, it is essential that the audience accept the picture as true; it cannot be permitted to feel that it is watching something "made up" or embellished. Hence the stripping down of the form and the elimination of effects that might be recognized as literary. For the first time too, in the realist drama, the accessories of the action are described at length by the playwright. The details must strike home and convince. The audience must be able to place the furniture, the carpets, the ornaments, the napery and glassware as "just what these people would have." This accounts for the importance of the stage set. Many critics who scornfully dismiss the "boxlike set" of the realistic drama, with its careful disposition of furniture, do not understand its function. This box is the box or "coffin" of average middle-class life opened at one end to reveal the corpse within, looking, as all embalmed corpses are said to do, "just as if it were alive." Inside the realist drama, whenever it is genuine and serious, there is a kind of double illusion, a false bottom: everything appears to be lifelike but this appearance of life is death. The stage set remains a central element in all true realism; it cannot be replaced by scrim or platforms. In *A Long Day's Journey into Night*, surely the greatest realist drama since Ibsen, the family living room, with its central overhead lighting-fixture is as solid and eternal as oak and as sad as wicker, and O'Neill in the text tells the stage designer what books must be in the glassed-in bookcase on the left and what books in the other by the entrance. The tenement of Elmer Rice's *Street Scene* (in the opera version) was a magnificent piece of characterization; so was the Bronx living room of Odets' *Awake and Sing* — his sole (and successful) experiment with realism. I can still see the bowl of fruit on the table, slightly to the left of stage center, and hear the Jewish mother interrupting whoever happened to be talking, to say, "Have a piece of fruit." That bowl of fruit, which

70 113

was the Jewish Bronx, remains more memorable as a character than many of the people in the drama. This gift of characterization through props and stage set is shared by Paddy Chayefsky in *Middle of the Night* and by William Inge in *Come Back, Little Sheba*, where an unseen prop or accessory, the housewife's terrible frowsty little dog, is the master-stroke of realist illusionism and, more than that, a kind of ghostly totem. All these plays, incidentally, are stories of death-in-life.

This urgent correspondence with a familiar reality, down to the last circumstantial detail, is what makes realism so gripping, like a trial in court. The dramatist is witnessing or testifying, on an oath never sworn before in a work of art, not to leave out anything and to tell the truth to the best of his ability. And yet the realistic dramatist, beginning with Ibsen, is aware of a missing element. The realist mode seems to generate a dissatisfaction with itself, even in the greatest masters: Tolstoy, for example, came to feel that his novels, up to *Resurrection*, were inconsequential trifling; the vital truth had been left out. In short, as a novelist, he began to feel like a hypocrite. This dissatisfaction with realism was evidently suffered also by Ibsen; halfway through his realist period, you see him start to look for another dimension. Hardly had he discovered or invented the new dramatic mode than he showed signs of being cramped by it; he experienced, if his plays are an index, that same sense of confinement, of being stifled, within the walls of realism that his characters experience within the walls of middle-class life. Something was missing: air. This is already plain in *The Wild Duck*, a strange piece of auto-criticism and probably his finest play; chafing, restless, mordant, he is searching for something else, for a poetic element, which he represents, finally, in the wild duck itself, a dramatic symbol for that cherished wild freedom that neither Ibsen nor his characters can maintain, without harming it, in a shut-in space. But to resort to symbols to make good the missing element becomes a kind of forcing, like trying to raise a wild bird in an attic, and the strain of this is felt in *Rosmersholm*, where symbols play a larger part and are charged with a more oppressive weight of meaning. In *The Lady from the Sea*, *The Master Builder*, and other late plays, the symbols have broken through the thin fence or framework of realism; poetry has spread its crippled wings, but the price has been heavy.

The whole history of dramatic realism is encapsulated in Ibsen. First, the renunciation of verse and of historical and philosophical subjects in the interests of prose and the present time; then the dissatisfaction and the attempt to restore the lost element through a recourse to symbols; then, or at the same time, a forcing of the action at the climaxes to heighten the drama; finally, the renunciation of realism in favor of a mixed mode or hodgepodge. The reaching for tragedy at the climaxes is evident in *Hedda Gabler* and still more so in *Rosmersholm*, where, to me at any rate, that climactic shriek "To the mill race!" is absurdly like a bad film. Many of Ibsen's big moments, even as early as *A Doll's House*, strike me as false and grandiose, that is, precisely, as stagey. Nor is it only in the context of realism that they appear so. It is not just that one objects that people do not act or talk like that — Tolstoy's criticism of King Lear on the heath. If you compare the mill-race scene in *Rosmersholm* with the climax of a Shakespearean tragedy, you will see that the Shakespearean heroes are far less histrionic, more natural and *ordinary*; there is always a stillness at the center of the Shakespearean storm. It is as if the realist, in reaching for tragedy, were punished for his *hubris* by a ludicrous fall into bathos. Tragedy is impossible by definition in the quotidian realist mode, since (quite aside from the question of the hero) tragedy is the exceptional action one of whose signs is beauty.

In America the desire to supply the missing element (usually identified as poetry or "beauty") seems to grow stronger and stronger exactly in proportion to the author's awkwardness with language. The less a playwright can write prose, the more he wishes to write poetry and to raise his plays by their bootstraps to a higher realm. You find these applications of "beauty" in Arthur Miller and Tennessee Williams; they stand out like rouge on a pitted complexion; it is as though the author first wrote the play naturalistically and then gave it a beauty treatment or face-lift. Before them, O'Neill, who was too honest and too philosophically inclined to be satisfied by a surface solution, kept looking methodically for a way of representing the missing element in dramas that would still be realistic at the core. He experimented with masks (*The Great God Brown*), with the aside and the soliloquy (*Strange Interlude*), with a story and pattern borrowed from the Greek classic drama (*Mourning Becomes Electra*). In other words, he imported into the American home or farm the machinery of tragedy. But his purpose was always a greater realism. His use of the aside, for example, was very different from the traditional use of the aside (a kind of nudge to the audience, usually on the part of the villain, to let them in on his true intent or motive); in *Strange Interlude* O'Neill was trying, through the aside, to make available to the realistic drama the discoveries of modern psychology, to represent on the stage the unconscious selves of his characters, at cross-purposes with their conscious selves but just as real if not realer, at least according to the psychoanalysts. He was trying, in short, to give a more complete picture of ordinary people in their daily lives. It was the same with his use of masks in *The Great God Brown*; he was appropriating the mask of Athenian drama, a ritual means of putting a distance between the human actor and the audience, to bring his own audience closer to the inner humanity of his character — the man behind the mask of conformity. The fact that these devices were clumsy is beside the point. O'Neill's sincerity usually involved him in clumsiness. In the end, he came back to the straight realism of his beginnings: *The Long Voyage Home*, the title of his young Caribbean series, could also be the title of the great play of his old age: *A Long Day's Journey into Night*. He has sailed beyond the horizon and back into port; the circle is complete. In this late play, the quest for the missing element, as such, is renounced; poetry is held to be finally unattainable by the author. "I couldn't touch what I tried to tell you just now," says the character who is supposed to be the young O'Neill. "I just stammered. That's the best I'll ever do. I mean, if I live. Well, it will be faithful realism, at least. Stammering is the native eloquence of us fog people." In this brave acknowledgment or advance acceptance of failure, there is something very moving. Moreover, the acceptance of defeat was in fact the signal of a victory. A *Long Day's Journey into Night*, sheer dogged prose from beginning to end, achieves in fact a peculiar poetry, and the relentless amassing of particulars takes on, eventually, some of the crushing force of inexorable logic that we find in Racine or in a Greek play. The weight of circumstance itself becomes a fate or nemesis. This is the closest, probably, that realism can get to tragedy.

The "stammering" of O'Neill was what made his later plays so long, and the stammering, which irritated some audiences, impatient for the next syllable to fall, was a sign of the author's agonized determination to be truthful. If O'Neill succeeded, at last, in deepening the character of his realism, it was because the missing element he strove to represent was not, in the end, "poetry" or "beauty" or "philosophy" (though he sometimes seems to have felt that it was) but simply meaning — the total significance of an action. What he came to conclude, rather wearily, in his last plays was that the total significance of an action lay in the accumulated minutiae of that action and could not be abstracted from it, at least not by him. There was no truth or meaning beyond the event itself; anything more (or less) would be a lie. This pun or tautology, this conundrum, committed him to a cycle of repetition, and memory, the mother of the Muses, became his only muse.

The younger American playwrights — Miller, Williams, Inge, Chayefsky — now all middle-aged, are pledged, like O'Neill, to verisimilitude. They purport to offer a "slice of life," in Tennessee Williams' case a rich, spicy slab of Southern fruitcake, but still a slice of life. The locus of their plays is the American porch or backyard or living room or parlor or bus station, presented as typical, authentic as home-fried potatoes or "real Vermont maple syrup." This authenticity may be regional, as with Williams and Paddy Chayefsky (the Jewish upper West side; a Brooklyn synagogue), or it may claim to be as broad as the nation, as with Arthur Miller, or somewhere rather central, in between the two, as with William Inge. But in any case, the promise of these playwrights is to show an ordinary home, an ordinary group of bus passengers, a typical manufacturer, and so on, and the dramatis personae tend to resemble a small-town, non-blue-ribbon jury: housewife, lawyer, salesman, chiropractor, working-man, schoolteacher. . . . Though Tennessee Williams' characters are more exotic, they too are offered as samples to the audience's somewhat voyeuristic eye; when Williams' film, *Baby Doll*, was attacked by Cardinal Spellman, the director (Elia Kazan) defended it on the grounds that it was true to the life that he and Williams had observed, on location, in Mississippi. If the people in Tennessee Williams were regarded as products of the author's imagination, his plays would lose all their interest. There is always a point in any one of Williams' dramas where recognition gives way to a feeling of shocked incredulity; this shock technique is the source of his sensational popularity. But the audience would not be electrified if it had not been persuaded earlier that it was witnessing something the author vouched for as a common, ordinary occurrence in the Deep South.

Unlike the other playwrights, who make a journalistic claim to neutral recording, Arthur Miller admittedly has a message. His first-produced play, *All My Sons*, was a social indictment taken, almost directly, from Ibsen's *Pillars of Society*. The coffin ships, rotten, unseaworthy vessels calked over to give an appearance of soundness, became defective airplanes sold to the government by a corner-cutting manufacturer during the Second World War; like the coffin ships, the airplanes are a symbol of the inner rottenness of bourgeois society, and the sins of the father, as *almost* in Ibsen, are visited on the son, a pilot who cracks up in the Pacific theater (in Ibsen, the ship-owner's boy is saved at the last minute from sailing on *The Indian Girl*). The insistence of this symbol and the vagueness or absence of concrete detail express Miller's impatience with the particular and his feeling that his play ought to say "more" than it appears to be saying. Ibsen, even in his later, symbolic works, was always specific about the where, when, and how of his histories (the biographies of his central characters are related with almost too much circumstantiality), but Miller has always regarded the specific as trivial and has sought, from the very outset, a hollow, reverberant universality. The reluctance to awaken a specific recognition, for fear that a larger meaning might go unrecognized by the public, grew on Miller with *Death of a Salesman* — a strong and original conception that was enfeebled by its creator's insistence on universality and by a too-hortatory excitement, *i.e.*, an eagerness to preach, which is really another form of the same thing. Miller was bent on making his Salesman (as he calls him) a parable of Everyman, exactly as in a clergyman's sermon, so that the drama has only the quality — and something of the canting tone — of an illustrative moral example. The thirst for universality becomes even more imperious in *A View from the Bridge*, where the account of a waterfront killing that Miller read in a newspaper is accessorized with Greek architecture, "archetypes," and, from time to time, intoned passages of verse, and Miller announces in a preface that he is not interested in his hero's "psychology." Miller does not understand that you cannot turn a newspaper item about Italian longshoremen and illegal immigration into a Greek play by adding a chorus and the pediment of a temple. Throughout Miller's long practice as a realist, there is not only a naïve searching for another dimension but an evident hatred of and contempt for reality — as not good enough to make plays out of.

It is natural, therefore, that he should never have had any interest in how people talk; his characters all talk the same way — somewhat funereally, through their noses. A live sense of speech differences (think of Shaw's *Pygmalion*) is rare in American playwrights; O'Neill tried to cultivate it ("dat ol' davil sea"), but he could never do more than write perfunctory dialect, rather like that of somebody telling a Pat and Mike story or a mountaineer joke. The only American realist with an ear for speech, aside from Chayefsky, whose range is narrow, is Tennessee Williams. He does really hear his characters, especially his female characters; he has studied their speech patterns and, like Professor Higgins, he can tell where they come from; Williams too is the only realist who places his characters in social history. Of all the realists, after O'Neill, he has probably the greatest native gift for the theater; he is a natural performer and comedian, and it is too bad that he suffers from the inferiority complex that is the curse of recent American realists —

the sense that a play must be bigger than its characters. This is really a social disease — a fear of being underrated — rather than the claustrophobia of the medium itself, which tormented Ibsen and O'Neill. But it goes back to the same source: the depreciation of the real. Real speech, for example, is not good enough for Williams and from time to time he silences his characters to put on a phonograph record of his special poetic long-play prose.

All dramatic realism is somewhat sadistic; an audience is persuaded to watch something that makes it uncomfortable and from which no relief is offered — no laughter, no tears, no purgation. This sadism had a moral justification, so long as there was the question of the exposure of a lie. But Williams is fascinated by the refinements of cruelty, which with him become a form of aestheticism, and his plays, far from baring a lie that society is trying to cover up, titillate society like a peepshow. The curtain is ripped off, to disclose, not a drab scene of ordinary life, but a sadistic exhibition of the kind certain rather specialized tourists pay to see in big cities like New Orleans. With Williams, it is always a case of watching some mangy cat on a hot tin roof. The ungratified sexual organ of an old maid, a young wife married to a homosexual, a subnormal poor white farmer is proffered to the audience as a curiosity. The witholding of sexual gratification from a creature or "critter" in heat for three long acts is Williams' central device; other forms of torture to which these poor critters are subjected are hysterectomy and castration. Nobody, not even the SPCA, would argue that it was a good thing to show the prolonged torture of a dumb animal on the stage, even though the torture were only simulated and animals, in the end, would profit from such cases being brought to light. Yet this, on a human level, is Tennessee Williams' realism — a cat, to repeat, on a hot tin roof. And, in a milder version, it is found again in William Inge's *Picnic*. No one could have prophesied, a hundred years ago, that the moral doctrine of realism would narrow to the point of becoming pornography, yet something like that seems to be happening with such realistic novels as *Peyton Place* and the later John O'Hara and with one branch of the realist theater. Realism seems to be a highly unstable mode, attracted on the one hand to the higher, on the other to the lower elements in the human scale, tending always to proceed toward its opposite, that is, to irreality, tracing a vicious circle from which it can escape only by repudiating itself. Realism, in short, is forever begging the question — the question of reality. To find the ideal realist, you would first have to find reality. And if no dramatist today, except O'Neill, can accept being a realist in its full implications, this is perhaps because of lack of courage. Ibsen and O'Neill, with all their dissatisfaction, produced major works in the full realist vein; the recent realists get discouraged after a single effort. *Street Scene; All My Sons; The Glass Menagerie; Come Back, Little Sheba; Middle of the Night;* perhaps *Awake and Sing* are the only convincing evidence that exists of an American realist school — not counting O'Neill. If I add *Death of a Salesman* and *A Streetcar Named Desire,* it is only because I do not know where else to put them.

THE PLAY IN THE THEATER

Although an occasional literary man insists that a play performed is only a play read aloud with gestures, almost everyone recognizes that performance transmutes the text.

George Bernard Shaw (1856-1950) knew that his plays were too valuable to be left to actors and directors. He often attended rehearsals and helped get his plays into shape on the stage. His basic idea is that a director best serves the play by keeping the actors on their toes, rather than by using actors and a script as a painter uses canvas and colors in order to create a work of art. For additional material on directing, see p. 208.

Konstantin Stanislavsky (1863-1938) was co-founder in 1898 of the Moscow Art Theater, where he put his theories into practice. In most of his writings he rejected "theatricalism" (he said he hated "the theater in the theater") and insisted on the illusion of reality. He was, of course, aware that the scenery, costumes, etc. were make-believe, but he insisted that true acting begins with a "feeling for truth"; the actor must have sufficient imagination and sufficient belief to say, "*If* this were real, I should do this scene in this way." For a brief summary of some of his main ideas, see p. 259.

Bertolt Brecht (1898-1956) achieved fame in Germany in the late twenties, especially for his *Three-Penny Opera* (1928). He left Germany in 1933 but returned after the Second World War, settling in East Berlin, where he directed the Berliner Ensemble's productions of his plays. Brecht rejected Stanislavsky's realism and insisted that the audience is not to be touched by a reproduction of life but is to be instructed and provoked into thought by a performance that is something of a demonstration. Stanislavsky tried to make people forget that they were in a theater; Brecht tried to make sure that they never forgot. The essay printed here is on the style of acting appropriate to Brecht's conception of "epic" drama, a form discussed on p. 213.

CHARLES LAMB (1775-1834) has been much accused of hostility to the theater because in his essay "On the Tragedies of Shakespeare" he suggested that King Lear "is essentially impossible to be represented on the stage." But in fact Lamb was an ardent play-goer as well as play-reader. The essay that follows, in which Lamb suggests that the desirable degree of dramatic illusion (see p. 210) varies with the kind of play presented, could never have been written by a man whose interest in the theater was not vital.

Rules for Directors

GEORGE BERNARD SHAW

Play directing, like orchestral conducting, became a separate and lucrative profession less than a century ago. The old stage manager who arranged the movements of the players, and called every actor Old Boy and every actress Darling, is extinct. The director has supplanted him. Yet there is no established method of directing and no handbook from which a novice can learn the technical side of the job. There is not even a tradition, because directors do not see one another at work as players do, and can learn only by experience at the expense of everyone else employed in the production.

These pages are an attempt to supply a beginners' guide. They are not concerned with direction as a fine art; but they cover the mechanical and teachable conditions which are common to all productions, without knowledge of which the novice will waste hours of rehearsal time that should be devoted to acting. All playwrights should study these.

The most desirable director of a play is the author.

Unfortunately, as playwriting is a solitary occupation which gives no social training, some playwrights are so lacking in the infinite patience, intense vigilance, consideration for others, and

*imperturbable good manners which directing requires, that their
presence at rehearsals is a hindrance instead of a help. None the
less, they should know how to write for the stage as playwrights,
and not as poets and novelists indulging their imaginations beyond the physical limits of "four boards and a passion."*

THE DIRECTOR, having considered the play, and decided to un-
dertake the job of directing it, has no further concern with its
literary merits or its doctrine (if any).

In selecting the cast no regard should be given to whether the
actors understand the play or not (players are not walking
encyclopedias); but their ages and personalities should be suitable, and their voices should not be alike. The four principals
should be soprano, alto, tenor, and bass. Vocal contrast is of the
greatest importance, and is indispensable for broadcasting.

The play should be read to the company, preferably by the
author if he or she is a competent dramatic reader: if not, by
the best available substitute. If none is available, no reading
is better than a bad one.

To the first rehearsals the director must come with the stage
business thoroughly studied, and every entry, movement, rising
and sitting, disposal of hat and umbrella, etc., is settled ready
for instant dictation; so that each player will be in the most
effective position to deliver his lines and not have to address
an intimate speech to a player at the other side of the stage,
nor to follow such a player without a line or movement to trans-
fer the attention of the audience accordingly. The exits must
be carefully arranged so that the players leave the stage immediately on their last word, and not hold up the play until
they have walked to the door. If the director arrives at the
first rehearsal without this blueprint, and proceeds to waste the
players' time improvising it at their expense, he will never gain
their confidence; and they will be perfectly justified in going
home after telling him not to call them again until they can
devote all the rehearsals to their proper function of acting.

To appreciate the necessity for this laborious planning one
has only to imagine a trial-at-law in a room without bench, bar,
or jury box, or a service in a cathedral without altar, choir, or

pews: in short, without an appointed place for anybody. This is what the stage is until the director has made a complete plan, called a prompt copy. Properly such a plan is the business of the author; for stage directions are as integral to a play as spoken dialogue. But the author may be dead. Or in view of the fact that writing dialogue (of Hamlet, for instance) is a pleasurable act of creation, whereas deciding whether the Ghost shall enter from the right or the left is pure drudgery, the author may leave the drudgery to the director. He mostly does.

It is not necessary to use a model stage for this job. All that is necessary is a chessboard with its chessmen, and a boy's box of assorted bricks. With these all scenes and furniture can be indicated and all movements made. Unless this is done some movements, especially exits, are likely to be forgotten by even the most experienced director.

The players should be instructed not to study their parts at this stage, and to rehearse, book in hand, without any exercise of memory.

When the movements are thoroughly rehearsed and mastered, the director should ask the players whether they are comfortable for them all, and if not, what is wrong.

All being satisfactorily arranged, books are discarded, and rehearsals called "perfect": that is, with the parts memorized. The director now leaves the stage and sits in the front of the house with an electric torch and a notebook; and from that moment he should watch the stage as a cat watches a mouse, but never utter a word nor interrupt a scene during its repetition no matter how completely the play goes to pieces, as it must at first when the players are trying to remember their parts and cues so desperately that they are incapable of acting. Nothing betrays the inexperienced director more than dismay at this collapse, with outbursts of reproach and attempts to get everything right at every rehearsal. The old hand knows that he must let the players memorize the words before they can act their parts.

At the end of each act, the director returns to the stage to explain or demonstrate such of his notes as may be judicious at the moment. But no fault should be mentioned or corrected unless and until its constant repetition shows that the player will not correct it in his or her own way as the play is gradually learnt. When all the players are letter-perfect their memorizing will be so mechanical that if one of them makes a slip by repeating an early cue later on, the rest will pick it up again and repeat what they have just been through, proving that the memorizing phase is over. The director can now return to the stage and interrupt as often as may be necessary.

The danger is that as the players can now utter their words without thinking they will catch one another's speed and tone, betraying to the audience that they are only gabbling off a prearranged list of words, each knowing what the other will say next and fielding their cues like cricketers. The director must accordingly take care that every speech contrasts as strongly as possible in speed, tone, manner, and pitch with the one which provokes it, as if coming unexpected as a shock, surprise, stimulant, offense, amusement, or what not. It is for the author to make this possible; for in it lies the difference between dramatic dialogue and epic narrative. A play by a great poet, in which every speech is a literary masterpiece, may fail hopelessly on the stage because the splendid speeches are merely strung together without provoking one another, whereas a trumpery farce may win an uproarious success by its retortive backchat.

The final phase of direction is that of "dress rehearsal" with costumes, scenery, and make-up all complete as for public performance, instead of everyday dress and a bare stage with the doors marked with a couple of chairs. It is now the director's turn to be more upset by the change than the actors. Everything seems to have become wrong and incredible. However, the director soon learns to be prepared for this, even if he never quite gets over the first shock of it. He is now back on the stage, going through the passages that need finishing, and generally doing what he likes. A bad last rehearsal need not alarm him: in fact he should connive at its failure lest the players should be too confident of success "on the night" and not do their utmost best.

The time needed for the direction of a full-length play on

this method is roughly a week for the stage movements book in hand, with the director on the stage; a fortnight for the memorizing, with the director off the stage silent, watching, and taking notes; and a week for the dress, with the director on the stage again, directing and interrupting *ad lib*.

Rehearsals should be most strictly private. No journalist or lay visitor of any kind should be present. When for some reason it may be necessary to allow strangers to witness a rehearsal, no instruction nor correction should be addressed in their presence to a player; and the consent of every player should be obtained before the permission is granted. To emphasize the fact that what the visitors are witnessing is only a rehearsal, a prearranged instruction should be addressed to a stage carpenter, never to a player.

During the memorizing phase a muffled passage must never be repeated on the spot, even if the players desire it. The director's word must be "No; you will not be able to repeat it on the night; and you must not make a habit of a mistake. Go right on." A director who says "We must go over and over this again until we get it right" is not directing; he is schoolmastering, which is the worst thing he can do. Repetitions on the spot do not improve: they deteriorate every time.

Never find fault until you know the remedy; and never discuss a passage with a player; show how the passage should be done as a suggestion, not an order; and exaggerate your demonstration sufficiently to prevent the player giving a mere imitation of it. A performance in which the players are all mimicking the director, instead of following his suggestions in their own different ways, is a bad performance. Above all, do not, instead of demonstrating a passage, say "This scene is essentially pathetic" (or comic as the case may be). If you do, the player will come to the next rehearsal bathed in tears from the first word to the last, or clowning for all he is worth all the time.

The notes taken by the director as he silently watches the players are a test of his competence. If, for example, he writes "Show influence of Kierkegaard on Ibsen in this scene," or "The Œdipus complex must be very apparent here. Discuss with the Queen," the sooner he is packed out of the theater and replaced the better. If they run "Ears too red," "Further up to make room for X," "Pleecemin," "Reel and Ideel," "Mariar Ann," "He, not Ee," "Contrast," "Change speed: Andante," "Shoe sole arches not blacked," "Unladylike: keep knees together," "More dialogue to give them time to get off," "This comes too suddenly," "?Cut this???" and the like, the director knows his job and his place.

When a play is by Shakespear such notes will crop up as "The green one red," "Tibbeeyrnottibeethat iz," "Become to Dunsinane," "Babbled," "Lo here I lenthee thishar pointed sword," meaning that the player should say "Making the green, one red," "To be? Or NOT to be? THAT is the question," "Though Birnam Wood BE come to Dunsinane," that Malone's silly "A babbled o' green fields" should be discarded for the original "His nose was as sharp as a pen on a table of green frieze," [1] and that consecutive consonants must be articulated, as in "lend thee" and "sharp pointed." Othello must not change chaste stars into chaste tars.

In arranging hours players with only a few lines to speak should not be kept hanging about all day whilst the principals are rehearsing. Late night rehearsals are most objectionable. Neither players nor directors should work when they ought to be in bed. If such rehearsals are unavoidable the players who are kept too late for their last trains or buses should be paid their taxi fares home.

A play may need to be cut, added to, or otherwise altered, sometimes to improve it as a play, sometimes to overcome some mechanical difficulty on the stage, sometimes by a passage proving too much for an otherwise indispensable player. These are highly skilled jobs, and should be done by the author, if available, or if not, by a qualified playwright, not by a player, nor by the callboy. Copyright in all such changes passes to the author. A player who reveals the plot or words of an unper-

[1] In *Henry* V, Mistress Quickly, in describing the dying Falstaff, says "His nose was as sharp as a pen, a table of green fields." Lewis Theobald (not Edmond Malone, as Shaw says) emended "a table" to "a' babbled," *i.e.*, "he babbled" [Editors' note].

formed play to the Press can be sued for breach of confidence at common law or under the Copyright Act.

These rules are founded on experience. They are of no use to a director who regards players not as fellow-artists collaborating with him, but as employees on whom he can impose his own notions of acting and his own interpretation of the author's meaning. He must let the players learn the play, and not expect them to know it all as well as he does at the first rehearsal. He must distinguish between born actors who should be let alone to find their own way, and spook actors who have to be coached sentence by sentence and are helpless without such coaching. There are so many degrees between these extremes that the tact and judgment of directors in their very delicate relations with players are sometimes strained to the utmost; and there is no effective check on the despotism of the director except his own conscience, because only the most ungovernable players dare risk being blacklisted by an authority so potent in the selection of casts as the director. This is why docile players are usually less often unemployed (which means running into debt) than better rebellious ones.

In stock companies, where the program changes from week to week or even from night to night, there can be no selection of the cast and no time to learn the play. Players have to "swallow" their speeches as best they can, and deliver them, not in the author's characterization, but in their specialties such as juvenile lead, ingénue, walking gentleman, light comedian, low comedian, singing chambermaid (soubrette), heavy old man (*père noble*), old woman, utility, and so forth. Each plays every part in the same way: there neither is nor can be any distinction between Polonius and Lafeu, Adam and old Gobbo, Countess Rousillon and Lady Macbeth, Juliet and Ophelia, Aguecheek and Roderigo. Each male player has one combat (sixes); and all have one stepdance for the Christmas pantomime. Obviously the foregoing directing method has a very limited application here; but the preparation beforehand of the director's prompt copy — if there be a director — is doubly necessary to save time.

Repertory companies which, instead of "supporting" touring

stars, rely on their own performances of the best plays they can get, are genuine prentice schools of acting, because the players are not "rats of the theater," in it only because as children of players they are born to it, but because they come from the educated laity, and have made their way into the theater against all prudent parental advice, for love of it. Stock players are a hereditary caste. Though their power of swallowing words in a few hours and improvising (ponging) and gagging is amazing, they finally become incapable of character study, and are never really word-perfect. When age brings loss of memory they have to be fed by the prompter word for word, as Italian actors are as a matter of course. They are obsessed with stage traditions and superstitions: to them all religious sages are Tartuffes or Malvolios, all old husbands cuckolds, all women either brides or Lady Wishforts, and all plays either fictitious police news of murders committed by Heavies (villains), or harlequinades, or an orotund but senseless variety of stage-work called shake-spear.

Some good players can act sobriety perfectly, though off the stage they are drunk and incapable. The same is true of fever temperatures, sciatica, lameness, and even partial paralysis. This curious fact, apparently unknown to psychologists, must be taken into account by directors lest they should sack an Edmund Kean or Frederick Robson (who both drank themselves into heroic fame and premature death) and retain a Gustavus Brooke (a great actor when sober, reeling and inarticulate when drunk, as he often was). In the logbooks of Drury Lane, when it was a patent theater in the eighteenth century, are such entries as "No performance: Mr. Kemble drunk."

When a player repeatedly omits some physical feat or movement, the director must conclude that it is made impossible by some infirmity which the player would rather die than disclose. In such cases the business must be altered.

A director sometimes has an antiquarian job. He may be called on to direct a play by, say, Euripides or Aristophanes as it was produced in Athens 2356 years ago. Or one of the pious Mysteries as the Church produced them in the Middle

Ages. Or an Elizabethan drama on an Elizabethan stage. Or a Restoration or early Victorian play on a stage with proscenium, wings, and flats.

He should know that the Athenian stage was an imposing tribune in the open air on which the actors, in mask, sock, and buskin, strutted in conventional hierarchic costumes, and that as scenery and curtains were undreamt of, and changes of place impossible, the action of the play had to pass in the same place on the same day. These conditions are called the Unities. On later stages and on the cinema screen they are negligible superstitions; but their observance still has great dramatic value. On the medieval stage unity of place was got rid of by a wide stage on which half a dozen different places were shown simultaneously. Heaven, the jaws of hell, the throne of the Blessed Virgin, the Garden of Gethsemane, the Mount of Olives, the Court of Pilate, the house of Caiaphas, were all in full view together, with the actors moving from one to the other as the story dictated. The Elizabethan stage, adaptable to innyards, had no scenery. The stage was surrounded on three sides by inn galleries, and had a balcony and an inner stage in the middle with curtains called traverses in which indoor scenes were played.

This inner stage, still in use at Oberammergau and elsewhere for Passion Plays, is important because it enables actors entering from the back at opposite sides to be seen by the audience before they can see one another, thus making possible such scenes as the first in Romeo and Juliet, in which the Montagues and Capulets talk out of sight of one another, and set the spectators wondering what will happen when they meet. The best example, however, is at Oberammergau, where the procession to Calvary starts upstage on the prompt side, and has to turn two corners before it passes out up the opposite avenue. At the first corner it is confronted with a comic character, Simon, going to market with his basket. He is seized by the soldiers, who compel him to help Jesus to carry the heavy cross. But as the fainting Christ in extreme exhaustion drags himself towards the second corner, the Virgin appears descending the avenue, and it is apparent that they must meet and turn the crude fun of the Simon encounter into the deepest tragedy.

It was for the sake of such effects that when the Elizabethan stage was succeeded by the Restoration stage, with painted scenery viewed through a proscenium acting as a picture frame, the scenes were pierced to provide avenues through which the actors could be seen before they could see one another. There were also doors in the proscenium through which the principal players could enter, with pages bearing the women's trains, not in historic costumes, but in the full court dress of the period. Old toy theaters preserve this type of stage. Every director should possess one; for effects are possible on it that are not possible in modern built-in sets. For instance, when there are three wide entrances between the wings on both sides of the stage a crowd can be cleared off it almost instantaneously. The very few who are old enough to have seen Queen Elizabeth and her court apparently sink into the earth and disappear when Ristori, as Marie Stewart, called her "the Bastard of England," will appreciate how a modern director is hampered by having to clear the stage through one door.

Modern direction includes film direction, in which there is no limit to scenic possibilities; and directors may spend millions of pounds profitably instead of a few thousands. The results so far include megalomaniac demoralization, disorganization, and waste of time and money. These evils will cure themselves. Meanwhile the art of the playwright and director remains basically the same. The playwright has to tell a good story, and the director to "get it across."

This is all that can be learnt by a director from anything but experience and natural vocation. Like all methods it depends for success on the taste and talent with which it is practiced.

There is no sex disqualification for directing. Women directors are at no disadvantage in comparison with men. As in marriage and queenship, the gray mare is often the better horse.

The Beginnings of My System

KONSTANTIN STANISLAVSKY

DURING one performance in which I was repeating a role I had played many times, suddenly, without any apparent cause, I perceived the inner meaning of the truth long known to me that creativeness on the stage demands first of all a special condition, which, for want of a better term, I will call the creative mood. Of course I knew this before, but only intellectually. From that evening on this simple truth entered into all my being, and I grew to perceive it not only with my soul, but with my body also. For an actor, to perceive is to feel. For this reason I can say that it was on that evening that I "first perceived a truth long known to me." I understood that to the genius on the stage this condition almost always comes of itself, in all its fullness and richness. Less talented people receive it less often, on Sundays only, so to say. Those who are even less talented receive it even less often, every twelfth holiday, as it were. Mediocrities are visited by it only on very rare occasions, on leap years, on the twenty-ninth of February. Nevertheless, all men of the stage from the genius to the mediocrity, are able to receive the creative mood, but it is not given them to control it with their own will. They receive it together with inspiration in the form of a heavenly gift.

Not pretending at all to be a god and to hand out heavenly gifts, I nevertheless put the following question to myself:

"Are there no technical means for the creation of the creative mood, so that inspiration may appear oftener than is its wont?" This does not mean that I was going to create inspiration by artificial means. That would be impossible. What I wanted to learn was how to create a favorable condition for the appearance of inspiration by means of the will, that condition in the presence of which inspiration was most likely to descend into the actor's soul. As I learned afterward, this creative mood is that spiritual and physical mood during which it is easiest for inspiration to be born.

Translated by J. J. Robbins.

"Today I am in good spirits! Today I am at my best!" or "I am acting with pleasure! I am living over my part!" means that the actor is accidentally in a creative mood.

But how was one to make this condition no longer a matter of mere accident, to create it at the will and order of the actor? If it is impossible to own it at once, then one must put it together bit by bit, using various elements for its construction. If it is necessary to develop each of the component elements in one's self separately, systematically, by a series of certain exercises — let it be so! If the ability to receive the creative mood in its full measure is given to the genius by nature, then perhaps ordinary people may reach a like state after a great deal of hard work with themselves — not in its full measure, but at least in part. Of course the ordinary, simply able man will never become a genius, but it will help him to approach and in time to become like the genius, of one school with the genius, the servant of the same art as the genius. But how was one to reach the nature and the component elements of the creative mood?

The solution of this problem had become the "regular enthusiasm of Stanislavsky," as my friends expressed themselves. There was nothing that I left undone in order to solve the mystery. I watched myself closely, I looked into my soul, so to say, on the stage and off. I watched other men and actors, when I rehearsed my new parts or their new parts with them. I also watched them from the auditorium. I performed all sorts of experiments with them and myself. I tortured them; they grew angry and said that I had turned the rehearsals into an experimental laboratory, and that actors were not guinea pigs to be used for experimentation. And they were right in their protests. But the chief object of my researches remained the great actors, Russian, and foreign. If they, oftener than others, almost always walked the stage in the midst of a creative mood, whom was I to study if not them? And that is what I did. And this is what I learned from what I saw: in Duse, Yermolova, Fedotova, Savina, Salvini, Chaliapin, Rossi, as well as in the actors of our Theater when they appeared to best advantage in their roles, I felt the presence of something that was common to them all, something by which they reminded me of each other. What was this quality, common to all great talents? It was easiest of all for me to notice this likeness in their physical freedom, in the lack of all strain. Their bodies were at the call and beck of the inner demands of their wills.

The creative mood on the stage is exceptionally pleasant, especially when it is compared with the state of strain to which the actor is subject when the creative mood is absent. It can be compared to the feelings of a prisoner when the chains that had interfered with all his movements for years have at last been removed. I luxuriated in this condition on the stage, sincerely believing that in it lay the whole secret, the whole soul of creativeness on the stage, that all the rest would come from this state and perception of physical freedom. I was only made anxious by the fact that none of the actors who played with me, or the spectators who saw me play, noticed the change which I believed had taken place in me, leaving out of consideration the few compliments I received about one or two poses, movements and gestures that I had stressed.

After the production of *The Drama of Life* I was free of new roles and the work of stage direction until the end of the season of 1906-1907. Playing my old parts, I continued my researches, my experiments, my public exercises and the study of the problems of the theory and the technique of our art. The habit of free physical creative mood on the stage grew stronger little by little, became dynamic, and gradually assumed the character of second nature.

And then, like Doctor Stockman, "I made a new discovery." I began to understand that I felt so pleasantly and comfortably on the stage because my public exercises centered my attention on the perceptions and states of my body, at the same time drawing my attention away from what was happening on the other side of the footlights, in the auditorium beyond the black and terrible hole of the proscenium arch. In what I was doing I ceased to be afraid of the audience, and at times forgot that I was on the stage. I noticed that it was especially at such times that my creative mood was most pleasant.

There was one fact that made me very happy. At one of the

performances given by a visiting star in Moscow, I watched his acting very closely. In my capacity of actor, I felt the presence of the creative mood in his playing, the freedom of his muscles in conjunction with a great general concentration. I felt clearly that his entire attention was on the stage and the stage alone, and this abstracted attention forced me to be interested in his life on the stage, and draw closer to him in spirit in order to find out what it was that held his attention.

In that moment I understood that the more the actor wishes to amuse his audience, the more the audience will sit in comfort waiting to be amused, and not even trying to play its part in the play on the stage before it. But as soon as the actor stops being concerned with his audience, the latter begins to watch the actor. It is especially so when the actor is occupied in something serious and interesting. If nobody amuses the spectator there is nothing left for him to do in the theater but to seek himself for an object of attention. Where can that object be found? On the stage, of course, in the actor himself. The concentration of the creating actor calls out the concentration of the spectator and in this manner forces him to enter into what is passing on the stage, exciting his attention, his imagination, his thinking processes and his emotion. That evening I discovered the greater value of concentration for the actor. Besides, I noticed at that performance that the concentration of the actor reacts not only on his sight and hearing, but on all the rest of his senses. It embraces his mind, his will, his emotions, his body, his memory and his imagination. The entire physical and spiritual nature of the actor must be concentrated on what is going on in the soul of the person he plays. I perceived that creativeness is first of all the complete concentration of the entire nature of the actor. With this in mind, I began the systematic development of my attention with the help of exercises I invented for that purpose. I hope to dedicate more than one chapter of my next book to these.

I looked at another great visiting star in his great roles. He pronounced the introductory words of his part. But he did not strike directly on true emotion, and yielding to the mechanical habit of the theater, fell back on false pathos. I looked at him carefully and saw that something was taking place in him. And really, he resembled a singer who used a sounding fork to find the true note. Now it seemed that he had found it. No, it was a trifle too low. He took a higher note. No, it was too high. He took a note a little lower. He recognized the true tone, came to understand it, to feel it, placed it, directed it, believed in it, and began to enjoy the art of his own speech. He *believed!*

The actor must first of all believe in everything that takes place on the stage, and most of all he must believe in what he himself is doing. And one can believe only in the truth. Therefore it is necessary to feel this truth at all times, to know how to find it, and for this it is unescapable to develop one's artistic sensitivity to truth. It will be said, "But what kind of truth can this be, when all on the stage is a lie, an imitation, scenery, cardboard, paint, make-up, properties, wooden goblets, swords and spears. Is all this truth?" But it is not of this truth I speak. I speak of the truth of emotions, of the truth of inner creative urges which strain forward to find expression, of the truth of the memories of bodily and physical perceptions. I am not interested in a truth that is without myself; I am interested in the truth that is within myself, the truth of my relation to this or that event on the stage, to the properties, the scenery, the other actors who play parts in the drama with me, to their thoughts and emotions.

The actor says to himself:

"All these properties, make-ups, costumes, the scenery, the publicness of the performance, are lies. I know they are lies, I know I do not need any of them. But *if* they were true, then I would do this and this, and I would behave in this manner and this way towards this and this event."

I came to understand that creativeness begins from that moment when in the soul and imagination of the actor there appears the magical, creative *if*. While only actual reality exists, only practical truth which a man naturally cannot but believe, creativeness has not yet begun. Then the creative *if* appears, that is, the imagined truth which the actor can believe as sincerely and with greater enthusiasms than he believes practical truth, just as the child believes in the existence of its doll and of all life in it and around it. From the moment of the appearance of *if* the actor passes from the plane of actual reality into the plane of another life, created and imagined by himself. Believing in this life, the actor can begin to create.

Scenic truth is not like truth in life; it is peculiar to itself. I understood that on the stage truth is that in which the actor sincerely believes. I understood that even a palpable lie must become a truth in the theater so that it may become art. For this it is necessary for the actor to develop to the highest degree his imagination, a childlike naïveté and trustfulness, an artistic sensitivity to truth and to the truthful in his soul and body. All these qualities help him to transform a coarse scenic lie into the most delicate truth of his relation to the life imagined. All these qualities, taken together, I shall call the *feeling of truth*. In it there is the play of imagination and the creation of creative faith; in it there is a barrier against scenic lies; in it is the feeling of true measure; in it is the tree of childlike naïveté and the sincerity of artistic emotion. The feeling of truth, as one of the important elements of the creative mood, can be both developed and practiced. But this is neither the time nor the place to speak of the methods and means of such work. I will only say now that this ability to feel the truth must be developed to such an extent that absolutely nothing would take place on the stage, that nothing would be said and nothing listened to, without a preparatory cleansing through the filter of the artistic feeling of truth.

If this was true, then all my scenic exercises in loosening the muscles as well as in concentration had been performed incorrectly. I had not cleansed them through the filter of spiritual and physical truth. I took a certain pose on the stage. I did not believe in it physically. Here and there I weakened the strain. It was better. Now I changed the pose somewhat. Ah! I understood. When one stretches himself in order to reach something, this pose is the result of such stretching. And my whole body and after it my soul, began to believe that I was stretching towards an object which I needed very much.

It was only with the help of the feeling of truth, and the inner justification of the pose, that I was able more or less to reach the loosening of the muscles in actual life and on the stage during performances.

From that time on all my scenic exercises in the loosening of muscles and in concentration passed under the strict control of my feeling of truth.

A New Technique of Acting

BERTOLT BRECHT

IN THIS short paper an attempt will be made to describe a technique of acting which has been used in the German theater to alienate the events being presented on the stage from the spectator. It has been the aim of this technique of alienation [*Verfremdung*] to make the spectator assume an enquiring, critical attitude towards events. The means employed are artistic.

If the A-effect is to achieve its aim, the stage and the auditorium must be cleared of "magic." No "hypnotic fields of action" must be set up. On the Epic stage, no attempt is made to create the atmosphere of a particular place (a room at evening, a street in autumn), or to generate a mood by a broken speech-rhythm. The actor does not warm the audience up by unloosing a flood of temperament, nor cast a spell over them by tightening his muscles. In short, no effort is made to put the audience in a trance and give them the illusion of witnessing natural, unrehearsed events. As will be seen, the audience's tendency to throw itself into such an illusion must be neutralized by definite artistic means.

If he is to bring off the A-effect, the actor must provide what he has to show the audience with clear gestures of "showing" (meaning by gestures our whole apparatus of expression). The idea of a fourth wall which is imagined separating the stage from the audience, an idea that produces the illusion that the stage action is actually taking place without spectators, must

Translated by Eric Bentley.

of course be abandoned. This being so, it is possible for the actors to turn directly to the audience.

Usually, as is well-known, contact between audience and stage is established by means of empathy. The conventional actor today concentrates so utterly on producing empathy that one can say, "He sees in it the principal goal of his art." As has already been suggested, the technique of the A-effect is diametrically opposed to that by which empathy is produced. The technique of the A-effect actually prevents the actor from producing empathy — at least to the usual extent.

In his efforts to portray people and show how they behave, the actor need not do without empathy altogether. He uses it to the extent that anyone without histrionic talent or ambition would use it to present another man, that is, to show how he behaves. Such "showing how other men behave" happens every day in countless situations (witnesses of an accident report to newcomers how the victim behaved, jokers imitate a friend's comical walk, etc.) without the people concerned trying to give their spectators any sort of illusion. Yet they do "feel themselves into" other people in order to take on their characteristics.

The actor, then, will make *some* use of empathy. But, whereas at present, the act of empathy is not completed till the actual performance, when the spectator is involved in the process, in Epic Theater it will be completed at an earlier stage — in fact, at some point in the course of rehearsals while the role is still being learned.

Lest the actors interpret the people and events of a play in too impulsive, frictionless, and uncritical a fashion, a larger than usual number of rehearsals must be held around a table. The actor will eschew all premature "living himself into" the role and as long as possible will just *read* it (though not as one reads aloud to an audience). One important procedure is the *memorizing of first impressions.*

In confronting his role, the actor's attitude should be that of someone who is astonished and resistant. He must carefully weigh, and grasp in all their specialness, not only the occurrence of the events in the story, but also the behavior of the person whom he is to represent. He cannot take any of the events as "given," as something that "couldn't be otherwise," that "was to be expected from the nature of the character." Before memorizing the words, he should memorize the things that astonished him and the ways in which he resisted them. He must hold on to these centers of energy. They belong to his interpretation.

In addition to what he does, he will at all essential points seek something to intimate what he is *not* doing. That is to say, he should play his part in such a way that one sees, and with the greatest possible clarity, the alternatives: his playing gives us an intimation of other possibilities, presents but one of the possible variants. He says, for instance: "I'll make you pay for this" and he does *not* say, "I forgive you." He hates his children, and it is not the case that he loves them. He is going down left and not up right. What he does *not* do must be contained in what he does and brought into relief by it. Hence all statements and gestures signify decisions. The character is kept under control and tested. Put it in terms of *not this but that —* such is the formula.

The actor does not let himself be transformed into the man he presents so that nothing of himself is left. He is not Lear, Harpagon, or the good soldier Schweik — he is "showing" them to an audience. He brings their words forward, and that as genuinely as possible. He indicates their way of living as well as his knowledge of men permits. But he does not delude himself (and therewith others) into the belief that he has completely transformed himself. Actors will know what is meant here if one cites as an example of "acting without being completely transformed" what a director does when showing an actor how to perform a certain passage. Such a director does not transform himself — since the role is not his. He underlines the technical side of the business, and preserves the attitude of some one just making a suggestion.

Giving up the idea of complete transformation, the actor brings forward his text, not as an improvisation, but as a *quotation*. At the same time, it is clear that he has to render, in this quotation, all the undertones, all the concrete, plastic detail

of full human utterance. His gestures, though they are frankly
a *copy* (and not spontaneous), must have the full corporeality
of human gestures.

In this sort of acting, where the transformation of the actor
is incomplete, three devices can contribute to the alienation of
the words and actions of the person presenting them:

1. The adoption of a third person.
2. The adoption of the past tense.
3. The speaking of stage directions and comments.

The adoption of the third person and the past tense enables
the actor to attain the correct, distanced attitude. In addition,
the actor seeks directions and comments on his text, and in
rehearsal he speaks them ("He stood up and said angrily, for
he hadn't eaten . . ." or, "He heard it for the first time, and
didn't know whether it was the truth" or, "He smiled and
said in all too carefree a manner . . ."). To speak stage directions or commentaries in the third person is to bring two
tonalities into collision in such a manner that the second (the
text proper) is alienated. The acting, also, is alienated in that
it actually happens after being expressed in words, after being
announced. The adoption of the past tense places the speaker
where he can look back at a statement. The statement is thereby
alienated without the speaker's having to assume an unreal
standpoint, for, in contrast to the listener, he has read the play
through already and (from the end backwards, from the consequences backwards) can better judge a statement than the
latter who knows less and is further away from (more "alien"
from) the statement.

Through this threefold process the text is alienated in rehearsal and in general will remain so in performance.

As to speaking of the lines, when the speaker addresses himself directly to the audience, he can and must vary his style —
in respect to the greater or lesser significance of his various
lines. The way witnesses talk in court affords an example; the
way they underline, insist on, what they say must be given a
special artistic form. If the actor turns to the audience, he must
turn the whole way. He must not use the technique of the aside
or the old-time soliloquy. To get the full A-effect out of the

verse the actor would do well to rehearse the content, for a time, in crude prose, sometimes together with the gestures that belong to the verse. A bold and beautiful verbal architecture itself alienates a text.

Gesture is a subject for further discussion, but it can be said here that feeling, when it is called for, should be *brought out;* that is, it should become gesture. The actor must find a sensuous outward expression for the emotions of his role — *an action,* wherever possible, which reveals what is going on inside. The emotion concerned must *come out,* must be set free, so that it can be given shape and greatness. Special elegance, strength, and charm of gesture have the A-effect. The Chinese actor handles gesture in a masterly fashion. In visibly observing his own movements, he achieves the A-effect.

Whatever the actor renders by way of gesture and verse-speaking must be *ready* and bear the stamp of readiness, finishedness, the stamp of rehearsal. An impression of ease, which means an impression of difficulties overcome, must be given. The actor must permit the audience to take acting — his own art, his mastery of technical problems — lightly. With consummate skill he presents events as in his opinion they may have happened — or may yet happen — in reality. He does not conceal the fact that he has studied all this any more than the acrobat conceals his training. And he underscores the fact that this is his, the actor's account, version, opinion of the events.

Since he does not identify himself with the man he presents, he can see him from a particular, chosen standpoint, can reveal his opinion of him, and bring the spectator, who also was not invited to identify himself with the character, to criticize him.

The standpoint thus assumed is that of social criticism. By his arrangement of events and his interpretation of his role, the actor gradually brings out those things, those traits, that belong to the social realm. His performance thus becomes a colloquy with the audience — to whom he turns — about social conditions. He induces the listener, according to his class, to justify or change these conditions.

It is the aim of the A-effect to alienate that "social gesture" which underlies all events. By "social gesture" is meant the mimetic and gestural expression of social relations between men in a particular epoch.

In recounting events for the benefit of society, in so ordering them that the key is placed in society's hands, a useful device is a written title for each scene. Such titles must have a historical character.

This brings us to a decisive technical feature, of Epic Theater, the "historification of everyday life."

The actor must play the events of a play as historical events. Historical events happen once for all and are over. They are bound up with particular epochs. People's behavior in these epochs is not merely human and invariable. It has special characteristics. It contains things, as history proceeds, which are repeated, or could be repeated. It is subject to criticism from the standpoint of the following epoch. Constant historical development estranges from us the behavior of those born earlier. Now, the actor has to assume that distance from occurrences and modes of behavior in the present which the historian assumes from occurrences and modes of behavior in the past. He has to alienate these events and people in the same way.

Events and people of the day, of the immediate environment, seem rather natural to us because we are used to them. To alienate them is to make them stand out. The technique of being irritated by customary, obvious, never-questioned events has been carefully built up by science, and there is no reason why art should not take over so infinitely useful an attitude. It is an attitude which, in the realm of science, resulted from a growth in human productivity. In the realm of art, it results from the same source.

As far as emotion is concerned, experiments with the A-effect in the German theater have demonstrated that even this kind of acting arouses emotions, if not the same emotions as those of the conventional theater. A critical attitude on the part of the spectator is a thoroughly artistic attitude. The A-effect is not as unnatural as it may sound.

Obviously this kind of acting has nothing to do with "stylization" as commonly understood. The leading preference of

Epic Theater, with its A-effect which has the single aim of showing how the world works, to the end that the world may be changed, is precisely for naturalness and earthiness, for humor, and for the renunciation of all the mysticism that still clings to the conventional theater, a relic of bygone days.

Stage Illusion

CHARLES LAMB

A PLAY is said to be well or ill acted, in proportion to the scenical illusion produced. Whether such illusion can in any case be perfect, is not the question. The nearest approach to it, we are told, is, when the actor appears wholly unconscious of the presence of spectators. In tragedy — in all which is to affect the feelings — this undivided attention to his stage business seems indispensable. Yet it is, in fact, dispensed with every day by our cleverest tragedians; and while these references to an audience, in the shape of rant or sentiment, are not too frequent or palpable, a sufficient quantity of illusion for the purposes of dramatic interest may be said to be produced in spite of them. But, tragedy apart, it may be inquired whether, in certain characters in comedy, especially those which are a little extravagant, or which involve some notion repugnant to the moral sense, it is not a proof of the highest skill in the comedian when, without absolutely appealing to an audience, he keeps up a tacit understanding with them: and makes them, unconsciously to themselves, a party in the scene. The utmost nicety is required in the mode of doing this; but we speak only of the great artists in the profession.

The most mortifying infirmity in human nature, to feel in ourselves, or to contemplate in another, is, perhaps, cowardice. To see a coward *done to the life* upon a stage would produce anything but mirth. Yet we most of us remember Jack Bannister's cowards. Could anything be more agreeable, more pleasant? We loved the rogues. How was this effected but by the exquisite art of the actor in a perpetual subinsinuation to us, the spectators, even in the extremity of the shaking fit, that he was not half such a coward as we took him for? We saw all the common symptoms of the malady upon him; the quivering lip, the cowering knees, the teeth chattering; and could have sworn "that man was frightened." But we forgot all the while — or kept it almost a secret to ourselves — that he never once lost his self-possession; that he let out, by a thousand droll looks and gestures — meant at *us*, and not at all supposed to be visible to his fellows in the scene, that his confidence in his own resources had never once deserted him. Was this a genuine picture of a coward; or not rather a likeness, which the clever artist contrived to palm upon us instead of an original; while we secretly connived at the delusion for the purpose of greater pleasure, than a more genuine counterfeiting of the imbecility, helplessness, and utter self-desertion, which we know to be concomitants of cowardice in real life, could have given us?

Why are misers so hateful in the world, and so endurable on the stage, but because the skillful actor, by a sort of subreference, rather than direct appeal to us, disarms the character of a great deal of its odiousness, by seeming to engage *our* compassion for the insecure tenure by which he holds his money-bags and parchments? By this subtle vent half of the hatefulness of the character — the self-closeness with which in real life it coils itself up from the sympathies of men — evaporates. The miser becomes sympathetic; *i.e.*, is no genuine miser. Here again a diverting likeness is substituted for a very disagreeable reality.

Spleen, irritability — the pitiable infirmities of old men, which produce only pain to behold in the realities, counterfeited upon a stage, divert not altogether for the comic appendages to them, but in part from an inner conviction that they are *being acted* before us; that a likeness only is going on, and not the thing itself. They please by being done under the life, or beside it; not *to the life*. When Gattie acts an old man, is he angry indeed? or only a pleasant counterfeit, just enough of a likeness to recognize, without pressing upon us the uneasy sense of a reality?

Comedians, paradoxical as it may seem, may be too natural.

It was the case with a late actor. Nothing could be more earnest
or true than the manner of Mr. Emery; this told excellently in
his Tyke, and characters of a tragic cast. But when he carried
the same rigid exclusiveness of attention to the stage business,
and willful blindness and oblivion of everything before the
curtain into his comedy, it produced a harsh and dissonant
effect. He was out of keeping with the rest of the *Personæ
Dramatis*. There was as little link between him and them, as
betwixt himself and the audience. He was a third estate —
dry, repulsive, and unsocial to all. Individually considered, his
execution was masterly. But comedy is not this unbending
thing; for this reason, that the same degree of credibility is not
required of it as to serious scenes. The degrees of credibility
demanded to the two things may be illustrated by the different
sort of truth which we expect when a man tells us a mournful
or a merry story. If we suspect the former of falsehood in any
one tittle, we reject it altogether. Our tears refuse to flow at a
suspected imposition. But the teller of a mirthful tale has
latitude allowed him. We are content with less than absolute
truth. 'Tis the same with dramatic illusion. We confess we love
in comedy to see an audience naturalized behind the scenes —
taken into the interest of the drama, welcomed as bystanders,
however. There is something ungracious in a comic actor holding
himself aloof from all participation or concern with those who
are come to be diverted by him. Macbeth must see the dagger,
and no ear but his own be told of it; but an old fool in farce
may think he *sees something*, and by conscious words and looks
express it, as plainly as he can speak, to pit, box, and gallery.
When an impertinent in tragedy, an Osric, for instance, breaks
in upon the serious passions of the scene, we approve of the
contempt with which he is treated. But when the pleasant impertinent of comedy, in a piece purely meant to give delight,
and raise mirth out of whimsical perplexities, worries the studi-
ous man with taking up his leisure, or making his house his
home, the same sort of contempt expressed (however *natural*)
would destroy the balance of delight in the spectators. To make
the intrusion comic, the actor who plays the annoyed man must
a little desert nature; he must, in short, be thinking of the audi-

ence, and express only so much dissatisfaction and peevishness as is consistent with the pleasure of comedy. In other words, his perplexity must seem half put on. If he repel the intruder with the sober set face of a man in earnest, and more especially if he deliver his expostulations in a tone which in the world must necessarily provoke a duel, his real-life manner will destroy the whimsical and purely dramatic existence of the other character (which to render it comic demands an antagonist comicality on the part of the character opposed to it), and convert what was meant for mirth, rather than belief, into a downright piece of impertinence indeed, which would raise no diversion in us, but rather stir pain, to see inflicted in earnest upon any unworthy person. A very judicious actor (in most of his parts) seems to have fallen into an error of this sort in his playing with Mr. Wrench in the farce of *Free and Easy*.

Many instances would be tedious; these may suffice to show that comic acting at least does not always demand from the performer that strict abstraction from all reference to an audience which is exacted of it; but that in some cases a sort of compromise may take place, and all the purposes of dramatic delight be attained by a judicious understanding, not too openly announced, between the ladies and gentlemen — on both sides of the curtain.

DRAMA, OPERA, AND CINEMA

Among the artistic forms that substantially resemble the drama are opera and cinema. An opera is sometimes thought of as a play that is sung, but in the best operas the music is primary, the words are secondary. (The success of *Otello*, in which music and words are perfectly matched, surely owes much to the fact that Verdi's librettist, Boito, was himself a composer.) The plot or fable, which Aristotle says is the soul of drama, is in opera commonly a vehicle that allows the performers to engage periodically in lyrical virtuoso pieces. The words of these lyrical moments are often obscured by musical requirements, and may be in a language unintelligible to many in the audience. The broad pantomimic gestures (in a play condemned as operatic) communicate the gist of the situation and contribute to the spectacle, which is usually lavish. The cinema, of course, relies even more heavily than opera on visual elements. At the beginning of this century, when motion pictures were in their infancy, the relationship between play and picture was indeed close, the camera projecting on the screen the melodramas and spectacular productions that the theater offered. The film, however, has increasingly made its own forms — most obviously the documentary and the animated cartoon, but also the screenplay, which, taking advantage of the camera's potentialities, is not merely a stage play on film. A good stage play, almost everyone has noticed, rarely makes a good movie unless heavily adapted.

W. H. Auden (1907-   ) has written several verse plays. His best known plays, *The Dog Beneath the Skin* (1935) and *The Ascent of F6* (1938) — both written with Christopher Isherwood — have recently appeared in a paperback reprint, but Auden has abandoned writing for the legitimate theater and has turned to the opera house. "Dramatic poetry, to be recognizable as poetry, must raise its voice and be grand. But a poet today," Auden says, "cannot raise his voice without sounding false and ridiculous." With Chester Kallman he has written two libretti, *The Rake's Progress* and *Elegy for Young Lovers,* and translated the libretto of *The Magic Flute.*

SIEGFRIED KRACAUER (1889-   ), educated in Germany, but now a resident of New York, is the author of *Theory of Film,* widely considered the best book on the aesthetics of the film. In the selecttion from his book printed here he suggests, among other things, that the theater excells in representing interrelationships between human beings, while the cinema excells in exploring the surrounding world and in presenting transient impressions.

A Public Art

W. H. AUDEN

WHY DO I want to write librettos? Because I have a passion for opera as an artistic genre. Any arguments I may advance to prove the virtues of opera are rationalizations to convince myself that my passion is not a mania.

One of the most striking changes in taste which has occurred during my lifetime has been the change in attitude towards opera among the musical highbrows in England and America. When I was young, it was very difficult for anyone who did not live within reach of Covent Garden or the Metropolitan to hear any operas; they were not, so far as I remember, broadcast, and there were no recordings of complete operas. But these facts do not really explain the change. I was brought up to believe that opera was a bastard art-form. The great Mozart operas might just do because Mozart was Mozart, but Wagner in one way and Verdi in another were considered vulgar; as for Rossini, Bellini, and Donizetti, they were simply beyond the pale. (Judging by some articles I have read, this prejudice still survives in certain English quarters.) In addition, we were put off, not en-

tirely without justification, by the kind of public which *did*
"go to the opera"; many of them seemed more interested in
appearing at the appropriate social event for the London Season
than in listening to music.

This attitude had an influence on the composers themselves.
Even as late as the thirties, no British or American composer,
I fancy, would have entertained the notion of being primarily
an operatic composer; he might write an opera as an experiment,
but he did not expect it to be taken as one of his major works.
All this, thank goodness, is past. The opera houses are packed
by an audience in which the socialite element is very small; the
broadcasts from Covent Garden, Glyndebourne, and the Metropolitan are listened to by tens of thousands; the record companies make a handsome profit from the sale of operatic recordings; almost every living composer of note has written more
than one opera with considerable critical and popular success.
A writer who shows the slightest talent for making a libretto
will find himself in demand.

There are two kinds of stage-work in which a poet can have
a hand, verse-drama and opera. If he chooses the first, he is responsible for everything except the interpretation; if he chooses
the second, then, though the librettist's contribution is not, I
believe, negligible, his role is obviously a subordinate one. Human egoism is such that no poet will prefer the subordinate role
unless he prefers opera to any verse-drama, even one he might
write himself. He must be convinced, that is to say, that there
are things opera can do which verse-drama cannot, and that
these are more valuable than anything which could be done in
the latter medium. He is thinking, of course, of the present,
not the past, of what can and cannot be done *now*.

For what it is worth, my personal conviction is this. Drama is
necessarily a public art. To be of public interest a human being
must be heroic; his or her actions, sufferings, emotions, must
be exceptional and in the grand manner. For a number of reasons the Public Realm is no longer a place where speech can
be authentic. Speech, the medium of the poet, is now the expressive medium of the intimate: the singular can address the
singular in poetry, but poetry cannot appear in public without

becoming false to itself. In our age there are only two public dramatic arts, opera and ballet. Ballet is wordless, but opera requires the singable word. (Let us not presume to call it poetry.) Outside his own proper sphere of the intimate, there is still something a poet, if he is prepared to submit to a librettist's limitations, can contribute to the Public Realm.

Dramatic poetry, to be recognizable as poetry, must raise its voice and be grand. But a poet today cannot raise his voice without sounding false and ridiculous. The modern poetic dramatist seems faced with these alternatives: either he writes the kind of verse which is natural to him, in which case he produces little closet dramas which can only make their effect if the audience is a small intimate one, or, if he wishes to write a public drama, he must so flatten his verse that it sounds to the ear like prose. Neither alternative seems to me satisfactory.

Opera and ballet, it will be noticed, are both virtuoso arts. Without an exceptional physical endowment, vocal cords or a body, granted to very few human beings, no amount of intelligence, taste, and training can make a great singer or dancer. It is this, I believe, that, in an age when all the other arts are restricted to the intimate, still allows the opera and the ballet to be public. When we listen to a great singer or watch a great dancer we feel him or her to be a heroic superhuman being even if the music or the choreography is sub-human trash.

Furthermore, there is still a tradition in opera-singing and in classical dancing of how things should be done which is handed on from generation to generation. That is why it is possible to compare the way one singer takes a particular phrase with the way another singer takes it. If there ever were such a tradition governing the speaking of English dramatic verse it has been lost. (The French theater may be different.) When I attend a performance of a Shakespeare play, most of the cast mangle the verse atrociously; there may be one or two who speak it well, but each has his own style which clashes with the style of the others.

Without going so far as to say that all opera must be *bel canto*, I am prepared to assert that in any satisfactory opera the voices must make as beautiful noises as the orchestra. (*Woz-*

zeck, in my opinion, fails in this respect.) It is up to the librettist to provide the composer with a set of characters and a kind of verse which make beautiful vocal noises plausible and possible. Before starting work, the librettist needs to know and be in sympathy with, firstly, the kind of sounds the composer is interested in making, and secondly the kind of voices, if possible the actual singers, the composer has in mind.

The suspicion which our modern sensibility has of the heroic, its quickness to detect the least trace of the fake-heroic, makes the discovery of a suitable plot and suitable characters much more difficult than it was in the past. It has, I believe, always been the case that, to be operatic, the principal characters must have a certain mythical significance which transcends their historical and social circumstances. (Violetta in *La Traviata,* for instance, is not merely a *grande cocotte*[1] living in Paris in the early 19th century; she is also an archetype which has fascinated our culture for centuries, the Magdalen, the harlot with the loving heart.) Where shall the modern librettist discover mythical figures which have not already been worked to death? That is the problem. But problems are fun.

If I may be excused for daring to make a suggestion to composers, I would hazard the guess that the serious opera possible in our age is *opera buffa,* not *opera seria.*

If it is difficult to get a new opera performed, it is surprising to me, and much to the credit of opera house managers, that any get performed at all. Producing an opera is an extremely expensive business; and an opera cannot, like a musical comedy, have a run. At best, if it is successful, it can become part of the repertory, where it has to compete with acknowledged masterpieces, and however good it is, the chances of it being a masterpiece are bound to be small. Moreover, a new opera has to overcome the unfortunate psycho-physical fact that the musical ear is a conservative organ, which prefers repetition to novelty. While most people would rather see a new play, even an inferior one, than a play they have seen before, most people would rather re-hear a symphony or an opera which they already know well than listen to an unfamiliar work, however good.

[1] A courtesan, kept luxuriously [Editors' note].

The Theatrical Story

SIEGFRIED KRACAUER

Form and content

The time-honored differentiation between form and content of artistic achievements affords a convenient starting-point for an analysis of story types. It is true that in any given case these two components of the work of art interpenetrate each other insolubly: each content includes form elements; each form is also content. (Hence the legitimate ambiguity of such terms as "comedy," "melodrama," and "tragedy"; they may point to the peculiar contents or the formal aspects of the genres they designate or cover both of them indiscriminately.) But it is no less true that the concepts "form" and "content" have a basis in the properties of the artistic work itself. And the near-impossibility of neatly validating these concepts in the material is rather a point in their favor. With complex live entities the accuracy of definitions does not suffer from the fact that they retain a fringe of indistinct meanings. Quite the contrary, they must be elusive to achieve maximum precision — which implies that any attempt to remove their seeming vagueness for the sake of semantically irreproachable concepts is thoroughly devious.

This chapter and the two following will be devoted to a breakdown of story types according to differences in form. Since these types should be expected to be relevant cinematically, they must be definable in terms which bear on the inherent affinities of film. They constitute types only if they reveal themselves as such from the angle of cinema.

An uncinematic story form

To begin with uncinematic story forms, only one such type stands out distinctly — the "theatrical story," so called because its prototype is the theatrical play. Uncinematic stories, then, are patterned on a traditional literary genre; they tend to follow

132

the ways of the theater. Significantly, the literature on film abounds with statements which place all the emphasis on the incompatibility of film and stage, while paying little attention, if any, to the obvious similarities between the two media. Thus Eisenstein, Pudovkin, and Alexandrov in their 1928 manifesto voice misgivings lest the advent of sound might engender a flood of " 'highly cultured dramas' and other photographed performances of a theatrical sort." In Proust the narrator compares the impression his grandmother makes on him after a long absence with a photograph picturing her as the sick, old woman she is. But this is not the way, he continues, in which we usually perceive the world, especially things we cherish. Rather, "our eye, charged with thought, neglects, as would a classical tragedy, every image that does not assist the action of the play and retains only those that may help us to make its purpose intelligible." He concludes by calling his lapse into photographic perception a chance event which is bound to happen when our eyes, "arising first in the field and having it to themselves, set to work mechanically like films." This passage is important because it specifies the sort of theater least amenable to cinematic treatment. Proust identifies it as the classical tragedy. To him the classical tragedy is a story form which, because of its tight and purposeful composition, goes the limit in defying the photographic media. By the way, the Eisenstein of 1928, who had not yet succumbed to the pressures of Stalinism, may have referred to this very compositional entity when he predicted an increase of "highly cultured dramas" in the wake of sound.

ORIGINS AND SOURCES

The trend in favor of the theatrical story was initiated as early as 1908 by *Film d'Art*, a new French film company whose first production, the much-praised and much decried *Assassination of the Duc de Guise*, represented a deliberate attempt to transform the cinema into an art medium on a par with the traditional literary media. The idea was to demonstrate that films were quite able to tell, in terms of their own, meaningful stories after the manner of the theater or the novel. An academician wrote the scenario of this ambitious film; actors of the *Comédie-Française* impersonated its historical characters; and dramatic critics of high repute published enthusiastic reviews. From the lower depths the cinema thus rose to the regions of literature and theatrical art. Cultured people could no longer look down on a medium engaged in such noble pursuits.

Duc de Guise, then, aimed at rehabilitating the cinema in the name of Art. And since its authors were saturated with stage traditions, it was natural for them to believe that, to be art, the cinema would have to evolve along much the same lines as the theater. The action of *Duc de Guise* is strongly reminiscent of historical dramas, as they unfold on the stage. And so is the *mise-en-scène.* Méliès' insistence on advancing the narrative with the aid of specifically cinematic devices seems forgotten; instead an immobile camera captures the drama from the angle of the spectator in the pit. The camera *is* the spectator. And the characters themselves move in settings which for all their realism never let you ignore that they are painted canvas — a *Château de Blois* intended to impress the theatergoer, not the moviegoer, as the real thing.[1]

It should be noted, though, that, its theatricality notwithstanding, *Duc de Guise* testifies to a certain awareness of the differences between the two media. The story of the conspiracy against the Duke and his ultimate liquidation appears to have been fashioned with a view to acclimatizing theatrical art to the screen. In any case, the jerky succession of isolated *tableaux vivants,* customary then, is here superseded by a sort of pictorial continuity which does not depend upon lengthy captions to make itself understood. Also, the actors play their parts with a sense of detailed characterization and a minimum of gestures, thus breaking away from stage conventions.[2]

A tremendous success, *Duc de Guise* fathered hosts of period pictures and "highly cultured dramas" in France. America followed suit. D. W. Griffith let himself be inspired by this first *film d'art;* and Adolph Zukor began to feature "famous players

[1] Cf. Sadoul, *Les Pionniers du cinéma,* p. 540.
[2] See ibid. pp. 540, 542; Langlois, "Notes sur l'histoire du cinéma," *La Revue du cinéma,* July 1948, vol. III, no. 15:13-14.

in famous plays." Producers, distributors, and exhibitors were quick to realize that Art meant big business. Films capitalizing on the prestige of literary works or imitating them attracted the culture-minded bourgeoisie which had shunned the moviehouses before. The moviehouses themselves became more and more sumptuous in the process.[3] Their cheap, if expensive, glamor was a condoning factor in as much as it denounced the falsity of these cultural aspirations. (Yet in stigmatizing the commercialization of art, the discerning critic will have to acknowledge that it does not necessarily do away with art. Many a commercial film or television production is a genuine achievement besides being a commodity. Germs of new beginnings may develop within a thoroughly alienated environment.)

The *film d'art* movement persists, unbroken, to the present day. As might be expected, numerous films of this type, such as *Pygmalion*, *Death of a Salesman*, etc., are actually theatrical adaptations. There is practically no Broadway hit that would not be exploited by Hollywood. Or think of the uninterrupted series of Shakespeare films, down to *Julius Caesar*, *Macbeth*, and *Richard III*. However brilliantly executed, in spirit and structure all such screen dramas can still be traced to *Duc de Guise*. They need not be theatrical adaptations. Films like *The Informer*, *The Heiress*, *Great Expectations*, and *Rouge et Noir* take their inspiration from novels and yet recall the stage as vividly as does any screen version of a play. About the same applies to *Moby Dick*; despite its cinematic elaborations it renders the Melville novel in terms of a dramatic action which would be a natural for the theater. Other theatrical films do not borrow from literary sources at all, as is illustrated by *Duc de Guise* itself. Similarly, Eisenstein's last films, *Alexander Nevsky* and *Ivan the Terrible*, are original screen works; nevertheless, they seem to be patterned after non-existent plays or operas. It is not by accident that shortly before his death Eisenstein directed Wagner's *Die Walküre*. He once rebelled against the theater; he reverted to it at the end.

[3] For this passage, see Jacobs, *The Rise of the American Film*, p. 9; Sadoul, op. cit. pp. 541-3, 573; Clair, "Le cinématographe contre l'esprit," in Lapierre, ed., *Anthologie du cinéma*, pp. 175-6.

Emphasis on human interaction

As viewed from both photography and film, one of the main features of the theatrical story form is its strong concern for human characters and human interrelations. This is in accordance with stage conditions. To repeat what has already been said, theatrical *mise-en-scène* cannot re-create full physical reality in all its incidents. Huge crowds transcend the given frame; tiny objects are lost in the total impression of it. Much must be omitted and much is an allusive substitute rather than the real thing. The stage universe is a shadowy replica of the world we live in, representing only such parts of it as sustain the dialogue and the acting and through them an intrigue which inevitably concentrates on events and experiences purely human.[4] But all this has a restrictive effect on film. The theatrical story limits the appropriate use of a medium which does not differentiate between humans and inanimate objects.

Complex units

The smallest elements of the stageplay — and consequently the theatrical story — are complex units as compared with the elements accessible to the camera. The reason is that, because of its dependence upon stage conditions and its concomitant emphasis on humanly significant action, the theatrical play does not admit indefinite breakdowns. Of course, it may suggest them in varying degrees. Shakespearean plays, for instance, are relatively transparent to unstaged nature, introducing characters and situations which might as well be dispensed with in a strictly compositional interest; and these seeming diversions and excursions evoke, somehow, life in the raw — its random events, its endless combinations.[5] Also, a *Kammerspiel** may come so close to its characters that it sensitizes the spectator to imperceptible psychological undercurrents and their physio-

[4] Cf. Cohen-Séat, *Essai sur les principes* . . . , pp. 94-5.
[5] See Auerbach, *Mimesis*, pp. 321-3.
* A private play given for a select audience [editors' note].

logical correspondences. Yet even the most subtle, most open-ended stage play is hardly in a position to implement its suggestions and carry analysis beyond a certain point.

The fact that the elements of which it consists — behavior patterns, passions, conflicts, beliefs — are highly complicated aggregates can easily be seen. Take the modern novel: Joyce, Proust, and Virginia Woolf coincide in decomposing the smallest units of older types of the novel — those which cover a series of developments as they occur in chronological time. These modern writers, says Erich Auerbach, "who prefer the exploitation of random everyday events, contained within a few hours and days, to the complete and chronological representation of a total exterior continuum . . . are guided by the consideration that it is a hopeless venture to try to be really complete within the total exterior continuum and yet to make what is essential stand out. Then too they hesitate to impose upon life, which is their subject, an order which it does not possess in itself." [6] But the theater goes far beyond any epic genre in forcing such an order on life in its fullness. A glance at the microscopic elements of, say, the Proust novel suffices to reveal the gross nature of the units which form the irreducible cells or nodal points of the stage play.

Film not only transcends human interaction but resembles the novel, modern or not, in that it tends to render transient impressions and relationships which are denied to the stage. From the angle of film the theatrical play is composed of units which represent a crude abbreviation of camera-life. To say the same in cinematic terms, the theatrical story proceeds by way of "long shots." How should it proceed otherwise? It is constructed for the theater, which indeed requires that analysis be curtailed for the sake of dramatic action and that the world onstage be visible from an inalterable, rather remote distance. This is what the young Eisenstein experienced when, as a theater director, he felt increasingly urged to stage the kind of reality germane to the cinema. He removed a wrestling match from the stage to the middle of the auditorium so as to transform it into a real-life event; he even tried — an impossible

[6] Ibid. p. 548.

artifice — to isolate hands, pillars, legs, house façades in an effort to create the illusion of close-ups. But it just did not work. So he left the stage for the screen, while at the same time turning his back on the story as such which, he then believed, was bound to feature individual destinies. His goal, a cinematic one, was the depiction of collective action, with the masses as the true hero.[7]

Complex units interfere with cinematic narration. Hence the jerkiness of films advancing a theatrical intrigue. It is as if they jumped from unit to unit, leaving unexplored the gaps in between — whereby it does not in the least matter whether the films are silent or follow the lead of dialogue. And each jump affects the spectator as an arbitrary change of direction, because the units which mark the joints of the intrigue are by far not the last elements at which cinematic analysis may arrive. In the play *Romeo and Juliet* the Friar's failure to pass on Juliet's letter in time is acceptable because it suggests the workings of Fate. But in *Romeo and Juliet*, the Castellani film, the same event does not stand for anything; rather, it appears as an outside intervention unmotivated by what goes before, a story twist which for no reason at all abruptly alters the course of action. The whole affair with the letter belongs at best to an ideological continuum, not the material one to which film aspires. It is a sham entity which would have to be broken down into its psychophysical components to become part of camera-reality. This does not imply, of course, that the cinema can afford completely to ignore units which, so to speak, are given only in long shots. These units, which resemble intricately structured molecules, transmit common thoughts, emotions, visions. If the film narrative did not occasionally avail itself of them as points of arrival or departure, the spectator would be at a loss how to assimilate the succession of camera revelations.

Detachable patterns of meanings

In progressing from complex unit to complex unit, the theatrical story evolves distinct patterns of meanings. From the angle of film these patterns give the impression of being prearranged

[7] See Eisenstein, *Film Form*, pp. 7, 14, 17.

because they assert themselves independently of the flow of visuals; instead of seeming to grow out of it, it is they which determine the direction of that flow, if flow it still is. Compare *Romeo and Juliet* with *Umberto D.*: the Shakespeare film relates a self-sufficient story which is significant in its own right, whereas the significance of the De Sica film lies in the penetration with which it pictures the everyday existence of an old man condemned to live on a pension which does not permit him to live; here the story consists in what the camera makes us see. Unlike this truly cinematic story, the theatrical intrigue is detachable from the medium; accordingly, the imagery conveying it illustrates rather than releases its meanings. When looking at a theatrical film, our imagination is in fact not primarily stimulated by pictures of physical reality so that, following their suggestions, it would work its way from them toward significant story contexts; conversely, it is first attracted by these contexts and only then takes cognizance of the pictorial material bearing them out.

A whole with a purpose

Much as theatrical intrigues may be given to meandering and thus acquire an almost epic quality, when compared with film they all appear to be modeled on the classical tragedy which, Proust has it, neglects "every image that does not assist the action of the play and retains only those that may help us to make its purpose intelligible." The story form he has in mind is not only a whole — all works of art are, more or less — but a whole with a purpose; its every element, that is, has the sole function of serving that purpose. Now the term "purpose," as used by Proust, evidently refers to the significance of the story. So one might as well say that, viewed from film, the theatrical intrigue revolves around an ideological center toward which all its patterns of meanings converge. In other words, it must be tightly organized; it is essentially a closed story.

From the early thirties on, when the individual hero began to supersede the heroic masses on the Soviet screen, Eisenstein under the pressure of terrorist totalitarianism expressly championed this story type and its compositional implications. He requested each fragment of a film to be "an organic part of an organically conceived whole."[8] And he declared toward the end of his life: "For us montage became a means . . . of achieving an organic embodiment of a single idea conception, embracing all elements, parts, details of the film-work."[9] In his youth Eisenstein had been less idealistic-minded, less totalitarian. Legitimately so, for a film built from elements whose only *raison d'être* consists in implementing the (pre-established) "idea conception" at the core of the whole runs counter to the spirit of a medium privileged to capture "the ripple of leaves in the wind." There is a nice observation by Béla Balázs to the effect that children linger over details while adults tend to neglect the detail in some big design. But since children see the world in close-ups, he argues, they are more at home in the atmosphere of film than in the long-shot universe of the theater.[10] The conclusion, not drawn by Balázs himself, would be that the theatrical film appeals to adults who have suppressed the child in themselves.

ATTEMPTS AT ADJUSTMENT

The "most marvelous things"

FEYDER'S DICTUM

Jacques Feyder, the French film director, once postulated that "everything can be transferred to the screen, everything expressed through an image. It is possible to adapt an engaging and humane film from the tenth chapter of Montesquieu's *L'Esprit des lois* as well as . . . a paragraph of Nietzsche's *Zoroaster*." Yet to do this, he cautiously adds, "it is indispensable to have the sense of the cinema."[11]

Assuming for the sake of argument that Feyder is right, the

[8] Ibid. p. 92.
[9] Ibid. p. 254. It should be noted that Pudovkin, *Film Technique and Film Acting*, part I, p. 90, advances a similar opinion: "A film is only really significant when every one of its elements is firmly welded to a whole."
[10] Balázs, *Der sichtbare Mensch*, p. 115.
[11] Feyder, "Transposition visuelle," in *Cinéma* (Les cahiers du mois, 16/17), 1925, p. 71.

theatrical story would certainly not resist cinematic treatment. But how can it be transformed into authentic cinema? In narrating such a story, any film maker who has the sense of the medium is obviously faced with two different, if not incompatible, tasks. He will have to put across the story as the purposeful whole it is — a task requiring him to reproduce its complex units and patterns of meanings in a straight manner. At the same time he will have to follow the realistic tendency — a task which prompts him to extend the story into the dimension of physical existence.

STRAIGHT REPRESENTATION OF THE INTRIGUE

Many theatrical films, among them some executed with consummate skill, live up to the first task without even trying to pursue the second. They adequately impart the intrigue, with all its inherent meanings but, as if completely absorbed in its straight representation, fail to explore the world around us. *The Informer, Glass Menagerie, Mourning Becomes Electra, Death of a Salesman, Rouge et Noir*, etc., are hardly more than custom-made adaptations of tightly composed stories detachable from the medium; they fit the story like a well-tailored suit. Hence an atmosphere which induces claustrophobia in the viewer. This must be laid to the way their imagery is handled.

In the old Griffith film, *Broken Blossoms*, the superb shots of the fog enveloping the Thames and the London East End streets seem to have no other function than to picture the environment in which the action takes place. Whatever they may contribute to establish the action, they do not exhaust themselves in supporting it. They really record city nature. What a contrast between this natural fog and the fog which plays so conspicuous a role in Ford's *The Informer*! It is a symbolic fog expressly selected or concocted to point beyond itself toward the "idea conception" of the intrigue.[12] Griffith's lens opens upon the world, while Ford shuts it out in the interest of theatrical composition. Yet at least *The Informer* does not pretend to

[12] Griffith, "The Film Since Then," in Rotha, *The Film Till Now*, p. 483, characterizes *The Informer* as a melodrama whose "pretentious, adolescent symbolism continued through the film."

camera-reality. Other films in the same vein do. Thus Kazan
leans over backward in an attempt to pass off his *On the Waterfront* as a semi-documentary. The film, a veritable *tour de force*,
is shot on location and utilizes techniques appropriate to a film
of fact. Actually it is nearly the opposite. Every shot of it is calculated to enhance the dramatic impact of a contrived intrigue.
There is no air about these shots. True, they let in material reality, but they do so only to drain it of its essence. Reality itself is
here employed to build a universe as hermetically closed as
that of *The Informer*.

In sum, films which aim at the straight implementation of a
theatrical story have the following, easily recognizable features
in common. They emphasize the actors and their interplay. In
keeping with this main concern, they further coincide in as-
signing to inanimate objects and environmental factors a subsidiary role. Finally and most important, they include practically
no image that would not serve the ends of story construction.
This is to say, each image, instead of being established as a
fragment of reality which may yield multiple meanings, must
assume a meaning derived from contexts alien to the medium
— contexts which gravitate toward an ideological center.

EXTENSION OF THE INTRIGUE

"I am rewriting Shakespeare," said Zecca, the contemporary
of Lumière and Méliès, to a friend who found him blue-pencil-
ing a manuscript. "The wretched fellow has left out the most
marvelous things." [13] Zecca had the feel of the medium; what
he did was simply to devote himself to the task of extending the
theatrical story in the direction of camera-life. There is little
doubt indeed that his "most marvelous things" are identical
with the specifically cinematic subjects treated in chapter 3:
objects moving, the small, the big, the familiar, etc. The necessity of incorporating these subjects, should even the script not
provide for them, has been recognized, if with less candor, by
modern film makers and critics as well. "The content of theater
material," said Hitchcock to an interviewer, "is much slighter

[13] Quoted by Bardèche and Brasillach, *The History of Motion Pictures*,
p. 46, and Sadoul, *Les Pionniers du cinéma*, p. 530n.

than that of the movies. One good movie may need as much material as four plays." [14] And Panofsky holds that "in a film it does not interrupt but rather intensifies the action if the shifting of the scene from one place to another — meaningless as it is psychologically — is thoroughly depicted as an actual transportation with car-driving through heavy street traffic, motorboating through a nocturnal harbor, galloping on horseback, or whatever the case may be." [15]

Not every extension of a theatrical intrigue, however, is an extension which causes "reality itself to participate in the action." [16] If, for instance, a play includes a verbal reference, indispensable for its understanding, to World War II, and the film version of that play shows a few typical battle scenes, these supplementary shots are unlikely to exert a noticeable impact; they illustrate rather than extend the verbal reference. The whole issue is intelligently paraphrased in the late Norbert Lusk's memoirs. Reminiscing about the silent 1923 adaptation of O'Neill's *Anna Christie*, Lusk observes that the film version comprises two episodes not given on the stage: Anna as a child in her Swedish native village and, somewhat later, Anna being raped by a degenerate. Are these additions in the nature of extensions?

The point he makes is that they are not. As he sees it, they just serve to tell in pictures what the play is able to convey through words — that Anna "was a foreigner but wholesome" and that "her subsequent life was no fault of her own." The playwright himself shared this view. "With quick perception of a medium new to him," relates Lusk, "Mr. O'Neill quietly pointed out that the interpolation was necessary to round out the story in terms of photographed action. He . . . accepted the film for the sincere transcription it was." [17] The two episodes, then, were added for the sole purpose of transcribing

[14] Turner, "On Suspense and Other Film Matters: An Interview with Alfred Hitchcock," *Films in Review*, April 1950, vol. I, no. 3:22, 47.
[15] Panofsky, "Style and Medium in the Moving Pictures," *transition*, 1937, no. 26:125.
[16] Quoted from Eisenstein, *Film Form*, p. 182.
[17] Lusk, "I Love Actresses!" *New Movies*, Jan. 1947, vol. XXII, no. 1:28, 30.

faithfully the intentions of the original in a medium which could not yet express them otherwise. For lack of sound, pictures were required not to extend the play but to reproduce it. The excess amount of visuals did not result from a concern with cinematic subjects.

Yet, more often than not, theatrical films do manifest such a concern. Their authors really extend the story to include the "most marvelous things." This may be achieved in a hundred of ways. A run-of-the-mill procedure, referred to by Panofsky, is the insertion of street scenes in films whose plots would be fully intelligible if the protagonists stayed indoors all the time. Whenever film makers want to "take an action out of stylized presentation (however effective) and make it completely natural," [18] they feel irresistibly attracted by the street and its extensions. Presumably the sharp contrast between unstaged street life and purposeful stage action is responsible for this common preference.

To mention also a few less typical efforts along similar lines, Laurence Olivier in his *Hamlet* has the camera incessantly pan and travel through the studio-built maze of Elsinore castle, with its irrational staircases, raw walls, and Romanesque ornaments, in an effort to expand the play into the twilight region of psychophysical correspondences. Or remember Eisenstein's script of *American Tragedy*, which clearly centers on an "idea conception": his desire to externalize Clyde's inner struggle in the form of a *monologue intérieur* marks an attempt to dissolve one of the most decisive complex units of his script into an all but unlimited succession of cinematic elements uncalled-for by the story construction. It sometimes is as if these extensions were considered more essential than the story itself. Stroheim confessed to an interviewer that he was possessed with a "madness for detail." [19] And Béla Balázs praises a silent American film for leaving on two occasions its story behind and indulg-

[18] Ferguson, "Life Goes to the Pictures," *films*, Spring 1940, vol. I, no. 2:21.

[19] Lewis, "Erich von Stroheim of the Movies . . . ," *The New York Times*, June 22, 1941.

ing instead in a "thin hail of small moments of . . . material life" [20] which were to bring the environment into play.

No doubt these cinematic elaborations have the function of adjusting the theatrical intrigue to the medium. But what about their relation to the intrigue proper? From the angle of the story they are much in the nature of gratuitous excursions. The story does not depend upon their inclusion to cast its spell over the audience.[21] On the one hand, then, such extensions prove desirable, if not indispensable, cinematically; on the other, they are inconsistent with a story form which for full impact requires straight representation. The concern for the extensions and the regard for the fabric of story motifs tend to conflict with each other. This conflict shows in two ways both of which press home the difficulty of a solution.

Two alternatives

THE STORY COMPOSITION OVERSHADOWING
THE CINEMATIC ELABORATIONS

"Nevsky I found too stylized and too prearranged," says Rotha. And comparing it with Eisenstein's earlier films, Potemkin and Ten Days, he adds: "The well-known Battle on the Ice never roused me to heights of response as did the Odessa Steps or the Storming of the Winter Palace." [22] His different reactions must be laid to a difference in story form between Nevsky and the two other films — a difference which Eisenstein himself tried to blur later on. At the time he made Nevsky, he still admitted, it is true, that Potemkin looks like a chronicle or a newsreel but then insisted that it was in reality a "tragic composition in its most canonic form — the five-act tragedy." [23]

[20] Balázs, Der sichtbare Mensch, pp. 46-7. Cf. also Greene, "Subjects and Stories," in Davy, ed., Footnotes to the Film, p. 69, about incidental life in We from Kronstadt. Similarly, Ferguson, op. cit. passim, emphasizes the importance for films to incorporate fleeting moments of physical life.
[21] Cf. Caveing, "Dialectique du concept du cinéma," Revue internationale de filmologie, Oct. 1948, vol. I, nos. 3-4:349-50.
[22] Rotha, "A Foreword," in Eisenstein, 1898-1948.
[23] Eisenstein, Film Form, pp. 162-3.

No definition of this film could be more misleading. Even though *Potemkin* culminates in moments of tragic suspense and is, all in all, a masterpiece of intense and deliberate cutting, it is anything but a tragedy in the sense of Proust — a theatrical composition, that is, which radically obstructs the photographic or cinematic approach. Evidence of this may be found in Eisenstein's sudden decision to change his script upon seeing the historic Odessa steps. The sight of them moved him to discard much of the work already done and concentrate on the mutiny of the *Potemkin* sailors, which is a nontheatrical episode rather than a classical drama.[24]

The testimony of his eyes seems to have convinced him that the cinema has a special affinity for episodes quivering with life in the raw. *Potemkin* is a real-life episode told in pictures. One must have seen the sailors' revolt or the sequence of the Odessa steps to grasp the action. The fact that these pictures embody the intrigue instead of merely illustrating it can be inferred from the indeterminacy of many shots. Not forced to lend color to given story lines, the rising mists in the harbor, the heavily sleeping sailors, and the moonlit waves stand for themselves alone. They are part and parcel of the wide reality involved; and they are under no obligation whatever to serve an extraneous purpose that would impinge on their essence. They are largely purposeless; it is they and their intrinsic meanings which *are* the action.

The same applies to the famous close-up of the surgeon's pince-nez dangling down the ship rope. A decade or so after *Potemkin* Eisenstein would refer to this particular close-up to exemplify the artistic merits of the *pars pro toto* method. By showing only part of an object or human figure, says he, the artist compels the spectator to retrogress to primitive modes of thinking — a state of mind where the part is at the same time the whole. "The pince-nez, taking the place of a whole surgeon, not only completely fills his role and place, but does so with a huge sensual-emotional increase in the intensity of the impression." [25] Here too Eisenstein overemphasizes the importance

[24] Seton, *Sergei M. Eisenstein*, pp. 74-5.
[25] Eisenstein, op. cit. p. 132.

of the whole at the expense of the parts and fragments. To be sure, the pince-nez caught up in the rope signifies the death of its owner. But the haphazard tangle, rich in contrasts, of materials — part rough, part fine — is also significant in its own right; it carries various implications and only one of them points in the direction which Eisenstein has in mind.

Now consider the Battle on the Ice in *Nevsky*. Unlike the Odessa steps, it marks the pictorial climax of an intrigue which conforms better than *Potemkin* to Eisenstein's misinterpretation of the latter — that *Potemkin* is not so much a "chronicle" as a "composition in its most canonic form." *Nevsky* is not strictly a five-act tragedy, yet it is a historical drama conceived in terms of the stage. It is a whole with a purpose. Its characters comprise a closed orbit; all its interlinked motifs radiate from an ideological center. *Nevsky* is utterly remote from a real-life episode. Within this self-contained universe, then, there appears the Lake Peipus Battle, a cinematic elaboration in grand style. It is definitely an extension of the intrigue; for all its thoroughness, however, it does not add anything essential to the story developments. Regarding its structural function, it resembles the battles in Shakespeare plays which need not be seen to produce a dramatic effect; summary eye-witness reports fully do the job. The whole extension is clearly intended to drag an otherwise theatrical narrative through the region of camera-reality. As a matter of fact, it is rather lifeless.

Far from reflecting transitory life, the imagery affects you as a (re-)construction meant to be life; each shot seems predetermined; none breathes the allusive indeterminacy of the *Potemkin* pictures. (This is not to belittle the incomparable beauty of the long-distance shot of the plain on which the sequence opens.) Yet the decisive point is the following: the patterns of motifs and themes which make up the *Nevsky* story are so pronounced that they subdue everything that comes their way. Hence, even assuming that the Battle on the Ice were cinematically on a par with the episode of the Odessa steps, these patterns which spread octopus-like would nevertheless corrode its substance, turning it from a suggestive rendering of physical events into a luxuriant adornment. Owing to the given compositional arrangements, the Battle sequence cannot possibly exert the impact of that *Potemkin* episode and thus on its part upset the theatricality of the action. It is nothing but an excrescence on the body of an intrigue imposed upon the medium. (Such "useless" [26] extensions are rather frequent. The battle in *Henry* V, for instance, is just a decorative pageant. And the final hunt of the whale in *Moby Dick* is under a cloud of symbolic references which nearly obscure it; its realism is wasted.)

CINEMATIC ELABORATIONS OVERSHADOWING
THE STORY CONSTRUCTION

The Griffith chase. A classic example of the other alternative — cinematic extensions overshadowing the story meanings — is the stereotyped chase sequence in D. W. Griffith films. Griffith indulges in theatrical intrigues; for long stretches he is content with rendering, one by one, dramatic actions and situations which are highly complex units from a cinematic point of view. Yet beginning with *The Lonely Villa*,[27] all his major films invariably conclude on a drawn-out chase which owes its particular thrill to the device of accelerated parallel cutting. While we are witnessing the agony of some innocent character doomed to death, we are at the same time permitted to watch the advance of his prospective rescuers, and these alternating scenes, or flashes of scenes, follow each other in ever shorter intervals until they ultimately merge, with the victim being redeemed. The Griffith chase dramatizes an intrinsically cinematic subject: objective physical movement.

More important, it is an ingenious attempt not only to extend theater into dimensions where material phenomena mean everything but to make the extension itself appear as an expression of the story's ideological climax. Griffith aspires to nothing less than to reconcile the requirements of the theater with those arising from the cinema's preference for physical reality and

[26] Marcel, "Possibilités et limites de l'art cinématographique," *Revue internationale de filmologie*, July-Dec. 1954, vol. V, nos. 18-9:170, applies the term "useless" in this sense. See also the passage on *Moby Dick* in Bluestone, *Novel into Film*, p. 206.
[27] Cf. Jacobs, *The Rise of the American Film*, pp. 105-6.

the flow of life. His attempt proves abortive, though. He does not, and cannot, succeed in bridging the gap between the theatrical and the cinematic narrative. True, his chases seem to transform ideological suspense into physical suspense without any friction; but upon closer inspection they represent an excess amount of the latter. Thus the "last-minute-rescue" in the "modern story" of *Intolerance* is by no means a translation into cinematic terms of the conclusion at which the story itself arrives; rather, this finale captivates and thrills the spectator as a physical race between antagonistic forces. It provides sensations which do not really bear on, and bring out, the "idea conception" of the story — the triumph of justice over the evil of intolerance. The Griffith chase is not so much the fulfillment of the story as a cinematically effective diversion from it. It drowns ideological suspense in physical excitement.[28]

Pygmalion. The screen adaptation of *Pygmalion* is a case in point also. This film adds to Shaw's comedy a montage of recording machinery in close shots, a detailed depiction of Eliza's phonetic education, including her suffering under its ruthlessness, and the whole embassy ball episode replete with amusing trifles — sequences, all of which feature the physical life and the environment of the stage characters. What is the good of them? Since Shaw states everything he wants to impart in his play, they are certainly not needed to clarify his intentions. Yet there they are. And the embassy ball and the sequence of Higgins pouncing on Eliza are easily the most impressive episodes of the film. Erwin Panofsky has it that "these two scenes, entirely absent from the play, and indeed unachievable on the stage, were the highlights of the film; whereas the Shavian dialogue, however severely cut, turned out to fall a little flat in certain moments." [29]

On the screen, then, the brilliant satire of middle-class morals

[28] Pudovkin, *Film Technique and Film Acting,* part I, p. 19, believes the Griffith chase fully to live up to the significance of the action whose climax it marks. As for Eisenstein's oblique interpretation of this standardized chase sequence, see his *Film Form,* pp. 234-5.
[29] Panofsky, "Style and Medium in the Motion Pictures," *Critique,* Jan.-Feb. 1947, vol. 1, no. 3:11.

loses much of its impact, and what remains of it at all affects us as a leftover from the theater rather than genuine cinema. Or in more general terms, the metamorphosis of the play into a film entails a shift of emphasis from the dimension of intellectual messages to that of photographable objects. Sociological notions are overwhelmed by environmental facts; conceptual reasoning succumbs to the ambiguous manifestations of nature. The stage play evolves, so to speak, *above* the level of physical existence, while the film tends to pass right *through* it in an effort to record it exhaustively. Unlike the film, which brings the embassy staircase, Eliza's nightmares, and Higgins' gadgets into focus, the play takes all this for granted as a background to sophisticated dialogue. It is as if the screen version sprang from a desire to retrieve the raw materials out of which Shaw has carved his comedy and as if this desire automatically weakened the concern with the topics and arguments which keep the comedy going. Those "most marvelous things" which Zecca tried to graft upon Shakespeare are evidently the most ephemeral ones. And sure enough, their insertion calls for a sacrifice.

Running controversy. The extensions of this second type have time and again been categorically rejected or wholeheartedly acclaimed — a smoldering controversy which confirms the depth of the conflict between theatrical and cinematic designs. In the camp of the theatrical-minded, who value above all the straight representation of the intrigue, elaborations which, *Pygmalion* fashion, becloud the intentions of the original are not readily tolerated. These critics condemn the spread of incidentals which do not seem to be integrant elements of the whole. "Is this the experts' way of telling a story?" asks one of them indignantly. And he answers: "The living story is told in people and the things they say, with an occasional essential prop necessary for the progress of the story." [30]

The cinematic-minded on their part are interested not so much in story composition as the incidence of "small moments of material life." They prefer a straying from the preordained

[30] Rawnsley, "Design by Inference," *The Penguin Film Review*, 1949, no. 9:34. Lindgren, *The Art of the Film*, p. 38, expresses a similar view.

course of action toward camera-reality to the rigidity of films which confine themselves dutifully to following that course. Lang's *Fury*, says Otis Ferguson, "has the true creative genius of including little things not germane to the concept but, once you see them, the spit and image of life itself." [31]

This perennial dispute acquires a peculiar poignancy if it comes into the open on occasion of one and the same film. Take the reviews of Vincente Minelli's 1945 film, *The Clock*: whether or not its boy-meets-girl story is a theatrical story proper, the cinematic excursions from it made themselves strongly felt as such at the time and gave rise to diametrically opposed opinions. The theatrical-minded Stephen Longstreet, angry at the director's apparently aimless indulgence in New York street life, requested of him that he should in future shoot scripts that have "honesty, density and depth," shoot them with "old standing sets, some lights and shadows, and a dumb cameraman." [32] Not so Louis Kronenberger. More cinematic-minded, he delighted in Minelli's gift for "incident and detail" and his ability to get "something into *The Clock* that transcends its formula." [33]

CONCLUSIONS

Insoluble dilemma

The upshot is that Feyder is wrong in contending that everything can be transferred to the screen in a cinematic spirit. His dictum breathes complacency; it is that of a man of all too catholic tastes. The theatrical story stems from formative aspirations which conflict irrevocably with the realistic tendency. Consequently, all attempts to adjust it to the cinema by extending its range into regions where the camera is at home result at

---

[31] Ferguson, "Hollywood's Half a Loaf," in Cooke, ed., *Garbo and the Night Watchman*, p. 257.

[32] Longstreet, "Setting Back the Clock," *The Screen Writer*, Aug. 1945, vol. I, no. 3:12.

[33] Kronenberger, "Meet One Day, Mate the Next," *PM*, May 4, 1945. There was the same division of opinions on occasion of Murnau's *Sunrise* (1927), with some critics enjoying the film's loose composition and others complaining about its lack of consistency.

best in some compromise of a sort. The extensions required for the adjustment either disintegrate the intrigue — the case of *Pygmalion* — or are, themselves, rendered ineffective by its indelible suggestions — the case of the *Nevsky* story themes overgrowing the Battle on the Ice.

In spite of these difficulties there are no end of films which follow the tradition of the *film d'art*. Their undeniable popularity, however, is by no means an indicator of their aesthetic validity. It only proves that a mass medium like the film is bound to yield to the enormous pressures of social and cultural conventions, collective preferences, and ingrained habits of perceiving, all of which combine to favor spectacles which may be high-level entertainment but have little to do with films. Within this context an argument by Pierre Bost, the well-known French scenarist, deserves mentioning.

Bost collaborated with Jean Aurenche on two scripts differing radically in cinematic quality — the script of *Gervaise*, an excellent film drawn from Zola's *L'Assommoir*, and that of *Rouge et Noir*, a Stendhal adaptation which is theater pure and simple. In a conversation with Bost, I was pleasantly surprised at learning that he was against using Stendhal in the first place and that he too does not consider *Rouge et Noir* true cinema, as are, say, *La Strada* or *Umberto D*. Yet the point of interest is one of his arguments in defense of the Stendhal film. Bost holds that adaptations from literary classics cater to a lasting demand of the public; at any rate, they are an established French film genre. And this would account for their relative legitimacy, even if they fall back on the ways of the stage. The yardstick by which to appraise them is not primarily their adequacy to the medium but their closeness to the essence of the original (and of course the quality of their execution).

D. W. Griffith's admirable nonsolution

Griffith is generally recognized as the first to narrate a given story — mostly a theatrical one — in cinematic terms. But perhaps his greatest merit is that, unlike many of his successors, he remains keenly aware of the gulf which separates the theatrical story from the cinematic narrative. Except for his chase finales in which he tries in vain to blend these two incompatible modes of representation, he always keeps apart what does not belong together. His films are full of fissures traceable to his cinematic instinct rather than technical awkwardness. On the one hand, he certainly aims at establishing dramatic continuity as impressively as possible; on the other, he invariably inserts images which do not just serve to further the action or convey relevant moods but retain a degree of independence of the intrigue and thus succeed in summoning physical existence. This is precisely the significance of his first close-up. And so do his extreme long shots,[34] his seething crowds, his street episodes and his many fragmentary scenes[35] invite us to absorb them intensely. In watching these pictures or pictorial configurations, we may indeed forget the drama they punctuate in their own diffuse meanings. Eisenstein did, for one. Years after having seen *Intolerance*, he no longer remembered who is who in the street sequences of this film's "modern story"; but the figure of a passer-by visible only "for a flashing glimpse" still stood vividly before his inner eye.

[34] Cf. Reisz, *The Technique of Film Editing*, pp. 24-5; Jacobs, *The Rise of the American Film*, pp. 111, 199.
[35] Jacobs, ibid. pp. 185, 192.

DRAMATIC CRITICISM

Most of the preceding essays are theoretical rather than critical: they study types rather than works, principles rather than plays. Criticism, it is commonly held, offers reasoned opinions about particular works; it analyzes and evaluates. Probably every piece of criticism rests on some theory, stated or not, but an essay that calls attention to the ways in which a specific play makes its effect — or which seeks to define a play's effect — can be said to be critical rather than theoretical. Aristotle is theoretical when he talks of the nature of the tragic hero, critical when he talks of Sophocles' and Euripides' use of the chorus.

H. D. F. KITTO (1897-   ) is Professor of Greek at the University of Bristol. In his two books on drama, *Greek Tragedy* and *Form and Meaning in Drama*, he assumes that a play "means" something, that its meaning is in its total impact, and that this meaning and impact can be best experienced by looking at the play's structure with care and imagination. In the essay printed here he attempts to see what sort of man Oedipus is, what sort of universe he lives in, and what sort of response the playwright elicits from an intelligent reader.

BERNARD KNOX (1914-   ), born in England, has been Professor of Greek at Yale University and is currently the director of the Center for Hellenic Studies, Washington, D.C. In addition to publishing a translation of *Oedipus the King* and a book on Oedipus, Mr. Knox has served as script-writer and lecturer for a series of four educational films on the play. More than any other essayist in this collection, he focuses on the language of a particular play. He shows how certain recurring words reveal and comment upon character and action — how, for example, the very name "Oidipous" combines the tragic protagonist's wisdom and weakness.

155

Sophocles: The *Oedipus Tyrannus*

H. D. F. KITTO

THE STORY of the *Tyrannus* is of a common Greek type; something unpleasant is predicted, the persons concerned try to avert it and think themselves safe, but in some natural though surprising fashion the prediction is fulfilled. Next to the *Tyrannus* itself, the most elaborate example is the story of Astyages and the infant Cyrus in Herodotus. What does Sophocles make of this ancient motif?

At the beginning of the play Oedipus is the great King who has saved Thebes in the past and is their only hope now; no one can compare with Oedipus in reading dark secrets. At the end, he is the polluted outcast, himself the cause of the city's distress, through crimes predicted by Apollo before he was born. Is this grim determinism? Is Sophocles telling us that Man is only the plaything of Fate? Or does he mean, as Bowra has recently suggested,[1] that the gods have contrived this awful fate for Oedipus in order to display their power to man and to teach him a salutary lesson? Or is Sophocles simply making exciting drama, leaving the philosophical implications unexplored? There is only one way of finding out. Whatever Sophocles meant, he put his meaning into the play, and to get it out again we must contemplate the play — all of it, in all its aspects; not bits of it, and some of its aspects.

As in the *Electra*, the action shows a certain duality. In the foreground are autonomous human actors, drawn vividly, and complete. Oedipus himself, Tiresias, Creon, Iocasta, and the two shepherds, are all as lifelike as characters in a play can be; and so, in their degree, are the remoter characters who do not appear — the hot-tempered Laius at the cross-road, and the unknown Corinthian who insulted Oedipus when he was half-drunk. The circumstances too are natural, even inevitable, granted these characters. Oedipus, as we see him time after time, is intelligent, determined, self-reliant, but hot-tempered and

[1] *Sophoclean Tragedy*, p. 175.

too sure of himself; and an apparently malignant chain of circumstances combines now with the strong, now with the weak side of his character to produce the catastrophe. A man of poor spirit would have swallowed the insult and remained safe in Corinth, but Oedipus was resolute; not content with Polybus' assurance he went to Delphi and asked the god about it, and when the god, not answering his question, repeated the warning given originally to Laius, Oedipus, being a man of determination, never went back to Corinth. It was a coincidence, but not an unnatural one, that Laius was on his way from Thebes to Delphi. They met at the cross-road, and as father and son were of similar temper the disaster occurred. Even so, he could have arrived at Thebes safely, had he not been a man of high intelligence; for then he could not have read the riddle of the Sphinx. But again, though intelligent, he was blind enough to marry a woman old enough to be his mother, certain that his mother was in Corinth. The story is not moralized. Sophocles could have put Oedipus in the wrong at the cross-road; he could have suggested that blind ambition made him accept the crown and Queen of Thebes. He does neither of these things; Oedipus is not being given his deserts by an offended Heaven. What happens is the natural result of the weaknesses and the virtues of his character, in combination with other people's. It is a tragic chapter from life, complete in itself, except for the original oracle and its repetition. Sophocles is not trying to make us feel that an inexorable destiny or a malignant god is guiding the events.

But we are made to feel, as in the *Electra*, that the action is moving, at the same time, on a parallel and higher plane.

The presence of some power or some design in the background is already suggested by the continuous dramatic irony — which seems overdone, if it is regarded as only a dramatic effect. In the matter of the Plague this hidden power is definitely stated; and its presence is most imaginatively revealed, as in the *Electra*, in the scene containing Iocasta's sacrifice. She who has been so skeptical of oracles surprises us by coming out with sacrificial offerings. She lays them on Apollo's altar, puts fire to the incense, and prays for deliverance from fear.

There is a moment of reverent silence, and this is broken by the arrival of the cheerful messenger from Corinth: Polybus is dead; fear is at an end; the prayer has been heard. But within the hour Iocasta has hanged herself. — And what of her offerings? Still there, on the altar, in full view of the audience; the incense, it may be, still carrying to the god a petition that he has so terribly answered.

This is no theatrical trick, but a revelation of the dramatist's thought. It is the action of the unseen god made manifest. But how does the god answer the pitiful prayer of Iocasta, the impious prayer of Clytemnestra? Not by any direct interposition. The Apollo of Sophocles is nothing like the Zeus of Aeschylus, who works his will by freezing the Strymon or by blasting a fleet. It was not Apollo who incited the Corinthian to come, but his own eagerness to be the first with the good news, and his own hopes (as Sophocles is careful to tell us) of standing well with the new King; for besides the news of his succession to the crown he has another and a much more exciting tale to tell — in his own good time. He, like the Paedagogus, is completely autonomous, yet in the coming of each the hand of the god is seen. The action moves on two planes at once.

Nevertheless, the whole texture of the play is so vividly naturalistic that we must be reluctant to interpret it as a bleak Determinism. These people are not puppets of higher powers; they act in their own right. Nor, I think, does this texture encourage us to accept Bowra's explanation.

In the first place, if Sophocles meant that the gods are displaying their power because they will, that they have ordained this life for Oedipus in order to read men a lesson, it was so easy for him to say so — to write an ode on the power and the mysterious ways of the gods. He conspicuously does not do this. Indeed, in the ode that immediately follows the catastrophe the chorus says not that the fate of Oedipus is a special display of divine power, but on the contrary that it is typical of human life and fortunes.

In the second place, although Oedipus is by far the greatest sufferer in the play he is not the only one. There are others

who suffer, not by any means in the same degree, but in the
same way; and we must take account of them too, not dismiss them as being parts of the dramatic economy but not of
the thought. If we contemplate, as we should, the whole play
and all its aspects, we see that Oedipus is not a special case,
except in the degree to which he suffers; he is, as the Chorus
says, typical; what has happened to him is part of the whole
web of human life. Why for example does Sophocles intro-
duce the children in the last act? Not simply because it is
"natural"; a good play isn't "nature," but art. One reason must
be that Oedipus may say to them what he does say: "What a
life must yours be! Who will admit you to the festivals? Who
will marry you — born as you were born?" Such is life, such
are the gods. The innocent suffer with the guilty.

We must contemplate also two other characters who form
no inconsiderable part of the play — the two shepherds. It
was not merely to liven up his play, or to indulge his talents,
that Sophocles drew them like this, with their motives, hopes,
fears, so sharply presented. The Corinthian, like the Paedagogus, makes no bones about expecting a tip; not for the
reason that Headlam so oddly gave,[2] that it was the oriental
custom to reward messengers (as if dramatists were only pho-
tographers), but because the point bears on the drama. The
news that this man brings is great news indeed, but he has
something much more astonishing in reserve and the moment
for producing it soon comes. "Polybus? He was no more your
father than I am. . . . Why, I gave you to him with my own
hands. . . . A hired shepherd? Yes, my son; but that day I
saved your life." A hired shepherd — but this is a great day
for him; he began by addressing Oedipus as "My Lord," but
now he can say "My son," "No, *that* I cannot tell you. . . .
You must find the Theban who gave you to me. . . ." Iocasta's last despairing shriek does not disturb him, for, as Oedipus
says, probably she is dismayed to find that her husband is of
low birth. The chorus is happy and excited; and when the
reluctant Theban is brought in, our friend becomes even more
bland and helpful, as he works up to his climax:

[2] See G. Thomson, *Oresteia*, II, 69 (note to v. 591).

"Here is the man, my friend, who was that baby!"
And this is his last speech. No reward for him; no glory in
Corinth — only bewilderment and utter dismay; for in a mo-
ment he hears, from his old companion,

> "I pitied it, my lord. I thought to send
> The child abroad, whence this man came. And he
> Saved it, for utter doom. For if you are
> The man he says, then you were born for ruin."

He sees his new King rush into the palace; and then — the
final ode? Not yet. These two actors have to make their exit,
by the long side-passages, in full view of the audience; some
forty yards of exit. And as we watch them stumbling out we
have time to reflect that this is the outcome, for them, of
their merciful interest in an abandoned baby.

Is not this too the work of Apollo? Here, as in the greater
case of Oedipus, is that conjunction of well-meant action with
a situation which makes it lead to disaster. An act of mercy,
tinged with a perfectly honest shrewdness, leads the Corinthian to the verge of what is, for him, greatness; as he stretches
out his hand, eagerly and with confidence, it turns into horror.

The other shepherd too is one who refused to kill a baby.
Part of his reward comes years later, when he sees the man
who killed Laius ascend his victim's throne and marry his
Queen — an event which sends him, for his own safety, into
half-exile[3]; the rest of his reward comes now, when a sudden
command brings him back at last to the city, to learn what
he learns here.

These minor tragedies, of the children and the shepherds,
are all of a piece with the major one. This is Apollo; this is
life. An awful sin is committed in all innocence; children
are born to a life of shame; virtuous intentions go awry. What
are we to think of it? Of course, moral and prudential lessons
can be drawn from it — though Sophocles draws very few —
but what do we think of it? Where is the explanation? What,
in other words, is the catharsis? That Oedipus accepts his

---

[3] For he, no bought slave, but reared in the palace (v. 1123), besought
Iocasta to send him into the fields, as far as possible from the city (vv.
758 ff.).

fate? But when you are knocked flat, you must accept it; and if you cannot get up again, you must be resigned. There is little illumination in this.

The catharsis that we are looking for is the ultimate illumination which shall turn a painful story into a profound and moving experience. It has been suggested by Professor Ellis-Fermor[4] that the catharsis of plays like the *Tyrannus* and *Macbeth* lies in the perfection of their form, which, by implication, represents the forces of righteousness and beneficence, of which Aeschylus speaks directly, in his choric odes. This is manifestly true of the *Tyrannus*.

Let us go back to Iocasta's sacrifice, and Apollo's swift and devastating answer. In the corresponding passage of the *Electra* the point was clear. Clytemnestra prayed that injustice, *adikia*, might triumph, and she got the answer she deserved. What of Iocasta? She has been denying the truth of oracles. Was Sophocles then so fiercely orthodox that he could equate Iocasta's skepticism with Clytemnestra's wickedness? Of course not; this was not the size of Sophocles' mind. He means much more than this. Iocasta has said "Why should we fear oracles, when there is no such thing as foresight (*pronoia*)? Best live at random, as one may" — a doctrine which would deny the very basis of all serious Greek thought; for while Greek life was still healthy and stable, the Greek believed, as if by instinct, that the universe was not chaotic and "irrational," but was based on a *logos*, obeyed Law. The Ionian philosophers did not discover, but rather postulated, this *logos*.

The tragic poets too think in this way — as Whitehead saw, when he said that they, rather than the Ionians, were the first scientific thinkers. In the *Oresteia* we find moral laws which have the same sort of validity as physical and mathematical laws. The doer must suffer; hybris leads to Atê; the problem there — a problem for gods as well as for men — is to find a system of Justice that will fit into this framework without disastrously contravening these laws. To the mind of Sophocles this *logos* shows itself (as we shall see more fully in the next chapter) as a balance, rhythm, or pattern in human affairs.

4 *Frontiers of Drama*, p. 133.

"Call no man happy until he is dead," for the chances of life
are incalculable. But this does not mean that they are chaotic;
if so they seem to us, it is because we are unable to see the
whole pattern. But sometimes, when life for a moment becomes
dramatic, we can see enough pattern to give us faith that there
is a meaning in the whole. In the *Antigone*, when Creon is
overwhelmed, it is by the natural recoil of his own acts, working themselves out through the minds and passions of Antigone and Haemon, and we can see in this a natural justice. In
the *Electra*, the vengeance that at last falls on the assassins
is linked to their crime by natural chains of cause and effect.
In the *Tyrannus* we have a much more complex picture. The
same *dikê* is at work, though this time the *adikia* which it
avenges was involuntary and indeed innocent. Oedipus — to repeat our image — is blasted as a man may be who inadvertently
interferes with the natural flow of electricity. *Dikê* here works
through many apparently casual and unrelated actions — of
the shepherds, of the charioteer who tried to push Oedipus
off the road, of the man at the banquet. . . . Things fall out
contrary to all expectation; life seems cruel and chaotic. Cruel,
perhaps; chaotic, no — for if it were chaotic no god could predict, and Iocasta would be right. "If these oracles are not manifestly fulfilled, why should I join in the sacred dance?" Piety
and purity are not the whole of the mysterious pattern of life,
as the fate of Oedipus shows, but they are an important part of
it, and the doctrine of chaos would deny even this. The pattern
may harshly cut across the life of the individual, but at least
we know that it exists, and we may feel assured that piety and
purity are a large part of it.

Every detail in the *Tyrannus* is contrived in order to enforce
Sophocles' faith in this underlying *logos*; that is the reason
why it is true to say that the perfection of its form implies a
world-order. Whether or not it is beneficient, Sophocles does
not say.

Sophocles' Oedipus

BERNARD KNOX

SOPHOCLES' Oedipus is not only the greatest creation of a major poet and the classic representative figure of his age: he is also one of the long series of tragic protagonists who stand as symbols of human aspiration and despair before the characteristic dilemma of Western civilization — the problem of man's true nature, his proper place in the universe.

In the earlier of the two Sophoclean plays which deal with the figure of Oedipus, this fundamental problem is raised at the very beginning of the prologue by the careful distinctions which the priest makes in defining his attitude toward Oedipus, the former savior of Thebes, its absolute ruler, and its last hope of rescue from the plague. "We beg your help," he says, "regarding you not as one equated to the gods, θεοῖσι . . οὐκ ἰσούμενον, but as first of men."

"Not equated to the gods, but first of men." The positive part of the statement at any rate is undeniably true. Oedipus is *tyrannos* of Thebes, its despotic ruler. The Greek word corresponds neither to Shelley's "Tyrant" nor to Yeats's "King": tyrannos is an absolute ruler, who may be a bad ruler, or a good one (as Oedipus clearly is), but in either case he is a ruler who has seized power, not inherited it. He is not a king, for a king succeeds only by birth; the tyrannos succeeds by brains, force, influence. "This absolute power, τυραννίς," says Oedipus in the play "is a prize won with masses and money." This title of Oedipus, tyrannos, is one of the most powerful ironies of the play, for, although Oedipus does not know it, he is not only tyrannos, the outsider who came to power in Thebes, he is also the legitimate king by birth, for he was born the son of Laius. Only when his identity is revealed can he properly be called king: and the chorus refers to him by this title for the first time in the great ode which it sings after Oedipus knows the truth.

But the word tyrannos has a larger significance. Oedipus, to quote that same choral ode, is a παράδειγμα, a paradigm, an

163

example to all men; and the fact that he is tyrannos, self-made ruler, the proverbial Greek example of worldly success won by individual intelligence and exertion, makes him an appropriate symbol of civilized man, who was beginning to believe, in the 5th century B.C., that he could seize control of his environment and make his own destiny, become, in fact, equated to the gods. "Oedipus shot his arrow far beyond the range of others" — the choral ode again — "and accomplished the conquest of complete prosperity and happiness."

Oedipus became tyrannos by answering the riddle of the Sphinx. It was no easy riddle, and he answered it, as he proudly asserts, without help from prophets, from bird-signs, from gods; he answered it alone, with his intelligence. The answer won him a city and the hand of a queen. And the answer to the Sphinx's riddle was — Man. In Sophocles' own century the same answer had been proposed to a greater riddle. "Man," said Protagoras the sophist, "is the measure of all things."

Protagoras' famous statement is the epitome of the critical and optimistic spirit of the middle years of the 5th century; its implications are clear — man is the center of the universe, his intelligence can overcome all obstacles, he is master of his own destiny, tyrannos, self-made ruler who has the capacity to attain complete prosperity and happiness.

In an earlier Sophoclean play, *Antigone*, the chorus sings a hymn to this man the conqueror. "Many are the wonders and terrors, and nothing more wonderful and terrible than man." He has conquered the sea, "this creature goes beyond the white sea pressing forward as the swell crashes about him"; and he has conquered the land, "earth, highest of the gods . . . he wears away with the turning plough." He has mastered not only the elements, sea and land, but the birds, beasts, and fishes; "through knowledge and technique," sings the chorus, he is yoker of the horse, tamer of the bull. "And he has taught himself speech and thought swift as the wind and attitudes which enable him to live in communities and means to shelter himself from the frost and rain. Full of resources he faces the future, nothing will find him at a loss. Death, it is true, he will not avoid, yet he has thought out ways of escape from desperate diseases. His knowledge, ingenuity and technique are beyond anything that could have been foreseen." These lyrics describe the rise to power of *anthropos tyrannos*; self-taught he seizes control of his environment, he is master of the elements, the animals, the arts and sciences of civilization. "Full of resources he faces the future"—an apt description of Oedipus at the beginning of our play.

And it is not the only phrase of this ode which is relevant; for Oedipus is connected by the terms he uses, and which are used to and about him, with the whole range of human achievement which has raised man to his present level. All the items of this triumphant catalogue recur in the *Oedipus Tyrannos*; the images of the play define him as helmsman, conqueror of the sea, and ploughman, conqueror of the land, as hunter, master of speech and thought, inventor, legislator, physician. Oedipus is faced in the play with an intellectual problem, and as he marshals his intellectual resources to solve it, the language of the play suggests a comparison between Oedipus' methods in the play and the whole range of sciences and techniques which have brought man to mastery, made him tyrannos of the world.

Oedipus' problem is apparently simple: "Who is the murderer of Laius?" but as he pursues the answer the question changes shape. It becomes a different problem: "Who am I?" And the answer to this problem involves the gods as well as man. The answer to the question is not what he expected, it is in fact a reversal, that *peripeteia* which Aristotle speaks of in connection with this play. The state of Oedipus is reversed from "first of men" to "most accursed of men"; his attitude from the proud ἀρκτέον "I must rule" to the humble πειστέον, "I must obey." "Reversal" says Aristotle, "is a change of the action into the opposite," and one meaning of this much disputed phrase is that the action produces the opposite of the actor's intentions. So Oedipus curses the murderer of Laius and it turns out that he has cursed himself. But this reversal is not confined to the action; it is also the process of all the great images of the play which identify Oedipus as the inventive, critical spirit of his century. As the images unfold, the enquirer turns into the object of enquiry, the hunter into the prey, the doctor into the patient, the investigator into the criminal, the revealer into the thing revealed, the finder into the thing found, the savior into the thing saved ("I was saved, for some dreadful destiny"), the liberator into the thing released ("I released your feet from the bonds which pierced your ankles" says the Corinthian messenger), the accuser becomes the defendant, the ruler the subject, the teacher not only the pupil but also the object lesson, the example. A change of the action into its opposite, from active to passive.

And the two opening images of the *Antigone* ode recur with hideous effect. Oedipus the helmsman, who steers the ship of state, is seen, in Tiresias' words, as one who "steers his ship into a nameless anchorage," "who" in the chorus' words "shared the same great harbor with his father." And Oedipus the ploughman — "How," asks the chorus, "how could the furrows which your father ploughed bear you in silence for so long?"

This reversal is the movement of the play, parallel in the imagery and the action: it is the overthrow of the tyrannos, of man who seized power and thought himself "equated to the gods." The bold metaphor of the priest introduces another of the images which parallel in their development the reversal of the hero, and which suggest that Oedipus is a figure symbolic of human intelligence and achievement in general. He is not only helmsman, ploughman, inventor, legislator, liberator, revealer, doctor — he is also equator, mathematician, calculator; "equated" is a mathematical term, and it is only one of a whole complex of such terms which present Oedipus in yet a fresh aspect of man tyrannos. One of Oedipus' favorite words is "measure" and this is of course a significant metaphor: measure, mensuration, number, calculation — these are among the most important inventions which have brought man to power. Aeschylus' Prometheus, the mythical civilizer of human life, counts number among the foremost of his gifts to man. "And number, too, I invented, outstanding among clever devices." In the river valleys of the East generations of mensuration and calculation had brought man to an under-

standing of the movements of the stars and of time: in the
histories of his friend Herodotus, Sophocles had read of the
calculation and mensuration which had gone into the building of the pyramids. "Measure" — it is Protagoras' word: "Man
is the measure of all things." In this play man's measure is
taken, his true equation found. The play is full of equations,
some of them incomplete, some false; the final equation shows
man equated not to the gods but to himself, as Oedipus is
finally equated to himself. For there are in the play not one
Oedipus but two.

One is the magnificent figure set before us in the opening
scenes, tyrannos, the man of wealth and power, first of men,
the intellect and energy which drives on the search. The other
is the object of the search, a shadowy figure who has violated
the most fundamental human taboos, an incestuous parricide,
"most accursed of men." And even before the one Oedipus
finds the other, they are connected and equated in the name
which they both bear, Oedipus. Oedipus — Swollen-foot; it
emphasizes the physical blemish which scars the body of the
splendid tyrannos, a defect which he tries to forget but which
reminds us of the outcast child this tyrannos once was and the
outcast man he is soon to be. The second half of the name
πούς, "foot," recurs throughout the play, as a mocking phrase
which recalls this other Oedipus. "The Sphinx forced us to
look at what was at our feet," says Creon. Tiresias invokes "the
dread-footed curse of your father and mother." And the choral
odes echo and re-echo with this word. "Let the murderer of
Laius set his foot in motion in flight." "The murderer is a man
alone with forlorn foot." "The laws of Zeus are high-footed."
"The man of pride plunges down into doom where he cannot
use his foot."

These mocking repitions of one-half the name invoke the
unknown Oedipus who will be revealed: the equally emphatic
repetition of the first half emphasizes the dominant attitude
of the man before us. *Oidi* — "swell," but it is also *Oida*, "I
know," and this word is often, too often, in Oedipus' mouth.
His knowledge is what makes him tyrannos, confident and decisive; knowledge has made man what he is, master of the

world. Οἶδα, "I know" — it runs through the play with the same
mocking persistence as πούς, "foot," and sometimes reaches an
extreme of macabre punning emphasis.

When the messenger, to take one example of many, comes
to tell Oedipus that his father, Polybus, is dead, he enquires for
Oedipus, who is in the palace, in the following words:

> "Strangers, from you might I learn where
>   is the palace of the tyrannos Oedipus,
>   best of all, where he is himself if you know where."

Here it is in the Greek:

> ἆρ' ἄν παρ' ὑμῶν ὦ ξένοι μάθοιμ' ὅπου (oimopou)
> τὰ τοῦ τυράννου δώματ' ἐστὶν Οἰδίπου (oidipou)
> μάλιστα δ' αὐτὸν εἴπατ' εἰ κάτισθ' ὅπου (isthopou)

Those punning rhyming line-endings, μάθοιμ' ὅπου, Οἰδίπου,
κάτισθ' ὅπου, "learn where," "Oedipus," "know where," un-
paralleled elsewhere in Greek tragedy, are a striking example
of the boldness with which Sophocles uses language: from the
"sweet singer of Colonus" they are somewhat unexpected, they
might almost have been written by the not-so-sweet singer of
Trieste-Zürich-Paris.[1]

Οἶδα, the knowledge of the tyrannos, πούς, the swollen foot
of Laius' son — in the hero's name the basic equation is already
symbolically present, the equation which Oedipus will finally
solve. But the priest in the prologue is speaking of a different
equation, ἰσούμενον, "We beg your help, not as one equated to
the gods. . . ." It is a warning, and the warning is needed. For
although Oedipus in the opening scenes is a model of formal
and verbal piety, the piety is skin-deep. And even before he
declares his true religion, he can address the chorus, which has
been praying to the gods, with godlike words. "What you pray
for you will receive, if you will listen to and accept what I am
about to say."

The priest goes on to suggest a better equation: he asks Oedipus to equate himself to the man he was when he saved Thebes
from the Sphinx. "You saved us then, be now the equal of

---

[1] *I.e.,* James Joyce [editors' note].

the man you were." This is the first statement of the theme, the double Oedipus; here there is a contrast implied between the present Oedipus who is failing to save his city from the plague and the successful Oedipus of the past who answered the riddle of the Sphinx. He must answer a riddle again, be his old self, but the answer to this riddle will not be as simple as the answer to the first. When it is found, he will be equated, not to the foreigner who saved the city and became tyrannos, but to the native-born king, the son of Laius and Jocasta.

Oedipus repeats the significant word, "equal," ὅστις ἐξ ἴσου νοσεῖ. "Sick as you are, not one of you has sickness equal to mine," and he adds a word of his own, his characteristic metaphor. He is impatient at Creon's absence. "Measuring the day against the time (ξυμμετρούμενον χρόνῳ), I am worried. . . ." And then as Creon approaches, "He is now commensurate with the range of our voices" — ξύμμετρος γὰρ ὡς κλύειν.

Here is Oedipus the equator and measurer, this is the method by which he will reach the truth: calculation of time and place, measurement and comparison of age and number and description — these are the techniques which will solve the equation, establish the identity of the murderer of Laius. The tightly organized and relentless process by which Oedipus finds his way to the truth is the operation of the human intellect in many aspects; it is the investigation of the officer of the law who identifies the criminal, the series of diagnoses of the physician who identifies the disease — it has even been compared by Freud to the process of psychoanalysis — and it is also the working out of a mathematical problem which will end with the establishment of a true equation.

The numerical nature of the problem is emphasized at once with Creon's entry. "One man of Laius' party escaped," says Creon, "he had only one thing to say." "What is it?" asks Oedipus. "One thing might find a way to learn many." The one thing is that Laius was killed not by one man but by many. This sounds like a problem in arithmetic, and Oedipus undertakes to solve it. But the chorus which now comes on stage has no such confidence: it sings of the plague with despair, but it makes this statement in terms of the same metaphor; it has its characteristic word which, like the priest and like Oedipus, it pronounces twice. The chorus' word is ἀνάριθμος, "numberless," "uncountable." "My sorrows are beyond the count of number," and later, "uncountable the deaths of which the city is dying." The plague is something beyond the power of "number . . . outstanding among clever devices."

The prologue and the first stasimon, besides presenting the customary exposition of the plot, present also the exposition of the metaphor. And with the entry of Tiresias, the development of the metaphor begins, its terrible potentialities are revealed. "Even though you are tyrannos," says the prophet at the height of his anger, "you and I must be made equal in one thing, at least, the chance for an equal reply," ἐξισωστέον τὸ γοῦν ἴσ' ἀντιλέξαι. Tiresias is blind, and Oedipus will be made equal to him in this before the play is over. But there is more still. "There is a mass of evil of which you are unconscious which shall equate you to yourself and your children."

ἅ σ' ἐξισώσει σοί τε καὶ τοῖς σοῖς τέκνοις.

This is not the equation the priest desired to see, Oedipus present equated with Oedipus past, the deliverer from the Sphinx, but a more terrible equation reaching farther back into the past, Oedipus son of Polybus and Merope equated to Oedipus son of Laius and Jocasta; "equate you with your own children," for Oedipus is the brother of his own sons and daughters. In his closing words Tiresias explains this mysterious line, and connects it with the unknown murderer of Laius. "He will be revealed, a native Theban, one who in his relationship with his own children is both brother and father, with his mother both son and husband, with his father, both marriage-partner and murderer. Go inside and reckon this up, λογίζου, and if you find me mistaken in my reckoning, ἐψευσμένον, then say I have no head for prophecy."

Tiresias adopts the terms of Oedipus' own science and throws them in his face. But these new equations are beyond Oedipus' understanding, he dismisses them as the ravings of an unsuccessful conspirator with his back to the wall. Even the chorus, though disturbed, rejects the prophet's words and resolves to stand by Oedipus.

After Tiresias, Creon: after the prophet, the politician. In Tiresias, Oedipus faced a blind man who saw with unearthly sight; but Creon's vision, like that of Oedipus, is of this world. They are two of a kind, and Creon talks Oedipus' language. It is a quarrel between two calculators. "Hear an equal reply," says Creon, and "Long time might be measured since Laius' murder." "You and Jocasta rule in equality of power." And finally "Am I not a third party equated, ἰσοῦμαι, to you two?" Creon and Oedipus are not equal now, for Creon is at the mercy of Oedipus, begging for a hearing; but before the play is over Oedipus will be at the mercy of Creon, begging kindness for his daughters, and he then uses the same word. "Do not equate them with my misfortunes."

μηδ' ἐξισώσῃς τάσδε τοῖς ἐμοῖς κακοῖς

With Jocasta's intervention the enquiry changes direction. In her attempt to comfort Oedipus, whose only accuser is a prophet, she indicts prophecy in general, using as an example the unfulfilled prophecy about her own child, who was supposed to kill Laius. The child was abandoned on the mountain-side and Laius was killed by robbers where three wagon roads meet. "Such were the definitions, διώρισαν, made by prophetic voices," and they were incorrect. But Oedipus is not, for the moment, interested in prophetic voices. "Where three wagon roads meet." He once killed a man at such a place and now in a series of swift questions he determines the relation of these two events. The place, the time, the description of the victim, the number in his party, five, all correspond exactly. His account of the circumstances includes Apollo's prophecy that he would kill his father and be his mother's mate. But this does not disturb him now. That prophecy has not been fulfilled, for his father and mother are in Corinth, where he will never go again. "I measure the distance to Corinth by the stars," ἄστροις . . . ἐκμετρούμενος. What does disturb him is that he may be the murderer of Laius, the cause of the plague, the object of his own solemn excommunication. But he has some slight ground for hope. There is a discrepancy in the two events. It is the same numerical distinction which was discussed before, whether Laius was killed by one man or many. Jocasta said robbers and Oedipus was alone. This distinction is now all-important, the key to the solution of the equation. Oedipus sends for the survivor who can confirm or deny the saving detail. "If he says the same number as you then I am not the murderer. For one cannot equal many."

οὐ γὰε γένοιτ' ἂν εἶs γε τοῖs πολλοῖs ἴσοs

which may fairly be rendered, "In no circumstances can one be equal to more than one." Oedipus' guilt or innocence rests now on a mathematical axiom.

But a more fundamental equation has been brought into question, the relation of the oracles to reality. Here are two oracles, both the same, both unfulfilled; the same terrible destiny was predicted for Jocasta's son, who is dead, and for Oedipus, who has avoided it. One thing is clear to Jocasta. Whoever turns out to be Laius' murderer, the oracles are wrong. "From this day forward I would not, for all prophecy can say, turn my head this way or that." If the equation of the oracles with reality is a false equation, then religion is meaningless. Neither Jocasta nor Oedipus can allow the possibility that the oracles are right, and they accept the consequences, as they proceed to make clear. But the chorus cannot, and it now abandons Oedipus the calculator and turns instead to those "high-footed laws, which are the children of Olympus and not a creation of mortal man." It calls on Zeus to fulfill the oracles. "If these things do not coincide," ἀρμόσει, if the oracles do not equal reality, then "the divine order is overthrown," ἔρρει τὰ θεῖα. The situation and future of two individuals has become a test of divine power: if they are right, sings the chorus, "why reverence Apollo's Delphi, the center of the world? Why join the choral dance?" τί δεῖ με χορεύειν; and with this phrase the issue is brought out of the past into the present moment in the theater of Dionysus. For this song itself is also a dance, the choral stasimon which is the nucleus of tragedy and which reminds us that tragedy itself is an act of religious worship. If the oracles and the truth are not equated the performance of the play has no meaning, for tragedy is a religious ritual. This phrase is a tour de force which makes the validity of the performance itself depend on the dénouement of the play.

The oracles are now the central issue; the murder of Laius fades into the background. A messenger from Corinth brings news, news which will be greeted, he announces, "with an equal amount of sorrow and joy." "What is it," asks Jocasta, "which has such double power?" Polybus is dead. The sorrow equal to the joy will come later; for the moment there is only joy. The oracles are proved wrong again: Oedipus' father is dead. Oedipus can no more kill his father than the son of Laius killed his. "Oracles of the gods, where are you now?" Oedipus is caught up in Jocasta's exaltation, but it does not last. Only half his burden has been lifted from him. His mother still lives. He must still measure the distance to Corinth by the stars, still fear the future.

Both Jocasta and the messenger now try to relieve him of this last remaining fear. Jocasta makes her famous declaration in which she rejects fear, providence, divine and human alike, and indeed any idea of order or plan. Her declaration amounts almost to a rejection of the law of cause and effect: and it certainly attacks the basis of human calculation. For her, the calculation has gone far enough: it has produced an acceptable result; let it stop here. "Why should man fear?" she asks. "His life is governed by the operation of chance. Nothing can be accurately foreseen. The best rule is to live blindly, at random, εἰκῇ, as best one can." It is a statement which recognizes and accepts a meaningless universe. And Oedipus would agree, but for one thing. His mother lives. He must still fear.

Where Jocasta failed the messenger succeeds. He does it by destroying the equation on which Oedipus' life is based. And he uses familiar terms. "Polybus is no more your father than I, but equally so." Oedipus' question is indignant: "How can my father be equal to a nobody, to zero? τῷ μηδενί" The answer — "Polybus is not your father, neither am I." But that is as far as the Corinthian's knowledge goes; he was given the child

Oedipus by another, a shepherd, one of Laius' men. And now the two separate equations begin to merge. "I think," says the chorus, "that that shepherd was the same man that you already sent for." The eyewitness to the death of Laius. He was sent for to say whether Laius was killed by one or many, but he will bring more important news. He will finally lift from Oedipus' shoulders the burden of fear he has carried since he left Delphi. Chance governs all. Oedipus' life history is the operation of chance; found by one shepherd, passed on to another, given to Polybus who was childless, brought up as heir to a kingdom, self-exiled from Corinth he came to Thebes a homeless wanderer, answered the riddle of the Sphinx, and won a city and the hand of a queen. And that same guiding chance will now reveal to him his real identity. Jocasta was right. Why should he fear?

But Jocasta has already seen the truth. Not chance, but the fulfillment of the oracle; the prophecy and the facts coincide (ἁρμόσει), as the chorus prayed they would. Jocasta is lost, but she tries to save Oedipus, to stop the enquiry. But nothing can stop him now. Her farewell to him expresses her agony and knowledge by its omissions: she recognizes but cannot formulate the dreadful equation which Tiresias stated. "ἰού, ἰού, δύστηνε, Unfortunate. This is the only name I can call you." She cannot call him husband. The three-day-old child she sent out to die on the mountain-side has been restored to her, and she cannot call him son.

Oedipus hardly listens. He in his turn has scaled the same heights of confidence from which she has toppled, and he goes higher still. "I will know my origin, burst forth what will." He knows that it will be good. Chance governs the universe and Oedipus is her son. Not the son of Polybus, nor of any mortal man but the son of fortunate chance. In his exaltation he rises in imagination above human stature. "The months, my brothers, have defined, διώρισαν, my greatness and smallness"; he has waned and waxed like the moon, he is one of the forces of the universe, his family is time and space. It is a religious, a mystical conception; here is Oedipus' real religion, he is equal to the gods, the son of chance, the only real goddess. Why should he not establish his identity?

The solution is only a few steps ahead. The shepherd is brought on. "If I, who never met the man, may make an estimate (σταθμᾶσθαι), I think this is the shepherd who has been the object of our investigation (ζητοῦμεν). In age he is commensurate σύμμετρος with the Corinthian here." With this significant prologue he plunges into the final calculation.

The movement of the next sixty lines is the swift ease of the last stages of the mathematical proof: the end is half foreseen, the process an automatic sequence from one step to the next until Oedipus tyrannos and Oedipus the accursed, the knowledge and the swollen foot, are equated. "It all comes out clear," he cries. τὰ πάντ' ἂν ἐξήκοι σαφῆ. The prophecy has been fulfilled. Oedipus knows himself for what he is. He is not the measurer but the thing measured, not the equator but the thing equated. He is the answer to the problem he tried to solve. The chorus sees in Oedipus a παράδειγμα, an example to mankind. In this self-recognition of Oedipus, man recognizes himself. Man measures himself and the result is not that man is the measure of all things. The chorus, which rejected number and all that it stood for, has learned to count; and states the result of the great calculation. "Generations of man that must die, I add up the total of your life and find it equal to zero." ἴσα καὶ τὸ μηδὲν ζώσας ἐναριθμῶ.

The overthrow of the tyrannos is complete. When Oedipus returns from the palace he is blind, and, by the terms of his own proclamation, an outcast. It is a terrible reversal, and it raises the question, "Is it deserved? How far is he responsible for what he has done? Were the actions for which he is now paying not predestined?" No. They were committed in ignorance, but they were not predestined, merely predicted. An essential distinction, as essential for Milton's Adam as for Sophocles' Oedipus. His will was free, his actions his own, but the pattern of his action is the same as that of the Delphic prophecy. The relation between the prophecy and Oedipus' actions is not that of cause and effect. It is the relation suggested by the metaphor, the relation of two independent entities which are equated.

Yet no man can look on Oedipus without sympathy. In his

moment of exaltation — "I am the son of fortune" — he is man at his blindest, but he is also man at his most courageous and heroic: "Burst forth what will, I will know." And he has served, as the chorus says, to point a moral. He is a paradigm, a demonstration. True, Oedipus, the independent being, was a perfectly appropriate subject for the demonstration. But we cannot help feeling that the gods owe Oedipus a debt. Sophocles felt it too, and in his last years wrote the play which shows us the nature of the payment, *Oedipus at Colonus*.

This play deals with Oedipus' reward, and the reward is a strange one. How strange can be seen clearly if we compare Oedipus with another great figure who also served as the subject of a divine demonstration, Job. After his torment Job had it all made up to him. "The Lord gave Job twice as much as he had before. For he had 14,000 sheep, and 6,000 camels and 1,000 yoke of oxen and 1,000 she-asses. He had also 7 sons and 3 daughters. And after this lived Job an hundred and forty years, and saw his sons and his sons' sons, even four generations." This is the kind of reward we can understand — 14,000 sheep, 6,000 camels — Job, to use an irreverent comparison, hit the patriarchal jackpot. Oedipus' reward includes no camels or she-asses, no long life, in fact no life at all, his reward is death. But a death which Job could never imagine. For in death Oedipus becomes equated to the gods. The ironic phrase with which the first play began has here a literal fulfillment. Oedipus becomes something superhuman, a spirit which lives on in power in the affairs of men after the death of the body. His tomb is to be a holy place, for the city in whose territory his body lies will win a great victory on the field where Oedipus lies buried. By his choice of a burial place he thus influences history, becomes a presence to be feared by some and thanked by others. But it is not only in his grave that he will be powerful. In the last hours of his life he begins to assume the attributes of the divinity he is to become; the second play, *Oedipus at Colonus*, puts on stage the process of Oedipus' transition from human to divine.

"Equated to the gods." We have not seen the gods, but we know from the first play what they are. That play demonstrated that the gods have knowledge, full complete knowledge, the knowledge which Oedipus thought he had. He was proved ignorant; real knowledge is what distinguishes god from man. Since the gods have knowledge their action is confident and sure. They act with the swift decision which was characteristic of Oedipus but which was in him misplaced. Only a god can be sure, not a man. And their action is just. It is a justice based on perfect knowledge, is exact and appropriate, and therefore allows no room for forgiveness — but it can be angry. The gods can even mock the wrongdoer as Athene does Ajax, as the echoes of his name mocked Oedipus. This sure, full, angry justice is what Oedipus tried to administer to Tiresias, to Creon, but his justice was based on ignorance and was injustice. These attributes of divinity — knowledge, certainty, justice — are the qualities Oedipus thought he possessed — and that is why he was the perfect example of the inadequacy of human knowledge, certainty, and justice. But in the second play Oedipus is made equal to the gods, he assumes the attributes of divinity, the attributes he once thought his, he becomes what he once thought he was. This old Oedipus seems to be equal to the young, confident in his knowledge, fiercely angry in his administration of justice, utterly sure of himself — but this time he is justified. These are not the proper attitudes for a man, but Oedipus is turning into something more than man; now he knows surely, sees clearly, the gods give Oedipus back his eyes, but they are eyes of superhuman vision. Now in his transformation, as then, in his reversal, he serves still as an example. The rebirth of the young, confident Oedipus in the tired old man emphasizes the same lesson; it defines once more the limits of man and the power of gods, states again that the possession of knowledge, certainty, and justice is what distinguishes god from man.

The opening statement of Oedipus shows that as a man he has learned the lesson well. "I have learned acquiescence, taught by suffering and long time." As a man Oedipus has nothing more to learn. With this statement he comes to the end of a long road. The nearby city whose walls he cannot see is Athens, and here is the place of his reward, his grave, his home.

The welcome he receives is to be ordered off by the first arrival; he has trespassed on holy ground, the grove of the Eumenides. He knows what this means, this is the resting place he was promised by Apollo, and he refuses to move. His statement recalls the tyrannos, a characteristic phrase: "In no circumstances will I leave this place." The terms of his prayer to the goddesses of the grave foreshadow his transition from body to spirit. "Pity this wretched ghost of Oedipus the man, this body that is not what it once was long ago."

As a body, as a man, he is a thing to be pitied; he is blind, feeble, ragged, dirty. But the transformation has already begun. The first comer spoke to him with pity, even condescension, but the chorus of citizens which now enters feels fear. "Dreadful to see, dreadful to hear." When they know his identity their fear changes to anger, but Oedipus defends his past. He sees himself as one who was ignorant, who suffered rather than acted. But now he is actor, not sufferer. He comes with knowledge, and power. "I come bringing advantage to this city."

He does not yet know what advantage. His daughter Ismene comes to tell him what it is, that his grave will be the site of a victory for the city that shelters him. And to tell him that his sons and Creon, all of whom despised and rejected him, now need him, and will come to beg his help. Oedipus has power over the future and can now reward his friends and punish his enemies. He chooses to reward Athens, to punish Creon and his own sons. He expresses his choice in terms which show a recognition of human limitations; Athens' reward, something which lies within his will, as an intention; his sons' punishment, something over which he has no sure control, as a wish. "May the issue of the battle between them lie in my hands. If that were to be, the one would not remain king, nor the other win the throne."

Theseus, the king of Athens, welcomes him generously, but when he learns that Thebes wants Oedipus back and that he refuses to go, Theseus reproaches the old man. "Anger is not what your misfortune calls for." And the answer is a fiery rebuke from a superior. "Wait till you hear what I say, before you reproach me." Oedipus tells Theseus that he bring victory over Thebes at some future time, and Theseus, the statesman, is confident that Athens will never be at war with Thebes. Oedipus reproaches him in his turn. Such confidence is misplaced. No man should be so sure of the future: "Only to the gods comes no old age or death. Everything else is dissolved by all-powerful time. The earth's strength decays, the body decays, faith dies, mistrust flowers and the wind of friendship changes between man and man, city and city." No man can be confident of the future. Man's knowledge is ignorance. It is the lesson Oedipus learned in his own person and he reads it to Theseus now with all the authority of his blind eyes and dreadful name — but he does not apply it to himself. For he goes on to predict the future. He hands down the law of human behavior to Theseus speaking already as a *daemon*, not one subject to the law but one who administers it. And with his confident prediction, his assumption of sure knowledge, goes anger, but not the old human anger of Oedipus tyrannos. As he speaks of Thebes' future defeat on the soil where he will be buried, the words take on an unearthly quality, a daemonic wrath.

> ἵν' οὑμὸς εὕδων καὶ κεκρυμμένος νέκυς
> ψυχρός ποτ' αὐτῶν θερμὸν αἷμα πίεται
> εἰ Ζεὺς ἔτι Ζεὺς χὼ Διὸς Φοῖβος σαφής.

"There my sleeping and hidden corpse, cold though it be, will drink their warm blood, if Zeus is still Zeus and Apollo a true prophet." What before was wish and prayer is now prediction. But the prediction is qualified: "if Apollo be a true prophet." He does not yet speak in the authority of his own name. That will be the final stage.

And when it comes, he speaks face to face with the objects of his anger. Creon's condescending and hypocritical speech is met with a blast of fury that surpasses the anger he had to face long ago in Thebes. The final interview is a repetition of the first. In both Creon is condemned, in both with the same swift vindictive wrath, but this time the condemnation is just. Oedipus sees through to the heart of Creon, he knows

what he is: and Creon proceeds to show the justice of Oedipus'
rejection by revealing that he has already kidnaped Ismene,
by kidnaping Antigone, and laying hands on Oedipus himself. Oedipus is helpless, and only the arrival of Theseus saves
him. This is the man who is being equated to the gods, not the
splendid tyrannos, the man of power, vigor, strength, but a
blind old man, the extreme of physical weakness, who cannot
even see, much less prevent, the violence that is done him.

Physical weakness, but a new height of spiritual strength.
This Oedipus judges justly and exactly, knows fully, sees clearly
— his power is power over the future, the defeat of Thebes, the
death of his sons, the terrible reversal of Creon. One thing
Creon says to Oedipus clarifies the nature of the process we
are witnessing. "Has not time taught you wisdom?" Creon expected to find the Oedipus of the opening scene of the play,
whom time had taught acquiescence, but he finds what seems
to be the tyrannos he knew and feared. "You harm yourself
now as you did then," he says, "giving way to that anger which
has always been your defeat." He sees the old Oedipus as equal
to the young. In one sense they are, but in a greater sense they
are no more equal than man is equal to the gods.

With the next scene the whole story comes full circle. A
suppliant begs Oedipus for help. Our last sight of Oedipus is
like our first. This suppliant is Polynices, his son, and the
comparison with the opening scene of the first play is emphasized by the repetitions of the priest's speech — words, phrases,
even whole lines — which appear in Polynices' appeal to his
father. It is a hypocritical speech which needs no refutation.
It is met with a terrible indictment which sweeps from accu-
sation through prophecy to a climax which, with its tightly
packed explosive consonants resembles not so much human
speech as a burst of daemonic anger:

> θανεῖν κτανεῖν θ'ὑφ' οὗπερ ἐξελήλασαι
> τοιαῦτ' ἀρῶμαι καὶ καλῶ τὸ Ταρτάρου
> στυγνὸν πατρῷον ἔρεβος ὥς σ' ἀποικίσῃ

"Kill and be killed by the brother who drove you out. This is
my curse, I call on the hideous darkness of Tartarus where

your fathers lie, to prepare a place for you. . . ." This is a
superhuman anger welling from the outraged sense of justice
not of a man but of the forces of the universe themselves.

Creon could still argue and resist, but to this speech no reply
is possible. There can be no doubt of its authority. When
Polynices discusses the speech with his sisters, the right word
for it is found. Oedipus speaks with the voice of an oracle.
"Will you go to Thebes and fulfill his prophecies? (μαντεύματα)"
says Antigone. Oedipus who fought to disprove an oracle has
become one himself. And his son now starts on the same road
his father trod. "Let him prophesy. I do not have to fulfill it."
Polynices leaves with a phrase that repeats his mother's de-
nunciation of prophets. "All this is in the power of the divinity
ἐν τῷ δαίμονι, it may turn out this way or that." In the power
of a god — in the power of chance — whatever he means, he
does not realize the sense in which the words are true. The
daemon, the divinity, in whose power it lies is Oedipus himself.

Oedipus has stayed too long. Power such as this should not
walk the earth in the shape of a man. The thunder and lightning summon him, and the gods reproach him for his delay.
"You Oedipus, you, why do we hesitate to go? You have delayed too long."

> ὦ οὗτος οὗτος Οἰδίπους τί μέλλομεν
> χωρεῖν; πάλαι δὴ τἀπὸ σοῦ βραδύνεται.

These strange words are the only thing the gods say in either
play. And as was to be expected of so long delayed and awful
a statement, it is complete and final. The hesitation for which
they reproach Oedipus is the last shred of his humanity, which
he must now cast off. Where he is going vision is clear, knowledge certain, action instantaneous and effective; between the
intention and the act there falls no shadow of hesitation or
delay. The divine "we" — "Why do we hesitate to go" — completes and transcends the equation of Oedipus with the gods;
his identity is merged with theirs. And in this last moment of
his bodily life they call him by his name, Oidipous, the name
which contains in itself the lesson of which not only his action
and suffering but also his apotheosis serve as the great example

— *oida* — that man's knowledge, which makes him master of the world, should never allow him to think that he is equated to the gods, should never allow him to forget the foot, *pous*, the reminder of his true measurement, his real identity.

DICTIONARY OF DRAMATIC TERMS

*L*IKE other dictionary-makers, we have sought to clarify the meanings of words. Some words — *e.g.*, "tragedy," "comedy," "scene" — are in common use, and yet such is their multiplicity of meanings that they require fairly lengthy definitions. We have tried to provide these, but we are uncomfortably aware of Dr. Johnson's warning to Boswell: "Sometimes things may be made darker by definition. I see a *cow*, I define her, *Animal quadrupes ruminans cornutum*. But a goat ruminates, and a cow may have no horns. *Cow* is plainer."

Because words like "farce," "humor," and "slapstick" can most clearly and most helpfully be defined by being placed in conjunction with each other, we have brought them (and others) together in an entry headed "comedy." They are also listed separately; the reader who looks for "farce" under "f" will find it listed there but will be referred to "comedy." "High comedy" and "low comedy," however, are not listed under "h" and "l" but only under "comedy," as, for example, "hand prop" and "set prop" are only under "property," and "Socratic irony" and "Sophoclean irony" are only under "irony."

Words defined are in **bold face**. In the course of a definition, a word preceded by the symbol ° is itself defined in its proper alphabetical position.

Absurd, Theater of the. Drama of such writers as Eugène Ionesco and Samuel Beckett in France and Harold Pinter in England that imitates the absurdity of man's existence. "Everything, as I see it, is an aberration," Ionesco has said. Though the plays are serious, they may contain extravagantly comic scenes in depicting a reality that is absurd, illogical, senseless, a world of futility and meaningless clichés. In Ionesco's *The Chairs* (1952), for example, an elderly couple rush about, filling a room with chairs for non-existent visitors. Old age is a fact, but an absurdity, too, and old people are incomprehensible. At the end of *The Chairs*, an orator, who is to deliver a solemn talk about the truths of life, turns out to be deaf and dumb and merely makes unintelligible noises and gestures to the invisible crowd. Ionesco summarizes (New York *Times*, 1 June 1958) the theme of *The Chairs*: "I have tried to deal . . . with emptiness, with frustration, with this world, at once fleeting and crushing. The characters I have used are not fully conscious of their spiritual rootlessness, but they feel it instinctively and emotionally." One basis of man's inability to communicate, and one which the "Absurd" dramatists seize upon, is the corruption of language. The absurdity of trying to communicate by means of a debased language is dramatized by Ionesco in *The Bald Soprano* (1950), where the characters speak in clichés. Because the characters are incomprehensible and the happenings illogical and baffling, the spectators cannot simply sit back in ease, but are continually challenged to grasp the play's meaning. Consult Martin Esslin, *The Theatre of the Absurd*.

acoustics. The qualities that govern the transmission of sound. It is sometimes said that the ancient Greeks used masks with distended mouths to serve as megaphones, but perhaps no such megaphones were needed, for the acoustics were reasonably good in Greek theaters: there was a barrier behind the performers, the flat hard ground in front of them reflected the sound upward, and the audience sat in tiers. Because the theater was unroofed, there was not enough reverberation to blur distinctness. (If there is too much reverberation in a theater, the audience will receive the direct waves uttered by a speaker in the midst of many reflected waves of sound uttered previously, and hearing will be unsure. Reverberation, however, is not always bad; reverberations perceived within one fifty-thousandth of a second after the direct sound is perceived do not blur distinctness but enhance the actor's voice. Hence reflecting surfaces carefully placed near the front of an auditorium and around the stage can build up an actor's voice and make it unnecessary for him to shout.) Some theaters in ancient Italy placed sounding vessels (*echeia*) under the seats, perhaps to supply reverberation that enhances vowel tones, perhaps to absorb (in order to reduce) reverberation. Consult Harold Burris-Meyer and Edward C. Cole, *Theatres & Auditoriums*, pp. 42-50.

act. (1) To perform. (2) A performance, as "a juggling act." (3) In Elizabethan usage, the interval (corresponding to our °intermission) during which players in a few higher-priced theaters briefly suspended their performance. (4) A main division in drama or opera. Act divisions probably arose in Roman theory and derive ultimately from the Greek practice of separating episodes in a play by choral interludes, but Greek (and probably Roman) plays were performed without interruption, for the choral interludes were part of the plays themselves. Consult George E. Duckworth, *The Nature of Roman Comedy*, Ch. 4. The division of Elizabethan plays into five acts is often the work of editors rather than authors. No play of Shakespeare's was published in his lifetime with divisions into five acts. Consult Wilfred T. Jewkes, *Act Division in Elizabethan and Jacobean Plays*. Today an act division is commonly indicated by lowering the curtain and turning up the house-lights. A **scene** is a smaller unit, either: (i) a division with no change of locale or abrupt shift of time, or (ii) a division consisting of an actor or a group of actors on the stage; according to the second definition, the departure or entrance of an actor changes the composition of the group and thus produces a new scene. In an entirely different sense, the scene is the locale where a work is set. The first speech in *Romeo and Juliet* informs the audience of the play's locale: "In fair Verona, where we lay our scene. . . ." Often the °décor lets the spectator know where the play is set, but during the last hundred years playwrights have tended, for the convenience of readers, to write long °stage directions describing the scene. Here is the beginning of the first stage direction in Shaw's *Candida*: "A fine morning in October 1894 in the north east quarter of London, a vast district miles away from the London of Mayfair and St James's, and much less narrow, squalid, fetid and airless in its slums. . . ." See °plot.

acting. See °actor, °Stanislavsky System, p. 110, and p. 116.

acting edition. See °prompter.

action. (1) The physical movement of an actor, whether he is leaping into Ophelia's grave or speaking softly to himself. That talk is action is easily seen in the Bastard's remark (*King John*, II.i.466): "Zounds! I was never so bethumped with words/ Since I first called my brother's father dad." See °stage business. (2) An incident in the °plot, an episode. (3) Aristotle's statement that a drama is an "imitation of an action" (*praxis*) has provoked considerable controversy; recently there has been a tendency to regard this action as the motive underlying the outward deeds of the plot. Francis Fergusson says (in *The Human Image in Dramatic Literature*, p. 116), for example, that the action of *Oedipus the King* "is the quest for Laius's slayer, . . . which persists through the changing circumstances of the play."

186

actor. A performer in a play. Thespis (sixth century B.C.) is said to have introduced the first actor into the choral performance from which drama developed; Aeschylus introduced the second, and Sophocles the third. The chorus-leader, with whom Thespis' one actor conversed, functioned as an actor, too. Furthermore, an actor could **double**, *i.e.*, play more than one role in one production. (Elizabethan actors, too, doubled; sometimes as few as eight performed a play with two dozen characters. Consult William J. Lawrence, *Pre-Restoration Stage Studies.*) In Rome, at least by the first century B.C., actors were disreputable, and were usually slaves. That in the first century A.D. the emperor Nero acted was simply a sign of his depravity. In the Middle Ages actors (aside from strolling minstrels) were amateurs—first priests, then guildsmen (see °medieval drama); in Renaissance England they had become professionals with a mixed reputation: they could be solid citizens, but legally the wandering actors were classified with "rogues, vagabonds, and sturdy beggars"; in eighteenth-century England an unlicensed player was still "a rogue and a vagabond." Catholic countries in the seventeeth century opposed the burial of actors in consecrated ground, even when they were as eminent as Molière. Prejudice against actors owed much to the Roman performers and much to the Christian hostility toward dissembling. "The Father of all truth," says Tertullian (160?-230? A.D.), "hates dissembling." Tertullian suggests that the greatest show will be on Judgment Day, when the tragic actors will howl louder than ever before.

An actor works with his body and his voice; he may have to fence with foils, and to thrust with words; sometimes he will strike another actor, sometimes he will bounce words off him. For the last two centuries there has been a good deal of controversy about the degree to which an actor "feels" his part. Dr. Johnson (1709-1784) said that any actor who felt Macbeth's emotions should be hanged. Talma (1763-1826) said he was once carried away, but was brought back to his job when the actress whom he was playing opposite warned, "Take care, Talma, you are moved!" Talma explained, "It is really from emotion that difficulties spring: the voice balks, the memory fails, and gestures become false; and the effect is destroyed." On the other hand, there are numerous statements by actors who claim to "feel" their role. Consult *Actors on Acting*, ed. Toby Cole (especially the selection from William Archer's "*Masks or Faces?*"); John R. Brown, "On the Acting of Shakespeare's Plays," *Quarterly Journal of Speech*, XXXIX (1953), 477-484; Bertram Joseph, *The Tragic Actor.* Alfred Harbage, in *Theatre for Shakespeare*, presents the case that Elizabethan acting was "formal," that is, stylized, rather than "natural." In formal acting, the actor represents, but in natural acting he impersonates; in formal acting he need not look at the actor to whom he is speaking, but in natural acting he must not look at the audience. Note that it does not follow that formal acting is unemotional, and natural acting emotional; a formal actor may feel his part, and a natural actor may unfeelingly impersonate. See °Stanislavsky System, and p. 110.

A **character actor** specializes in imitating idiosyncrasies of types, *e.g.*, the Deaf Old Man, who is a **character part.** Usually a character actor imitates characteristics not his own, *e.g.*, a young actor plays old men. A **bit actor** has a small role; a **supernumerary** (or **super**) or **extra** has so small a role—he is part of a crowd or he carries a spear—that he need have no professional training or gift. An **actor-manager** is a performer who runs a °company, in which he usually stars. Consult Hesketh Pearson, *The Last Actor-Managers.* **Ensemble acting** stresses the performance of the group rather than of the individual; it is sometimes especially apparent in crowd scenes, the crowd behaving as a unit rather than as a chaotic collection of units.

actress. Actresses were unknown in ancient Greece, female roles being played by men. Actresses appeared on the Roman stage, and were regarded as debauched. The Elizabethan theater, like the Greek theater, did not have actresses, but used boys to play female roles. Women took part in Elizabethan °masques, but professional actresses (an early seventeenth-century innovation in Spain, Italy, and France) did not appear in the English public theaters until the °Restoration (1660). In the Orient female parts have usually been played by males; Japan's °kabuki drama was originated by a woman but soon became an all-male performance.

ad-lib. To add (especially to improvise) words or gestures (from Latin *ad libitum*: at pleasure).

aesthetic distance, or **psychical distance.** The detachment between the receptor and the work of art. The concept is chiefly associated with Edward Bullough (see the essay in his *Aesthetics*, reprinted in Melvin Rader, *A Modern Book of Aesthetics*). Bullough explains that there must be some sort of psychical "distance" (gap) between our practical self (our personal needs) and the work of art. Thus, a jealous man who suspects his wife may be unable to divorce his personal feelings from *Othello*. He may be too involved with the piece as life to see it as art. But "distance" does not mean that the receptor is totally detached or objective. Rather, he is detached from his usual personal involvements, and because of this detachment he can look with a new vigorous interest — he can look with a new sort of passion born of his new personality — at the work of art as art. Persons who do not understand the need for distance between themselves and a work, Bullough explains, commonly say that they do not wish to see a °tragedy because there is enough suffering in real life. But the more sophisticated spectator at a tragedy realizes that as a picture is distanced by the frame, a play is distanced (the characters may speak verse, they perform behind footlights, and their deeds cohere to make a unified harmonious pattern); the feelings it evokes in him are not the feelings evoked by a roughly similar event in real life. In the theater we feel "rapturous awe" at what in life would be depressing. Consult John Dolman, Jr., *The Art of Play Production*, Ch. 3; for the view that both °arena staging and °epic staging destroy the necessary distance, consult Oscar Büdel, "Contemporary Theater and Aesthetic Distance," *Publications of the Modern Language Association*, LXXVI (1961), 277-291. See also °dramatic illusion, °empathy, and p. 122.

affective memory. See °Stanislavsky System.

after-piece. See °one-act play.

agon (Greek: contest). For its traditional meaning see °comedy. In the last few decades the term has been used (*e.g.*, by Francis Fergusson, *The Idea of a Theater*) to designate a scene of conflict in °tragedy, such as the agonizing struggle between Oedipus and Teiresias.

agroikos. See °character.

alarums and **excursions.** The alarum (modern "alarm") is an °off-stage °sound effect of trumpets, drums, and guns in Elizabethan drama, used to indicate battle or (occasionally) the approach of an army. The excursion is an onstage combat of a few men. Consult Paul A. Jorgensen, *Shakespeare's Military World*.

alazon. See °character.

alienation effect. See °epic drama.

allegory. When St. Augustine noted that we derive pleasure from thinking of holy men as sheep, he was commenting on the pleasure afforded by allegory. Frequently an allegory is a narrative wherein abstractions (*e.g.*, virtue, fear) are made concrete (Mr. Virtue, Giant Fear), for the purpose of effectively communicating a moral, but in essence an allegory is merely a system of equivalents. Though allegory need not personify abstractions, allegoric drama almost always does. *Everyman* (c. 1500), an allegoric °morality play, includes among its °dramatis personae Death, Good Deeds, Beauty, and, of course, Everyman. But morality plays may also include allegoric castles (standing for strength or chastity), roses (standing for love or virtue), etc. Consult Bernard Spivack, *Shakespeare and the Allegory of Evil*.

anagnorisis. See °plot, °tragedy.

analysis. See °criticism.

antagonist. See °plot, °protagonist.

antecedent action. See °plot.

anticlimax. A descent, the lines or happenings being markedly less important or less impressive than their predecessors. In °melodrama, a decrease in tension may cause disappointment and loss of interest; in °comedy, a sharp descent (the beautiful princess opens her mouth and sounds like a burlesque queen) may get a desirable laugh. On the desirability of a gradual decrease in tension in °tragedy (*i.e.*, a "quiet ending"), consult Max Beerbohm, "Last Acts," in *Around Theatres*.

antimasque. See °masque.

antistrophe. See °tragedy.

apocrypha. See °canon.

Apollo, Apollonian. See °Dionysus.

apron. The part of the stage extending beyond the °proscenium curtain toward the audience; the **forestage.** In proscenium theaters built in the nineteenth and early twentieth centuries, it is commonly only two or three feet, but in English theaters of the °Restoration (*i.e.*, the late seventeenth century) it was some ten or fifteen feet — almost equal to the portion of the stage behind the curtain. See °Elizabethan playhouse, °proscenium stage, °Restoration playhouse.

arena stage. (1) In British usage, a stage with a back wall and with an audience on three sides. (2) In American usage, a playing space surrounded by spectators, **theater-in-the-round.** Proponents of arena staging (in the American sense) stress the intimacy afforded by having actors in the midst of the audience, but opponents suggest that at least for some plays the intimacy ought not to be very great. (See °aesthetic distance.) It has been noted, too, that even in arena staging the audience normally feels set apart from the actors, for the audience is in the dark while the actors are in an illuminated playing area. Critics of arena staging cite the following difficulties: °soliloquies, °asides, and °direct addresses are hard to deliver in such a theater; °directors, aware that the back of an actor's head is not very expressive, tend to have the actors gyrate disturbingly and meaninglessly; entrances and exits are often cumbersome; little use can be made of elevation and of groupings of actors. Consult the note by Marston Balch and John Woodruff, and the essay by Kelly Yeaton, in John Gassner, *Producing the Play*. Because arena staging has disadvantages as well as advantages, several new theaters have been constructed with a **flexible stage,** i.e., the seats can be redistributed, allowing the playing space to be enlarged or shifted from one end of the theater to the center of the theater. Consult Walden P. Boyle, *Central and Flexible Staging*. Finally, it should be mentioned that arena staging is not new; it (or something close to it) was used in the Middle Ages. Consult Richard Southern, *The Medieval Theatre in the Round*. Leslie Hotson, in *Shakespeare's Wooden O*, claims that in the Elizabethan playhouse the actors were entirely surrounded, but most scholars hold that the audience was on only three sides.

arras. See °Elizabethan playhouse.

aside. See °soliloquy, °convention.

audience. The viewers and hearers of a performance. The influence of the audience on popular drama is immense; Dr. Johnson was scarcely exaggerating when he said,

> The stage but echoes back the public voice;
> The drama's laws, the drama's patrons give,
> For we that live to please, must please to live.

For an examination of Elizabethan taste and its influence on the drama, consult Alfred Harbage, *Shakespeare and the Rival Traditions*. Consult also J. L. Styan, *The Elements of Drama*, Ch. 11. See the essays in this book by Wilder, Brecht, and Lamb.

audition. A demonstration, usually competitive, enabling a performer seeking a °role to show his ability. As a verb, to try out for a role.

auditorium. See °theater.

auto sacramental. See °medieval drama.

backcloth, backdrop, backscene. A screen (usually sliding in grooves) or a curtain hanging behind the performers, often painted with a sky or a landscape. See °scenery, °set.

backstage. See °stage, °theater.

ballet. See °dance.

barnstorm. To tour, playing in barns and provincial makeshift theaters. An actor in such a touring troupe is a **barnstormer.**

baroque. First used, in the eighteenth century, pejoratively, to describe a kind of architecture that flourished throughout the seventeenth century. The word has increasingly lost its pejorative tone, and has come to denote a style whose chief characteristic is a degree of explosive elaboration which almost obscures the underlying order or pattern: there is elaborate balance, but also a decided sense of strain or contortion. Thus, the baroque tragic heroes of, say, Pierre Corneille (1606-1684) are passionate but they retain a formal grandeur. Baroque heroes are intensely aware of life's littleness and also of its grandeur; one of the common baroque themes is that the world is (to quote from Shakespeare's *The Tempest*, c. 1611) an "insubstantial pageant." In Calderón's *La Vida es sueño* (*Life is a Dream*, c. 1635), a prince who has been imprisoned is

191

drugged and tested, and then cast back into prison, where he wonders if his experience has been a dream and if his wondering is itself a dream. The baroque's combination of glory and a sense of transience is often said to be largely due to advances in science — especially astronomy (which showed man that the earth was not the glorious center about which the heavenly bodies moved) — and to the rise of the modern state (which brought into being a powerful centralized bureaucracy and drastically reduced the power of local lords). Consult Wylie Sypher, *Four Stages of Renaissance Style,* and *Journal of Aesthetics and Art Criticism,* V (1946) and XIV (1955) for several articles on the meaning of baroque. On baroque scene design of the seventeenth and eighteenth centuries, consult James Laver, *Drama*, Ch. IX.

batten. A length of timber or metal pipe, commonly used to stiffen an edge of cloth (*e.g.*, at the bottom of a °backdrop), or as a mount for lights.

benefit. A performance given for a charitable purpose. In the eighteenth and early nineteenth centuries, benefit performances were held for the author or actor. Today, the two chief kinds of benefits are (i) performances for the residents of charitable institutions; (ii) performances to raise money to aid such institutions. Persons who attend the theater in a group in order to aid an institution form a **theater party.** Because they are often homogeneous and noisily interested in each other, members of theater parties, actors feel, make a bad audience.

les bienséances. See °neoclassicism.

blackout. A sudden extinguishing of the lights on the stage, often to conclude a °skit in a °revue.

block out. To work out the gestures, positions, entrances and exits of actors; blocking out usually begins fairly early in the °rehearsal schedule. For °blocking rehearsal, see °rehearsal.

bombast. From a word meaning "cotton stuffing"; rant, speech that is too inflated for the occasion. In Marlowe's *Tamburlaine* (c. 1587), Tamburlaine brags thus:

> Our quivering lances, shaking in the air,
> And bullets, like Jove's dreadful thunderbolts,
> Enrolled in flames and fiery smoldering mists,
> Shall threat the gods more than Cyclopian wars:
> And with our sun-bright armor as we march,
> Will chase the stars from Heaven and dim their eyes
> That stand and muse at our admirèd arms.

bomolochos. See °character.

book. See °musical comedy.

border. See °scenery.

borderlights. See °lighting.

Boulevard dramatist. See °melodrama.

bourgeois drama. A serious play with middle-class °dramatis personae. There are a few Elizabethan tragedies of middle-class life, but bourgeois drama, with its emphasis on °pathos, is more or less an eighteenth-century invention. Bourgeois dramas were written in the eighteenth and nineteenth centuries, apparently in response to the middle class's desire to see itself on the stage; the bourgeois by the eighteenth century regarded himself as a suitable replacement for the nobleman of earlier tragedy. Speaking generally, the characteristics of these plays are: middle-class dramatis personae, virtue in distress, °sentimentality, and an unreasonably high moral tone. Eighteenth-century critics, not sure what to do with pathetic plays on middle-class life, used the terms *drame, drame bourgeois, comédie larmoyante* (tearful comedy), *tragédie bourgeoise, bürgerliches Trauerspiel* (bourgeois tragedy) interchangeably. (Note that a *comédie larmoyante* need not end happily, nor a *tragédie bourgeoise* end sadly.) In England, George Lillo's *The London Merchant* (1731), "a tale of private woe. A London 'prentice ruined," depicted an apprentice who murdered his benefactor. In France, Diderot compared *The London Merchant* to plays by Sophocles and Euripides. In Germany, it moved Lessing to write *Miss Sara Sampson* (1755), a play set in England: Sara, inveigled into eloping with a blackguard, is poisoned by his former mistress, causing him to repent his villainy in the presence of Sara's lamenting father. Unlike Miss Sara, bourgeois drama does not die in the eighteenth century; it lives on into the nineteenth century to become melodrama in many hands and tragedy in Ibsen's hands. Consult Fred O. Nolte, *Early Middle Class Drama*; and Eric Auerbach, *Mimesis*, Ch. 17. On Ibsen as a bourgeois dramatist, consult Eric Bentley, *The Playwright as Thinker*. See °domestic tragedy, °sentimental, and the essays in this book by Miller and McCarthy.

box. See °theater.

box office. See °theater.

box set. See °set.

braggart soldier. The boastful, vain, cowardly soldier is a stock figure in much comedy. As a braggart, he belongs to the class *alazon* (see °character). The *miles gloriosus* (plural *milites gloriosi*), to give him his Latin name, in Roman comedies usually is in a position to buy the girl desired by the young lover; he is thus an obstacle to joy, but his cowardice makes him easily conquered. He is the *capitano* in the °*commedia dell' arte*, Shakespeare's Pistol (and even a part of Falstaff), and, by slight extension, Synge's

193

Christy Mahon (who claims to have killed his father). Consult Daniel Boughner, *The Braggart in Renaissance Comedy*.

Broadway. An avenue passing through the theater district in New York City; by metonymy, the commercial theater. **Off-Broadway** pertains to the smaller, allegedly more artistic or *avant-garde* theaters, often located in lofts, church cellars, etc. Recently there has been a tendency to think of Broadway plays as "entertainment," off-Broadway plays as more serious art.

built scenery. See °scenery.

burla. See °*commedia dell' arte*.

burlesque. Any imitation which, by distortion, aims to amuse. Its subject matter is sometimes said to be faults rather than vices, and its tone is neither shrill nor savage. Thus, in distinction from °satire it can be defined as a comic imitation of a mannerism or a minor fault (either in style or subject-matter), contrived to arouse amusement rather than indignation. In the theater, a burlesque may be a play that amusingly criticizes another play by grotesquely imitating aspects of it, as Gay's *The Beggar's Opera* (1728) mimicked serious °operas, Buckingham's *The Rehearsal* (1671) mimicked °heroic drama, and Sheridan's *The Critic* (1779) mimicked (among other things) °sentimental drama. In England, a burlesque may be a musical °extravaganza in which fantasy has almost entirely ousted criticism. In America, burlesque (especially popular in the late nineteenth and first half of the twentieth century) is usually a sort of vaudeville or variety show stressing bawdy humor and sex. The sexual theme is most fully revealed in the strip-tease, introduced about 1920. Consult V. C. Clinton-Baddeley, *The Burlesque Tradition in the English Theater after 1660*; Gypsy Rose Lee, *The G-String Murders*. See °comedy, °satire.

burletta. See °legitimate drama.

business. See °stage business.

buskin. See °sock.

canon. The undoubted works of a particular author or authors. Doubtful works are the **apocrypha**. Thus, most scholars include thirty-seven plays in the Shakespeare canon, but other plays, attributed to him on uncertain evidence, belong to the Shakespeare apocrypha. Consult Marchette Chute, *Shakespeare of London*, Appendix 3.

carpenter's scene. See °curtain.

cast. (1) The performers in a play. (2) As a verb, "to cast" means to assign roles to actors. To **type-cast** is to assign actors to roles similar to those which they are accustomed to performing.

See °character and °stock company. Consult Edith J. Isaacs, "Type casting," *Theatre Arts*, XVII (February, 1933), 131-138. An agency that supplies actors for roles in a play is a **casting office.**

catastrophe. See °plot.

catharsis. See °tragedy.

cellar. See °Elizabethan playhouse, °stage.

character. (1) One of the °dramatis personae, *e.g.,* Hamlet. (2) The personality of such a figure. Characters are sometimes divided into **flat** and **round characters.** The former have only one "side," representing a single trait (*e.g.,* the faithful wife, the genial drunkard); the latter have many traits and are seen, as it were, from all sides, in the round. The behavior of flat characters is thoroughly predictable, that of round characters is sometimes unexpected though credible. The term "flat" is not necessarily pejorative, for it is sometimes desirable to show only one aspect of a single character, but E. M. Forster suggests (*Aspects of the Novel*) that "flat people are not in themselves as big achievements as round ones, and also . . . they are best when they are comic." See °comedy of humors. A **stock character** is a type that recurs in many works. For example, from Greek comedy to the present there have been numerous braggart soldiers, stubborn fathers, jealous husbands. Northrop Frye finds four chief types of comic figures: (i) the *alazon,* the impostor, boaster, hypocrite; (ii) the *eiron* (see °irony), the man who deprecates himself and exposes the boaster; (iii) the *bomolochos,* the buffoon, or more generally, the man who entertains by his mannerisms and talk; (iv) the *agroikos,* the straightman who is the unwitting butt of humor. Each of these types appears in many dresses; the *alazon,* for example, is most commonly the °braggart soldier (*miles gloriosus*), but he is also the pedant, the crank, or anyone who is full of ideas that have no relation to reality. (See °*commedia dell' arte*; consult Northrop Frye, *Anatomy of Criticism*, pp. 171-176.) Stock characters are not limited to comedy: the proud tragic hero is a stock character, as are, for example, the cruel stepmother and the son who wishes to avenge his father. See also °motivation, °plot, °stock company. Consult J. L. Styan, *The Elements of Drama*, Ch. 8.

character actor. See °actor.

choregus. See °Greek theater.

chorus. In Greek drama, a group of performers who play a role, *e.g.,* Old Men of Corinth. (The chorus leader is the *coryphaeus.*) In Aeschylus' *The Suppliants* (c. 490 B.C.), perhaps the earliest extant play, the chorus consists of the heroines, but in most Greek plays the chorus consists of subsidiary figures who comment rather helplessly on what is happening to the important people.

Aeschylus reduced the chorus of fifty to twelve; Sophocles increased it to fifteen, where it remained. The Greek chorus, it is often said, is a sort of middle-man between the unusual main figures and the humdrum spectators. Elizabethan dramas occasionally had a chorus of one actor who, not a participant in the story, commented on it. The Chorus (or °prologue) in Shakespeare's *Henry V* urges the audience to:

> Think when we talk of horses that you see them
> Printing their proud hoofs i' the receiving earth;
> For 'tis your thoughts that now must deck our kings,
> Carry them here and there, jumping o'er times,
> Turning the accomplishment of many years
> Into an hour-glass: for the which supply,
> Admit me Chorus to this history:
> Who prologue-like your humble patience pray,
> Gently to hear, kindly to judge, our play.

A **chorus character** (or *raisonneur*), however, such as Enobarbus in *Antony and Cleopatra*, is a character who participates in the story yet seems to be the author's mouthpiece, intelligently commenting (often with °irony) on the actions of the other characters. But Alfred Harbage, in *As They Liked It*, skeptically and aptly calls such a figure "The Unreliable Spokesman." The use of the chorus, in one form or another, continues into our times, for example in T. S. Eliot's *Murder in the Cathedral*, whose "Chorus of Women of Canterbury," like a Greek chorus and like the audience, "are forced to bear witness"; and in Tennessee Williams' *The Glass Menagerie*, whose Tom Wingfield tells the audience he is "the narrator of the play, and also a character in it."

chronicle play. A dramatization of historical material, often with an emphasis on depicting the chief events in a ruler's life. Examples: Shakespeare's *Henry V* (c. 1599), and Laurence Housman's *Victoria Regina* (1934). Chronicle plays were especially popular with the Elizabethan general public; some of the plays were unified merely by the central figure, the king whose reign was depicted, but others — such as *Richard II*—were pretty much organized as tragedies. The line between a chronicle play and an historical tragedy can be shadowy. Alfred Harbage suggests (in *As They Liked It*) that the chronicle plays—unlike, for example, *Macbeth* and *King Lear*, which also draw their material from history — are concerned more with political situations than with moral evil. He points out, too, that the end of a Shakespearean tragedy brings universal sorrow, the end of a Shakespearean comedy brings universal joy, but the fall of Richard II mainly brings the rise of Bolingbroke. Consult, also, Irving Ribner, *The English History Play in the Age of Shakespeare*; E. M. W. Tillyard, *Shakespeare's*

History Plays. For the Roman play dealing with historical events, see °*fabula praetexta.*

City Dionysia. See °Greek theater.

classic. For the Romans of the second century A.D., classic meant "a first-class author." For the Middle Ages and the Renaissance, it meant "a writer read in the classroom," *i.e.,* an ancient author, not necessarily first class. Today it commonly means an author or work whose greatness is universally recognized. See °neoclassicism.

climax. See °plot.

cloak-and-sword play. See °Golden Age.

closet drama. A play suited only for reading, not for acting. Most nineteenth-century English poetic dramas (*e.g.,* Coleridge's, Shelley's, Tennyson's) fit into this category, although Byron's plays have recently been moving out of the closet. Consult Moody Prior, *The Language of Tragedy.*

clown. A humorous figure, found in much drama. He is usually the simpleton whose comments are unconsciously funny, and he often reminds us of the realities of this workaday world by an uninhibited simplicity. The clown merges into the **fool,** a jester who (licensed to speak truth in the guise of folly) sometimes has a wisdom that others lack. Feste (in *Twelfth Night*) is "wise enough to play the fool." Among Shakespeare's notable clowns in comedies are Bottom (*A Midsummer Night's Dream*) and Dogberry (*Much Ado About Nothing*); among the fools are Touchstone, in *As You Like It,* and Feste. Nor should one forget the clowns in such tragedies as *Hamlet* (the grave-diggers) and *Antony and Cleopatra* (the country-fellow who brings Cleopatra the asp), and the fool in *King Lear.* About 1583 Sir Philip Sidney complained that Elizabethan dramatists "thrust in clowns by head and shoulders, to play a part in majestical matters," but in the next decades Shakespeare was to show what heights could thus be attained. See °comic relief. Consult Enid Welsford, *The Fool;* Robert H. Goldsmith, *Wise Fools in Shakespeare.*

comedia de capa y espada. See °Golden Age.

comedy. Most broadly, anything amusing — a literary work or a situation — is a comedy. More specifically, comedy is (in Dr. Johnson's words) "such a dramatic representation of human life, as may excite mirth." Dramatic comedies generally depict a movement from unhappiness to happiness, from (for example) young lovers frustrated by their parents to young lovers happily married. The unhappy situation is so presented that it entertains rather than distresses the spectator; it is ridiculous and/or diverting rather than painful.

Comic drama seems related to fertility rituals; it celebrates generation, renewal, variety (laughing away any narrow-minded persons who seek to limit life's abundance), and it celebrates man's triumphs over the chances of life. Irate parents and shipwrecks cannot prevent journeys from ending with lovers meeting. Greek comedy (from *komos:* revel) is usually divided into Old Comedy, Middle Comedy, and New Comedy. All are in verse. **Old Comedy,** exemplified by Aristophanes (448?-380? B.C.), combines fantastic elements (*e.g.,* a utopia founded by birds) with raucous political °satire. It usually concludes with expressions of joy, after the obstreperous people have been hooted out. An Old Comedy usually has the following parts: *prologos* (a scene or monologue in which a situation or problem is sketched); *parodos* (entrance song of the fantastically dressed chorus); *agon* (contest or debate between two speakers, with interlarded choral lyrics); *parabasis* (literally a "coming-forward," an address by the members of the chorus to the audience, usually on a subject connected with the theme of the play); *epeisodia* (episodes, happenings dramatizing the theme, interlarded with choral lyrics); *exodos* (the final scene of rejoicing). **Middle Comedy** flourished about 400 B.C., but the only surviving example is Aristophanes' last extant comedy, *Plutus* (388 B.C.). Middle Comedy seems to have been transitional to **New Comedy** — exemplified by Menander (343?-291? B.C.) — which is of the boy-meets-girl sort, often combining adventure with scenes of ordinary life; there are obstacles to a union, but finally the lovers are brought together. Substantial fragments of three of Menander's plays survive, and a fourth play, *Dyskolos (The Grouch)* is virtually complete. Here is the gist of *Dyskolos:* a misanthropic farmer, Cnemon, lives in the mountains with his daughter. Sostratus, a young Athenian, sees the girl and desires her, but he and his servant are driven away. Sostratus adopts the disguise of a poor rustic and rescues Cnemon, who has accidentally fallen down a well. Cnemon, thus, converted from his misanthropy, offers his daughter to Sostratus; Sostratus' father approves and offers his own daughter to Cnemon's son. Rejoicing. In short, where Old Comedy was satiric and political (and therefore inclined to depict individuals), New Comedy is romantic and social (and therefore inclined to depict types). Note, too, that New Comedy does not employ a chorus. Consult Katherine Lever, *The Art of Greek Comedy;* for a translation of *Dyskolos* consult Lionel Casson, *Masters of Ancient Comedy.* The basic formula of New Comedy was continued in Rome by Plautus (254?-184 B.C.) and Terence (190?-159? B.C.). Consult Philip W. Harsh, *A Handbook of Classical Drama.* For basic types of comic characters, see °character.

Most comedies since the Renaissance fall roughly into three sorts: (i) **romantic comedies,** such as most of Shakespeare's, where the stage-world is a delightful never-never land (Illyria, the Forest of Arden, Belmont) and where the chief figures are lovers; (ii) **critical** or **satiric comedies,** such as Molière's, where the chief figures, who

198

often interfere with the lovers, are ridiculed; (iii) **rogue comedies,** such as Jonson's *The Alchemist,* where the chief figures are pleasant scoundrels who, by outwitting their less astute neighbors, entertain us, perhaps because they represent a fulfillment of our rebellious instincts. The second of these types, satiric comedy, is probably the commonest; its authors usually defend it on the grounds that it is therapeutic. See, for example, Shaw's comment, under °satire. **Comedy of humors** is a term sometimes applied to plays — notably those of Ben Jonson — wherein the characters, though somewhat individualized, obviously represent types or moods (the jealous husband, the witless pedant). A humor was a bodily liquid (blood [Latin: *sanguis*], phlegm, yellow bile, black bile) thought to control one's behavior. Allegedly, a proper mixture produced a well adjusted man, but a preponderance of any one humor produced a distorted personality. The old sense of the word survives in the phrase, "He is in a bad humor"; "sanguine," "choleric," "phlegmatic," and "bilious" are also modern survivals of the old psychology of humors. **Humor characters** are common in **situational comedy;** they are engineered by a clever plot into a situation that displays their absurdity: the man who craves silence is confronted with a talkative woman; the coward is confronted by the braggart; the hypochondriacal lady meets a veterinarian and asks for medical advice. **Farce,** a sort of comedy based not on clever language or subtleties of character, but on broadly humorous situations (a man mistakenly enters the ladies' locker room), is lucidly defended by Eric Bentley in his introduction to *"Let's Get a Divorce" and Other Plays,* where he suggests that farce, like dreams, shows "the disguised fulfillment of repressed wishes." Farce is usually filled with surprise, with swift physical action, and with assault; character is unsubtle, being subordinated to plot. **Slapstick** (named for an implement made of two slats which resound when slapped against a posterior) is farce that relies on physical assault. Farce and slapstick are **low comedy,** as is comedy that depends on obscenity.

At the other extreme from low comedy is **high comedy;** intellectual rather than physical, it requires the close attention of a sophisticated audience, flourishing (says George Meredith in his *Essay on Comedy* [1877]) in a "society of cultivated men and women . . . wherein ideas are current, and the perceptions quick." Etherege, Wycherley, Congreve, and other playwrights of the decades following the Restoration of Charles II to the throne of England (1660) wrote **Restoration comedy,** high comedy of a particular sort, often called **comedy of manners** or **comedy of wit.** Their plays abound in witty **repartee** (what Dr. Johnson called "gay remarks and unexpected answers"), and often strike modern audiences as cynical. Example (from Congreve's *The Way of the World* [1700]): "Marriage is honorable, as you say; and if so, wherefore should cuckoldom be a discredit, being derived from so honorable a root?" The common assumption in much comedy of wit, that love, marriage, and conventional notions of romance are humbug, caused George Meredith to speak of "our so-called Comedy of Manners, or comedy of the manners of South-Sea islanders under city veneer." Recently, however, it has been seen that the Restoration dramatists were not merely flippant and without values, but were forcefully presenting a view of man as selfish, pleasure-loving, and skeptical of irrational traditions. Furthermore, in *The Way of the World*, Congreve satirizes the "affected wit" of most of his characters, and rejects the view that love is a fiction. Restoration comedy has no precise terminal date, but can be said to end about 1700, when satire came to be directed against heartless cleverness rather than against deviations from manners. Coincident with the decline of comedy of manners is the development of °sentimental comedy, plays of venerable parents and middle-class dutiful sons who love pure young things. Example: Richard Steele's *The Conscious Lovers* (1722). Consult Thomas H. Fujimura, *The Restoration Comedy of Wit*; Louis Kronenberger, *The Thread of Laughter*; Norman N. Holland, *The First Modern Comedies*.

Comedy in the sense of the laughable has been the subject of innumerable analyses. One common distinction is that between wit and humor: Wit, from Old English *witan*, "to know," has had several meanings, but behind them there is usually the shadow of John Locke's definition: "The assemblage of ideas, and putting those together with quickness and variety." Thus, in the Restoration court, a wit was an intellectual. Wit has come, however, to be associated particularly with one variety of cleverness; it is no longer merely Locke's quick assemblage of ideas, but an assemblage that, by its striking observation and phraseology — usually compressed and mocking — evokes laughter or amusement. (See comedy of wit, above). In short, wit today commonly means clever raillery. Often contrasted with comic wit — and with °satire, for satire like comic wit is aggressive — is **humor**. In this sense, humor is genial, joshing at eccentricities, including one's own. George Meredith says, "If you laugh all round him [*i.e.*, a ridiculous person], tumble him, roll him about, deal him a smack, and drop a tear on him, own his likeness to you, and yours to your neighbor, spare him as little as you shun, pity him as much as you expose, it is a spirit of Humor that is moving you." Saroyan, then, is a humorist, and so usually are Kaufman and Hart, who seem to have a fondness for the zanies in *You Can't Take It With You*. Sometimes wit is said to be the perception of resemblances, humor the perception of incongruities. Sigmund Freud, in "Wit and its Relation to the Unconscious" (reprinted in the Modern Library's *Basic Writings of Sigmund Freud*) distinguishes between wit (twenty-three varieties), humor, and comedy, but these distinctions have gained little currency among dramatic critics. (Freud's essay is difficult; the student will be aided by D. H. Monro's analysis of it in *The Argument of Laughter*.)

Taking the laughable as a whole, theories analyzing it commonly fall into one of two categories: (i) laughter is evoked by (in Hobbes's famous phrase) "a kind of sudden glory," wherein the spectator abruptly perceives his superiority to others, as when he sees the awkward posture of someone who slips on a banana peel; (ii) laughter is evoked by (in Kant's famous phrase) a "transformation of a strained expectation into nothing," as when we laugh at the comedian who says "I have enough money to last me the rest of my life — provided I die a week from Tuesday." In this second example the alleged humor consists in a statement that causes us abruptly to release the tension we generate thinking that we are in the presence of a wealthy man. See °burlesque and °satire, and consult L. J. Potts, *Comedy*; Thomas M. Parrott, *Shakespearean Comedy*; Albert Cook, *The Dark Voyage and the Golden Mean*; D. H. Monro, *The Argument of Laughter*; William K. Wimsatt, Jr. and Cleanth Brooks, *Literary Criticism: A Short History*; Athene Seyler and Stephen Haggard, *The Craft of Comedy*.

comic relief. Humorous episodes in tragedy, alleged to alleviate or lighten the tragic effect. Some comic scenes in °tragedy, however, not only provide "relief" but enlarge the canvas of tragedy, showing us a fuller picture of life. The clown who brings Cleopatra the poisonous asp sets her tragedy against the daily world. Critics have increasingly noted that the comic scenes (such as the macabre comments of the grave-diggers in *Hamlet*) often deepen rather than alleviate the tragic effect. See °tragicomedy. Although Aristotle stressed "unity of action," some Greek comedies include figures that seem comic to us, *e.g.*, Okeanos in Aeschylus' *Prometheus Bound*. Calderón's °cloak-and-sword plays customarily include a clownish servant, the **gracioso,** and the Japanese °kabuki drama often includes comedy — sometimes relevant and sometimes not — in its romantic melancholy plays. See °clown. Consult A. P. Rossiter, *Angel with Horns*, Ch. 14.

commedia dell' arte. Italian drama, more or less improvised, performed by professionals in Italy and abroad, mostly in the sixteenth century but still alive in the early eighteenth century. In contrast to the classically-inspired written drama (**commedia erudita**) performed by actors who memorized their lines, *commedia dell' arte* (perhaps best translated as "professional drama") employed sketches of plots (**scenario;** pl. **scenarii**) specifying entrances and exits and the gist of the dialogue; in performance these *scenarii* were fleshed out with stock bits of comic °stage business (**lazzi**) or larger pieces of business (**burle**) such as practical jokes. (The singulars are **lazzo** and **burla.**) Thus, a *scenario* may call for the *lazzo* of anger, or the *burla* of chasing a fly, and leave it to the actor to work out the swats and the smile when at last he munches the fly. Though these plays are said to have been improvised, the °stock characters, stock situations, and stock °stage business make them something more — or less — than improvised. The origin of the *commedia dell' arte* is much disputed. It may be a reflowering of the °mimes who, through the Dark Ages, perhaps carried on the tradition of the ancient °*fabula Atellana,* which used masked characters. In any case, the chief characters — most of whom wore masks — in the *commedia dell' arte* are Pantalone, an elderly Venetian merchant wearing a little cap, a red jacket, loose trousers (hence our word "pants"), and slippers: his age, amours, and avarice make him ridiculous; Dottore, a Bolognese doctor wearing a black academic gown: his age and his pedantry make him ridiculous; Capitano, a soldier, ridiculous because a braggart and a coward; several servants called *zanne* (singular: °*zanni,* from *Gianni,* "Johnny") including Arlecchino (later Harlequin), who in the sixteenth century wore patches that in the next century were represented by triangles or diamonds; Brighella, a rather cruel and crafty rogue; Pulcinella, noted for his resourcefulness and his disguises; Pedrolino, a naive valet who becomes the melancholy Pagliacci and Pierrot; Colombina, who later becomes Columbine and loves Harlequin. Further, there are usually four lovers, children of the two Old Men. Consult Allardyce Nicoll, *Masks, Mimes and Miracles,* and *The World of Harlequin;* and K. M. Lea, *Italian Popular Comedy.*

commedia erudita. See °*commedia dell' arte.*

Commonwealth Period, or **Puritan Period.** In England, from the end of the Civil War (1649) to the °Restoration (1660), when England was ruled not by a king but by a Parliament under Puritan control. Although the theaters were closed, °drolls were occasionally performed in improvised theaters in houses and occasionally in the old theaters. Consult Leslie Hotson, *The Commonwealth and Restoration Stage.*

community theater. A theater operated by and for the entertainment and edification of people in a given town or city. On December 22, 1958, *Life* magazine reported there were then some 13,000 non-professional groups in the United States engaged in regular production of plays. Consult *Organizing a Community Theatre,* ed. Samuel Selden; Robert E. Gard and Gertrude S. Burley, *Community Theatre: Idea and Achievement.*

company. A group of actors who perform together; sometimes the word includes stagehands and all others connected with the production. A company may also be called a **troupe,** especially if it tours. See °repertory.

complication. See °plot.

confidant (feminine: **confidante**). A character in whom a principal character confides, revealing his state of mind and often furthering the °exposition. Horatio is Hamlet's confidant; Oenone is Phèdre's. Although Horatio and Oenone are memorable, the confidant is sometimes absurdly vapid; though the French defended the device as more plausible than the °soliloquy, the confidant may be more trouble than he is worth. In *The Critic* (1779), Sheridan ridiculed it thus: "Enter Tilburina stark mad in white satin, and her confidante stark mad in white linen." See °neoclassicism.

conflict. See °plot.

Confrérie de la Passion. The Confraternity (or Brotherhood) of the Passion was an association of artisans formed in Paris in 1402 to put on religious plays. It obtained a monopoly on dramatic activity in Paris, but from the mid-sixteenth century onward its importance was chiefly that it leased its playhouse, the Hôtel de Bourgogne, to visiting professional troupes.

constructivism. A movement, chiefly associated with Meyerhold and Tairov in Russia in the second and third decades of this century; it rejected painted scenery and other realistic (*i.e.,* "illusionistic") scenery, and substituted constructions of ladders, platforms, planes, etc., letting the performers move in three dimensions instead of two. The theater was a machine for acting (and perhaps a representation of Soviet materialism). At the rear, the bare wall of the stage was visible. In Meyerhold's production (1924) of Ostrovsky's *The Forest* (1871), girders and ramps represented the forest, but in a slight retreat from hard-core constructivism the back wall was covered with canvas. Consult Mordecai Gorelik, *New Theatres for Old*; Norris Houghton, *Moscow Rehearsals.*

convention. An unrealistic device that the public agrees to tolerate. Thus, a character in a drama may express his thoughts aloud and not be heard by other characters (the **aside**), or he may speak his thoughts aloud on the empty stage (the °soliloquy). Italian characters (*e.g.,* Romeo and Juliet) speak English, yet are understood to be speaking Italian. On the Roman comic stage, a character entering at the left was conventionally understood to be coming from the harbor, and one entering at the right from the forum. In motion pictures, one image fades out, another fades in, and through this convention the audience knows that there is a shift in time or place. More generally any character-type, any theme, or motif (*e.g.,* the suspected butler) widely used in literature or drama is a convention. Consult Harry Levin, *Contexts of Criticism*; M. C. Bradbrook, *Themes and Conventions of Elizabethan Tragedy.* See p. 1.

Corpus Christi play. See °medieval drama.

coryphaeus. See °chorus.

cosmic irony. See °irony.

costume. Because drama involves impersonation, the performers almost always disguise themselves in some way. The Greek tragic actors wore °masks, and long Asiatic sleeved robes. A Greek comic actor, wearing a mask, was grotesquely padded and equipped with a large phallus. Actors who imitated foreigners, *e.g.*, Persians, probably wore the traditional stage costume with a turban. Roman garments for tragedy and comedy seem to have been based on Greek ones, but the mask was not at first used in Rome. (The females who performed in the lewd Roman °pantomimes were sometimes entirely uncostumed.)

In the Middle Ages costumes were basically fine specimens of the clothing of the day with some additions: the serpent's costume had a tail, an angel's costume had wings. Elizabethan performers mostly wore elaborate Elizabethan clothing, but the costumes of those playing Romans, Turks, Jews, etc. included a few identifying touches. An Elizabethan list of theatrical costumes has a tantalizing reference to "the robe to go invisible in." (On Elizabethan costume consult Allardyce Nicoll, *The Development of the Theatre*, Appendix A.) Costumes in the eighteenth century, like those of Elizabethan England, tended to be of the contemporary period rather than that in which the play was set, though plays set in ancient Greece and Rome used a conventionalized "classic" costume; in the middle of the century, however, David Garrick moved toward historical accuracy, or, put differently, toward °realism. By the late nineteenth century, costumes were as accurate as research could make them. (Consult Raymond Mander and Joe Mitchenson, *Hamlet through the Ages*, and the articles on Hamlet's costume in *Shakespeare Survey* 9 and 11, ed. Allardyce Nicoll.) Costumes are in the care of the **wardrobe mistress,** who collects and stores them. A **costume plot** is a list of a play's characters indicating the costumes each wears; a **costume parade** is a try-out of costumes by the cast. Consult Fairfax Proudfit Walkup, *Dressing the Part*; Lucy Barton, *Historic Costume for the Stage*.

costume piece, costume play. A play (usually set in a remote time or place) requiring eye-catching costumes.

costume plot. See °costume.

cothurnus. See °sock.

counterweight system. See °flies.

coup de théâtre. A surprise, especially a striking turn of events in the °plot. Consult Alan R. Thompson, *The Anatomy of Drama*.

craft cycle. See °medieval drama.

create a role. To perform a °role in the first production of a work.

criticism. The art (or science) of criticizing. "To criticize" is, etymologically, "to judge," or, even further back, "to cut" or "to analyze." But the standards by which critics judge or cut or analyze vary greatly. It has been neatly said, for example, that one judges by asking three questions: What did the dramatist intend to do? How well has he done it? Was it worth doing? But we are balked at the start; how do we know what the author intended? We have the play, not the intention. We have *Hamlet*, not Shakespeare's mental plan when he sat down to write it. Perhaps Shakespeare intended to make money, or to provide Richard Burbage with a °vehicle, or to imitate the plays of Thomas Kyd. The standard proposed by the three questions is in fact unworkable. "Criticism," Dr. Johnson said, "has not yet attained the certainty and stability of a science." Most critics engage in **analysis** — the examination of the parts and their relation to the whole — but they vary in what they analyze. Some analyze a dramatist's alleged intention, some his artistry, some his politics, etc. Kenneth Tynan, in a controversy with Eugène Ionesco, held that "every play worth consideration is a statement," and he found that he did not care for Ionesco's statement, though he applauded Ionesco's "verbal audacity." A critic commonly analyzes and then evaluates. Probably most critics would agree that their job is (in T. S. Eliot's words) "to promote the understanding and enjoyment" of a work; to understand a work "comes to the same thing as to enjoy it for the right reasons." Consult *The English Dramatic Critics*, ed. James Agate; *An Experience of Critics*, ed. Christopher Fry; *European Theories of the Drama*, ed. Barrett H. Clark. Some important recent critical works by authors not represented in the collection of essays in this book are Eric Bentley, *The Playwright as Thinker*; Francis Fergusson, *The Idea of A Theater*; Kenneth Tynan, *Curtains*.

cue. A signal, usually a gesture or the last few words of a line, to which an actor or a member of the °stage crew must respond.

cup-and-saucer drama, or **drawing-room drama.** A play (or plays) depicting domestic life, in which there is not much more physical action than the serving of tea. The term was chiefly applied to the plays of T. W. Robertson (1829-1871), which were much concerned with the foibles of Victorian society. Part of a stage direction in his *Caste* (1867) runs as follows: "Polly meantime has poured out tea in two cups, and one saucer for Sam, sugars them, and then hands cup and saucer to Hawtree, who has both hands full. He takes it awkwardly, and places it on table. . . . Polly stirs her own tea, and drops spoon into Hawtree's cup, causing it to spurt in his eye. He drops eyeglass and wipes his eyes."

curtain. (1) A drapery used to conceal part of the stage. The Greek theater had no curtain, but in the first century B.C.

the Roman theater (outdoors, like the Greek theater) had a curtain at the front of the stage that was *lowered* into a trench when the performance began, and raised when it ended. Consult W. Beare, *The Roman Stage*. Some °masques of the seventeenth century are known to have used a falling curtain to reveal a scene; the Japanese °kabuki play occasionally uses a falling curtain to reveal a colorful setting, and regularly uses a black curtain to indicate night or nothingness. Strolling players in the Middle Ages seem to have sometimes used a traveling stage equipped with a °backcloth, through which entrances and exits were made, and a curtain that dropped at the end of the performance. The Elizabethan actor, too, apparently made some exits and entrances through a curtain at the rear. The °proscenium theater is now normally equipped with an asbestos curtain, behind which is a **house curtain** or **front curtain.** Sometimes behind the house curtain there is an **act curtain** that descends after each act. In the °Restoration theater the curtain rose at the start and did not fall until the end of the epilogue; the custom of lowering the house curtain or act curtain at the end of each act arose in the mid-eighteenth century. Some curtains fly (*i.e.*, rise above the stage); others, divided down the middle, are **traverse curtains** moving off to the sides. Consult James Laver, *Drama*. A scene played near the front of the stage, before a painted backcloth or large °set behind which a new scene is being prepared, is a **carpenter's scene.** A short play that precedes a longer one is a **curtain-raiser.** (2) "Curtain" is sometimes used to denote the last few lines or the situation at the end of a scene or act on which the curtain descends. Thus, in Ibsen's *Ghosts* (1881) there is a "strong curtain" (*i.e.*, a theatrically effective one) at the end of Act II, when it is announced that the orphanage is burning. See °stage business for a description of one of Henry Irving's attempts to provide a strong curtain for *The Merchant of Venice.*

      curtain-raiser. See °curtain, °one-act play.

      curtain set. See °set.

      cycle. See °medieval drama.

      cyclorama, cyc, or **sky-dome.** A shell-shaped structure at the rear of the stage, bending at the sides and top toward the audience. Properly lighted, it gives an illusion of infinite depth. The device was instituted at the beginning of this century. A full cyclorama is a quarter-sphere, usually with a whitewashed surface of roughened plaster, but because such a device takes a great deal of space at the sides of the stage and is an obstruction to °fly lines, a curtailed cyclorama (basically a flat backwall that curves forward at the top and sides) is more common. A **rolling cyclorama** is a cloth which when unused is kept rolled on a vertical pillar; when it is to be used, it is unrolled along a curved track at the rear of the stage. A **panorama,** or **panoramic cloth,** is either a painted °backcloth whose ends curve forward, or one which by unrolling from one pillar to another presents a moving background.

dance. The rhythmic movement of the body, especially of the limbs, usually to the accompaniment of music. There is, of course, much drama without dance, and there is much drama in which dance plays only a small part (*e.g.*, in Ibsen's *A Doll's House*, Nora dances a tarantella). Dance played a substantial part in Greek tragedy, but the exact nature of the dances is uncertain. Consult Margarete Bieber, *The History of the Greek and Roman Theater.* In °musical comedy (see °music) dance plays a substantial part, in the °masque dance is more important than words, and in the ballet dance utterly displaces words. A **ballet** is traditionally a dramatic spectacle in which performers dance and mime a story to the accompaniment of music. Ballets of the last few decades, however, like some in the early eighteenth century, have occasionally dispensed with narrative content; in George Balanchine's "Danses Concertantes" (1944), for example, dancers perform intricate choreographic patterns to Stravinsky's music, but communicate no story.

Though dance has long been associated with dramatic works, Molière (1622-1673) was the first important modern dramatist to incorporate ballet sequences into the framework of his plays. Under the patronage of Louis XIV, and with the collaboration of Louis' court musician, Lully, Molière wrote several *comédies-ballets. Le Bourgeois Gentilhomme* (1670) includes several dance sequences, the most notable of which is the elaborate mock initiation of M. Jourdain into a supposed Turkish order. Today, primarily as a result of Agnes de Mille's dances for *Oklahoma!* (1943), few American musical comedies, for better or worse, are without a ballet.

décor. See °set.

denouement. See °plot.

designer. One who makes plans from which things may be constructed. The theater employs costume designers, scenic designers, and even theater designers.

deus ex machina. Literally, a god out of a machine. (1) In Greek drama a god who descends by a crane-like arrangement and solves a problem in the story, thus allowing the play to end. It was much used by Euripides; Sophocles in his old age borrowed the idea and introduced Heracles at the end of *Philoctetes* to induce the title-character to go to Troy. (2) Any unexpected and improbable device (*e.g.*, an unexpected inheritance from a long-lost uncle in Australia) used to unknot a problem and thus conclude the work.

deuteragonist. See °protagonist.

dialogue. The speech exchanged between characters, or, loosely, even the speech of a single character. Dialogue is sometimes contrasted to °action, but Elizabeth Bowen aptly says that dialogue is what the characters *do* to each other, and Shaw aptly says that his plays are all talk just as Beethoven's symphonies are all music. **Stichomythia** is a special form of dialogue, wherein two speakers in a verbal duel thrust and parry in alternating lines. Example:

> *Queen.*   Hamlet, thou hast thy father much offended.
> *Hamlet.*   Mother, you have my father much offended.
> *Queen.*   Come, come, you answer with an idle tongue.
> *Hamlet.*   Go, go, you question with a wicked tongue.

The Elizabethans probably got stichomythia from °Seneca, who doubtless got it from the Greeks. In Greek tragedy it often consists of questions and answers. See °action, °soliloquy. Consult J. L. Styan, *The Elements of Drama*, Chs. 1-2.

diction. (1) Choice of words, wording. Dr. Johnson objected to the "knife" ("an instrument used by butchers and cooks," he said) which Lady Macbeth says she will use to murder the King. "Words too familiar, or too remote," Johnson said, "defeat the purpose of a poet." See °neoclassicism. Consult Moody Prior, *The Language of Tragedy*. (2) A performer's manner or style of speaking, including pronunciation and phrasing.

dimmer. See °lighting.

Dionysus. Greek god of wine, the phallus, the surge of growth, and (to join all these) irrational impulse. It is commonly held that Greek °tragedy grew from choral celebrations in his honor; in any case, from the sixth century B.C. tragedies were performed in Athens at the **Great** (or **Greater,** or **City**) **Dionysia,** a festival in Dionysus' honor. (The Dionysiac origin is interestingly rejected by H. D. F. Kitto, in *Theatre Survey*, I [1960], 3-17.) Friedrich Nietzsche suggested in *The Birth of Tragedy* (1872) that Greek tragedy, usually considered calm and poised, was not the product of quiet minds. If tragedy, Nietzsche said, showed light and beauty (over which the god **Apollo** presided), it was nevertheless also indebted to Dionysus, who represented the frenzied, buried self-assertions of the mind. That is, Greek tragedy was the product of **Dionysian** ecstatic and violent self-assertion tamed by (or fused with) the **Apollonian** sense of reason, of moderation, and of external order. "Apollonian" is often associated with classicism, and "Dionysian" with romanticism (see °neoclassic).

direct address. See °soliloquy.

director or (especially in Germany and Russia) **régisseur.** The co-ordinator of author, actors, designers, and technicians. Stark Young says (in *The Theatre*) that "the director has the same relation to the theatre that the orchestra conductor has to music. . . . He uses his actors as the conductor uses his musicians, and is related to the play as the conductor is to the score." He decides (as Orson Welles did) to set *Macbeth* in Haiti during the reign of Henri Christophe (1811-1820), or decides (as numerous directors since the nineteenth century have) to play Shakespeare's comedy of *The Merchant of Venice* as *The Tragedy of Shylock*. In short, he **mounts** the play — gets it off the author's pages, out of the designer's mind, out of the scene-painters' shop, and into the sights and sounds on the stage that the audience experiences. The full-time director is a late-nineteenth-century innovation: in earlier ages the author directed the play (Sophocles is said to have done so, Molière is known to have done so) or the °star actor did (David Garrick is notable here), or the °company was sufficiently united not to need a director. But the later nineteenth century saw the rise of independent theaters run by strong-minded men (*e.g.*, André Antoine's Théâtre Libre, and Otto Brahm's Freie Bühne) who had new ideas about the purpose of the drama; this period also saw Edison's invention (1879) of the incandescent-filament lamp, which made lighting important. The first important director or *régisseur* is George II, Duke of Saxe-Meiningen (1826-1914), who stressed ensemble playing in crowd scenes (see °actor). In Russia in the early twentieth century, Meyerhold and Tairov were notorious for reducing the actors to puppets. Norris Houghton reports in *Moscow Rehearsals* that Meyerhold's approach was summed up in his command to an actor: "Observe me and do likewise." The profession has been fertile; a play may now have a musical director, a dance director, and a technical director (the last supervises the construction of scenery and machinery, the construction or acquisition of °properties, the rigging of the stage, etc.). In England and Ireland the director is called the **producer,** but in America the producer is an entrepreneur, chiefly concerned with raising money to buy the play, rent the theater, and finance the production; often the producer hires the director and sometimes the stars, and thus is ultimately responsible for what gets on to the stage. Consult Toby Cole and Helen K. Chinoy, *Directing the Play* (a collection of statements by directors); John Dolman, Jr., *The Art of Play Production*; and Hugh Hunt, *The Director in the Theatre*. Many of the Dell paperback editions of Shakespeare's plays have interesting prefaces by directors. See p. 100.

   disclosure, or **discovery.** For the Aristotelian meaning, see °plot, °tragedy. "To discover" is to reveal a °scene or an °actor, as by raising a curtain.

   dithyramb. See °tragedy.

   domestic tragedy. A serious play showing the misfortunes (especially within the family) of a private citizen rather than of a man of high rank who is involved in events that shake a realm.

See °bourgeois drama. Consult Henry H. Adams, *English Domestic or Homiletic Tragedy 1575 to 1642*.

domus. See °medieval drama.

double. See °actor.

double plot. See °plot.

down left, down center, down right, down stage. See °stage.

drama (from Greek *dran:* to do). (1) A play, a work that tells a story by means of impersonators. (2) The whole body of work written for the theater. (3) A serious but untragic play (see °drame). (4) Events containing conflict, tension, surprise ("life is full of drama"; "the first act lacks drama"). See °closet drama, °comedy, °melodrama, °tragedy. A play is written by a **dramatist;** the art of writing plays is **dramaturgy.** A man who writes plays is also a **playwright.** (Note that the last syllable is not "-write" but "-wright," denoting a maker, as a shipwright is a maker of ships.) Consult Kenneth T. Rowe, *Write That Play*; Walter Kerr, *How Not to Write a Play*; Bernard Grebanier, *Playwriting*.

drama of ideas. See °*pièce à thèse.*

dramatic illusion. The notion that the reader or spectator voluntarily enters into the world of the piece of literature, disclaiming (as Coleridge says in *Biographia Literaria,* Ch. 22) "denial or affirmation." This state, between delusion (the spectator thinks the world on the stage is real), and full awareness (the spectator never forgets he is looking at scenery and actors), Coleridge characterized (Ch. 14) as "that willing suspension of disbelief for the moment, which constitutes poetic faith." In *A Midsummer Night's Dream,* Bottom fears that delusion will occur unless the audience is carefully warned: "Write me a prologue, and let the prologue seem to say we will do no harm with our swords, and that Pyramus is not killed indeed. And, for the more better assurance, tell them that I Pyramus am not Pyramus, but Bottom the Weaver. This will put them out of fear." See °aesthetic distance, and Lamb's comments, p. 122.

George Henry Lewes (1817-1878) introduced into English dramatic criticism the term *optique du théâtre,* taken from the French actor François René Molé (1734-1802). A spectator must have this "theater view," this understanding of "scenic illusion," if he is to enjoy the theater; if he lacks it, he will complain that Hamlet ought to be speaking Danish (see °convention). *Optique du théâtre* requires that we be given not reality but a symbolic representation of it. A stage miser should finger his gold differently from a real miser; a stage character must be heard, even though in real life the character he is playing might speak softly.

Staging that aims at delusion or a high degree of illusion is *representational staging*. Here the stage-characters eat real food on stage, speak with their backs to the audience, etc. (See °naturalism, °realism, °Stanislavsky System.) When David Belasco staged *The Governor's Lady* in 1912, he was representational, placing on the stage an exact duplicate of a particular (Child's) restaurant. On the other hand, **presentational staging** is anti-realistic; in Thornton Wilder's *Our Town* (1938), a drugstore counter, for example, consisted of a board across the backs of two chairs. The staging in musical comedies, ballets, and puppet shows is, of course, presentational. Presentational staging is sometimes called **theatrical staging. Theatricalism,** by its unreality, continually reminds us that we are in the theater, not in the street. On theatricalism, see °style. See also Brecht, p. 116. A derogatory way of saying a work is theatrical is to say it is **stagy.**

dramatic irony. See °irony.

dramatis personae (Latin: literally, the masks of the play). The characters in a play, or a list of them.

dramatist. See °drama.

dramaturgy. See °drama.

drame. A solemn but untragic play, especially an eighteenth-century play that, quietly glorifying the bourgeois virtues, preaches and appeals to the audience's emotions. See °bourgeois drama. Consult Alan R. Thompson, *The Anatomy of Drama,* which classifies most °naturalistic and °realistic plays (*e.g.,* Ibsen's and Chekhov's) as drames.

drawing-room drama. See °cup-and-saucer drama.

dress rehearsal. See °rehearsal.

drolls. Short comic sketches (popular during the °Commonwealth Period) taken from well known plays, *e.g., The Grave-Digger,* from *Hamlet.* The word comes from the French *drole,* "rascal," derived from Dutch *drol,* "stout fellow," literally "bowling pin." For a collection of drolls, consult Francis Kirkman, *The Wits,* ed. John J. Elson.

drop. A cloth that hangs from the °flies to the stage floor, furnishing the back of the setting.

dumb show. See °mime.

eccyclema. See °Greek theater.

effect machine. A contrivance to produce sounds (*e.g.,* thunder) or images (*e.g.,* moving clouds) or even smells. A **thunder-sheet,** for example, is a suspended iron sheet which when shaken provides the background noise to King Lear as he raves in the storm. See °sound effect.

Einfühlung. See °empathy.

eiron. See °character, °irony.

Elizabethan playhouse. The first permanent structure built in England for plays was The Theater, built outside the city limits of London in 1576 by James Burbage. It soon had several competitors, but little is known about any of these playhouses. The contract for one, The Fortune (built in 1600), survives; it tells us that the three-storied building was square, 80′ on the outside, 55′ on the inside. The stage was 43′ broad and 27½′ deep. It has been calculated that about 800 people (the **groundlings**) could stand around the three sides of the stage on the ground that was called the **yard,** and another 1500 could be seated in the three galleries. The other chief pieces of evidence concerning the physical nature of the theater are (i) the "De Witt drawing" (see frontispiece), a copy of a sketch made by a visitor (c. 1596) to The Swan, and (ii) bits of evidence that can be gleaned from the plays themselves, such as "Enter a Fairy at one door, and Robin Goodfellow at another." Conclusions vary and scholarly tempers run high; the following statements are not indisputable. Most theaters were polygonal or round structures (Shakespeare calls the theater a "wooden O") with three galleries; the yard was open to the sky. From one side a raised stage (or open **platform**) jutted into the middle. A sort of wooden canopy (the **heavens,** or the **shadow**) projected over the stage and in some theaters rested on two pillars; these pillars could conveniently serve as a hiding place for an actor supposed to be unseen by the other characters. At the rear of the stage was probably a curtained alcove or booth or pavilion, which when uncurtained might represent a room or a cave. The curtain is often called an **arras,** and it was probably behind this curtain that Polonius hid, only to be stabbed. (John Cranford Adams, in *The Globe Playhouse,* assumes a permanent alcove or **inner stage;** the Swan drawing, however, is against him. But because there are some clear references to a sort of chamber at the rear, a temporary curtained booth, erected for some performances, has intelligently been conjectured.) At the rear of the stage (flanking the curtained space?) there were perhaps also two or three doors, through which entrances and exits were made. Probably the **tiring house** ("attiring house," *i.e.,* dressing room) was behind the rear of the stage. Above the alcove or booth was an **upper stage** (used, for example, in scenes of people standing on a city's walls); flanking the upper stage were windows, one of which may have served Juliet for her misnamed balcony scene. Some scholars argue that in a yet higher place were musicians, and at the very top — called the **top** — was an opening from which an actor could look; in *Henry VI, Part I,* Joan of Arc appears "on the top, thrusting out a torch burning." Most of the acting was done on the main stage (the platform), but the "inner stage," "upper stage," "windows," and "top" must have been useful occasionally (if they existed); and there is some evidence that actors occasionally vaulted off the platform stage into the audience. The **cellar** (beneath the stage) was used, for example for the voice of the ghost in *Hamlet*, and for Ophelia's grave. Though some °scenery was used, the absence of a front curtain precluded many elaborate scenic effects (much, however, could be done by carrying banners) and encouraged continuous action. The stage that was a battlefield could in an instant, by the introduction of a throne, become a room in a palace. Two readable books are A. M. Nagler, *Shakespeare's Stage*, and C. Walter Hodges, *The Globe Restored*. Nagler (Ch. 12) also gives information about a second kind of Elizabethan theater — basically a platform at one end of a hall — that catered to a courtly group. Interesting specialized items on playhouses are in *Shakespeare Survey* I and XII, ed. Allardyce Nicoll.

empathy. The projection of one's feelings into a perceived object. The Germans call it *Einfühlung* — "a feeling into." Vernon Lee, one of the formulators of the idea, claimed that when we say "the mountain rises" we do so not because the mountain rises (it doesn't) but because we have often raised our eyes, head, and total muscular structure to look at mountains or other tall objects. In perceiving a mountain, we merge (unawares) its image with the previously accumulated idea of rising. We are said to empathize with a character if we flinch at a blow directed at him, or if we feel bowed with his grief; if, in short, we *experience* as well as *see* his behavior. Empathy is often distinguished from **sympathy:** we empathize if we feel *with* the character; we sympathize if we feel *for* the character. See °aesthetic distance. Consult Vernon Lee's essay in *A Modern Book of Aesthetics*, ed. Melvin Rader; Herbert S. Langfeld, *The Aesthetic Attitude*. See p. 117.

ensemble acting. See °actor.

entr' acte. See °intermission.

entremés. In sixteenth-century Spain, a short comic piece performed between the acts of a longer play, but the term later came to denote any °one-act comic play.

epeisodion (pl.: *epeisodia*). See °comedy, °tragedy.

epic drama. Bertolt Brecht (1898-1956) labeled "Aristotelian" most drama before his own. He held that it aimed at enthralling the spectators by building up to a climax, thus arousing and then purging their emotions. In contrast, Brecht said, epic drama (he borrowed the phrase from Erwin Piscator) aims at arousing the audience's detached thought; it teaches, keeping the spectators alert by preventing any emotional involvement. The epic drama (probably so-called because it resembles the epic in its abundance of loosely connected scenes and its tendency to deal with a society rather than merely with a few individuals) achieves this estrangement or **alienation effect** (German: *Verfremdungseffekt*) by many means: the epic play (*e.g.*, Brecht's *Puntilla*, or his *Mother Courage*) commonly consists of a series of loosely connected scenes rather than a tightly organized plot with a climax; the settings are not realistic but merely suggest the locale, and they are often changed in full view of the audience, preventing any entrancing illusion (a night scene may be done on an illuminated stage, again to prevent the audience from emotionally entering into the play); the actor may address the audience directly, sometimes in song, and he aims not at becoming the character (Brecht had little sympathy for the °Stanislavsky System) but at presenting him, or, to put it differently, at making a comment on him, as we might do when we put aside a cigarette and say, "He said to me, '. . . .' "; loudspeakers, films, and placards may be used, and the whole is something of a lecture-demonstration, aimed not at arousing and then quieting the audience's emotions, but at making things somewhat strange to the audience so that the audience will look sharply and will think. Consult Bertolt Brecht, "A Short Organum," in *Playwrights on Playwriting*, ed. Toby Cole; John Willett, *The Theatre of Bertolt Brecht*; Ronald Gray, *Brecht*; *The Tulane Drama Review*, VI, No. 1 (September 1961). See °living newspaper, and p. 116.

epilogue. (1) An appendix (usually a concluding address) to a play; (2) the actor who recites such an appendix (*e.g.*, Rosalind, at the close of Shakespeare's *As You Like It*).

episkenion. See under °Greek theater, °Hellenistic theater.

epode. See °tragedy.

excursions. See °alarums.

exodos. See °comedy, °tragedy.

exposition. See °plot.

expressionism. An anti-°naturalistic movement chiefly associated with Germany just after World War I, but which was foreshadowed by Strindberg, notably in his trilogy, *To Damascus* (1898-1904), and in his *A Dream Play* (1902). Expressionism does not seek to present reality dispassionately imitated, but reality passionately felt. Thus, when Mr. Zero shakes his employer (in Elmer Rice's *The Adding Machine* [1923]), the office spins; when he is on trial, the walls of the courtroom veer crazily. Speaking broadly, expressionist plays (in addition to being unrealistic) usually (i) depict types or classes (Rice's Mr. Zero; the Man, the Woman, the

Nameless One in Ernst Toller's *Man and Masses* [1921]), (ii) employ dream sequences, often making concrete and obvious the forces working on the protagonist (in Kaufman and Connelly's *Beggar on Horseback* [1924] the young composer who is about to marry for money dreams that his bride's bouquet consists of banknotes), (iii) assume that man is responsible for his troubles, and can remake the world if he frees himself from his self-enslavement. Though Arthur Miller's *Death of a Salesman* (1949) is in many ways "realistic," it also is indebted to expressionism, especially in the scenes involving Ben. Consult Richard Samuel and R. Hinton Thomas, *Expressionism in German Life, Literature, and the Theatre*; H. F. Garten, *Modern German Drama*; John Gassner, *The Theatre in Our Times*.

extra. See °actor.

extra-dramatic speech. See °soliloquy.

extravaganza. A dramatic entertainment consisting chiefly of a flimsy plot (often a traditional fairy tale) that is °mounted with music and spectacle. In England the type is especially associated with J. R. Planché, who in the earlier nineteenth century wrote extravaganzas that combined a fairy-tale atmosphere with burlesque and satire. Planché's extravaganzas doubtless helped to shape Gilbert and Sullivan's operettas.

fable. See °plot.

fabula. A play, story, fable. The term is used with various adjectives to denote kinds of Roman plays. *Fabula Atellana* denotes Atellan °farce (named for Atella, modern Averna, a town between Capua and Naples). The *fabulae Atellanae* were short farcical rustic performances (sample title: *The Vine-dressers*), probably obscene, chiefly containing four °stock characters: Maccus, the fool; Bucco or Manducus, the big-mouthed glutton or braggart; Pappus, the foolish old man; Dossenus (perhaps a hunchback), the swindler. The performers were all males and were masked. The genre was brought to Rome in the third century B.C.; in the first century B.C. it was popular with amateurs of good families, as well as with professionals, but no complete farces of this period survive. The *Atellanae* may have lived on through the Dark Ages and influenced the °*commedia dell' arte* in Italy and the °puppet show in Germany and England. The *phlyakes* (singular *phlyax*) are sometimes identified with the *Atellanae*, but are more often said to be Greek farces that early influenced the *Atellanae*. The *fabula palliata* (from the *pallium*, a Greek mantle) is a Roman comedy imitated from the Greek, *i.e.*, derived from Greek New Comedy (see °comedy), as the plays of Plautus and Terence were. The *fabula togata*, which replaced the *palliata* at about the time of Terence's death (159? B.C.) was a comedy in Roman dress (the toga), depicting the life of ordinary people; only fragments survive. The *fabula praetexta* (the name comes from the *toga praetexta*, a white garment with a purple stripe, worn by magistrates) was a drama whose subject was drawn from Roman history. It seems to have been invented in the third century B.C. and is chiefly associated with Gnaeus Naevius. Consult W. Beare, *The Roman Stage*; George E. Duckworth, *The Nature of Roman Comedy*.

falling action. See °plot.

false proscenium. See °proscenium stage.

farce. See °comedy.

feather-dusting scene. A scene of °exposition (see °plot), so-called because it commonly presents gossiping maid-servants dusting furniture.

feature billing. See °star.

flat, flat scene. See °scenery.

flexible stage. See °arena stage.

flies. The space above the stage concealed by the °proscenium arch. To hoist scenery is to **fly** it. The commonest system is this: ropes (called "lines") run from the strip of wood at the top of the scenery up to a **grid** or **gridiron** (framework of beams above the playing area), across pulley-blocks to the **fly-men** who stand on the **fly gallery** (a balcony, also called the **fly floor,** at one side of the stage). The fly gallery has a **pin rail,** which has two rows of belaying pins. For a performance, the scenery is lowered to the stage and the line is tied to the lower rail (the **tie-off rail,** or the **trim rail**). To fly scenery, the fly-man pulls the rope and fastens it to the upper row (the **fly rail** or **working rail**). A theater that thus depends on hauling ropes is a hand-worked house or a rope house; in contrast, a counterweight house uses a **counterweight system**: cables run across pulley wheels on the grid over to an iron frame (holding weights to counterweight the scenery) that runs in tracks at the side of the stage. When the scenery is in position on the stage, the counterweight is up near the grid. To raise the scenery, the counterweight is pulled down. See °scenery, °theater.

floodlight. See °lighting.

fly, fly floor, fly gallery, fly men, fly rail. See °flies.

foil. A character who sets off another, as Laertes and Fortinbras — young men who, like Hamlet, have lost a father — help to set off Hamlet, or as a °braggart soldier helps to set off a courageous one.

folio. A book consisting of sheets folded once, each sheet thus providing two leaves, *i.e.*, four pages. The first collected edition of Shakespeare is a folio, published in 1623. If the sheets are folded twice, each supplying four leaves, *i.e.*, eight pages, the book is a **quarto.** Before the folio of Shakespeare's plays was issued, seventeen of the plays had been issued in quartos, some providing good texts but some filled with serious errors. Consult Karl J. Holzknecht, *The Backgrounds of Shakespeare's Plays*, Ch. 14.

folk play. (1) A play of unknown authorship, probably derived from an ancient ritual which has been passed down, performed by rural people as a traditional activity. Such a play is also called a **mummer's play,** perhaps a term from Low German *Mumme*, "a mask," but in the late Middle Ages any play could be called a **mumming.** Consult E. K. Chambers, *The English Folk-Play*, which studies plays of death and rebirth, of the sort Thomas Hardy describes in *The Return of the Native*, Book II, Chs. 4 and 5. (2) A play, commonly in dialect, dealing with rural life. Example, Synge's *The Playboy of the Western World* (1907). (3) Recently in America "folk play" has been applied to plays which, stressing pageantry and local tradition, are put on by amateurs in towns (especially in the South) celebrating historical events such as the settling of Jamestown, Virginia. Consult Paul Green, *Dramatic Heritage*.

fool. See °clown.

footlights. See °lighting.

foreshadowing. See °suspense.

forestage. See °apron.

fourth wall. The wall imagined to be at the °proscenium, through which the audience looks at the play; when mentioned by Diderot (1713-1784), it denoted the wall behind the audience. See p. 116.

gallery. See °theater.

the gods. See °theater.

Golden Age (Spanish: *siglo de oro*). Spanish high culture from the middle of the sixteenth century to the late seventeenth century. Among the notable dramatists are Lope de Vega (1562-1635), Tirso de Molina (1584-1648), and Calderón de la Barca (1600-1681). The chief dramatic genre was the *comedia de capa y espada* (**cloak-and-sword play**), depicting the swift adventures, trials, and excitements of lovers. There are near-disasters, swords are flourished, but things end happily, chiefly because men rise above themselves and act honorably. The form was invented by Lope de Vega, who, finding his colleagues' plots (influenced by Roman writers) too slow-moving for the public's taste, decided to pack his plays with excitement, °suspense, and surprise. For example, in

Castelvines y Monteses, Lope's version of *Romeo and Juliet,* all ends well: Juliet, recovered from her death-like trance, tells her father she is an angel and then works things out. Note that a Spanish *comedia* is not a comedy; it may include comic scenes, but it is simply a play, usually dealing with contemporary life. See °baroque. Consult A. A. Parker, "An Approach to the Spanish Drama of the Golden Age," *Tulane Drama Review,* IV (1959), 42-59.

gracioso. See °comic relief.

Grand Guignol. A nerve-racking horror play, so called from the Théâtre du Grand Guignol in Paris, which specializes in terrifying the spectators with plays of rape, torture, etc. Guignol had earlier been the name of a marionette.

grease paint. See °costume and make-up.

Great (or **Greater,** or **City**) **Dionysia.** See °Greek theater.

Greek and **Hellenistic theater.** The great age of the Greek drama was the fifth century B.C. The audience sat on wooden benches in tiers on a hillside, looking down at a flat circular dancing-place (the **orchestra**), in the middle of which was an altar to °Dionysus; behind the dancing place was a playing-area, which logic (but no concrete evidence) suggests may have been slightly elevated; visible behind the playing-area was the *skene,* a wooden "scene-building" introduced about 458 B.C. that served as a background, as a place for actors to make entrances from and exits to, and as a dressing room. To speak of these elements in a little more detail: the seating-area, which held as many as 16,000 people, was the *theatron* ("seeing-place"); fan-shaped or horse-shoe shaped, it swept around the orchestra in a segment a little greater than a semicircle. The chorus, entering by an aisle (*parodos*) at each side of the *theatron,* danced in the orchestra. The front (*i.e.,* the façade) of the *skene* (or perhaps a temporary screen) and sometimes the playing-area in front of it seem to have been called the *proskenion.* Though the *skene's* façade perhaps suggested the front of a palace, there were further efforts at indicating locale: Sophocles is said to have invented scene-painting (a painted cloth or screen in front of the *skene?*), and there are allusions to *periaktoi,* upright prisms bearing a different decoration on each side. Apparently when a new locality in the same town was to be indicated, the *periaktos* at the right was turned, when an entirely new locality was to be indicated, both *periaktoi* were turned. Other machines were the *eccyclema,* a platform that was rolled out of the *skene* to indicate a scene indoors, and the *mechane,* a crane from which a god could descend or by means of which a character could soar through the air. (See °*deus ex machina.*)

It should be added that plays were put on chiefly during two holidays, the **Lenaea** (Feast of the Wine-press) in January, and the **Great** (or **Greater,** or **City**) **Dionysia** in March or April. The Lenaea was chiefly associated with comedy, the Great Dionysia with tragedy. At the latter, on each of three mornings a tragic dramatist presented three tragedies and one satyr-play. The expense was born by a *choregus,* a wealthy citizen ordered by the state to assume the financial burden. See °comedy, °satyr-play, °tragedy.

The **Hellenistic theater** (*i.e.,* theaters of, say, the third and second centuries B.C. erected in towns to which Greek culture had been spread by Alexander's conquests) seems to have been much like the Greek theater, though now the *proskenion* is apparently more highly decorated, having pillars a few feet in front of it and being fitted with painted panels called *pinakes.* And the *skene,* now of stone rather than of wood, may have had projections at the sides (*para-skenia*) and an upper story (*episkenion*). The playing-area on this upper level is the *logeion.* Consult Margarete Bieber, *The History of the Greek and Roman Theater.* See °actor, °comedy, °costume, °mask, °tragedy.

> **green room.** See °theater.
>
> **grid, gridiron.** See °flies.
>
> **groundlings.** See °Elizabethan playhouse.
>
> **ground row.** See °scenery.
>
> **ham, ham actor.** An incompetent performer, especially one who overacts.
>
> *hamartia.* See °tragedy.
>
> *hanamichi.* See °kabuki drama.
>
> **harlequinade.** A lavishly produced entertainment with a Harlequin (the name of a masked comic character traditionally attired in parti-colored tights); the second part of an English °pantomime is customarily a harlequinade. (On Harlequin's origin, see °*commedia dell' arte.*) Consult Richard Findlater, *Grimaldi.*
>
> **heavens.** See °Elizabethan playhouse.
>
> **heavy, heavy lead, heavy woman.** A solemn major character, especially a villain. See °character.
>
> **Hellenistic theater.** See °Greek theater.
>
> **hero, heroine.** (1) The central character, the °protagonist. (2) The leading romantic character.
>
> **heroic drama.** A serious play, usually in rhymed couplets, involving the noble °protagonist in a grandiose conflict between love and honor. °Poetic justice rules, and the hero usually ends up with both love and honor. The genre, popular in °Restoration Eng-

219

land, is well exemplified in Dryden's *The Conquest of Granada* (1669, 1670), and well burlesqued in Buckingham's *The Rehearsal* (1672) and Sheridan's *The Critic* (1779). Heroic drama owed much to **cavalier drama**, plays by and for English courtiers around the middle of the seventeenth century. Cavalier drama is filled with magnanimous men and virtuous ladies, whose behavior expressed the court's ideal. There are wars, pirates, rival lovers, and lost children, but things end well. Consult Alfred Harbage, *Cavalier Drama*.

hubris. See °tragedy.

humor character. See °comedy.

hybris. See °tragedy.

imitation (Greek: *mimesis*). Not a pejorative term in much criticism, for it often implies a "making" or "re-creating" or "re-presenting" of a form in a substance not natural to it. Thus Michelangelo reproduced or imitated the form of Moses, in stone. For Aristotle, °tragedy is the imitation (*i.e.*, representation, re-creation) by means of words, gesture, music, and scenery, of an important action. See p. 15.

improvisation. Invention of °lines and °stage business by performers. See °*commedia dell' arte*, °Stanislavsky System.

induction. An Elizabethan word for a °prologue or introductory scene, especially one in which the characters are presented to the audience and their relationships established, or in which the theme or atmosphere of the play is quickly set forth. The beginning of *Macbeth*, showing the witches, can be considered an induction.

ingenue. The °role of an innocent young woman, or the actress who plays it. See °stock company.

inner justification. See °Stanislavsky System.

inner stage. See °Elizabethan playhouse.

interlude. (1) A light entertainment, usually musical, introduced into a play, sometimes while scenery is being shifted. (2) In mid-sixteenth-century England, the word is used to describe so many sorts of short plays, from °farces to °moralities, that it is virtually equivalent to "play," though some scholars hold that it describes a professionally performed play, or a play (*ludus*) put on between (*inter*) halves of a banquet. Consult E. K. Chambers, *The Mediaeval Stage*, Volume II, Book IV; T. W. Craik, *The Tudor Interlude*.

intermezzo (pl. *intermezzi*). See °intermission.

intermission. A period between acts or scenes. An *intermezzo* (pl. *intermezzi*) is a light entertainment (usually musical and/or spectacular) during this interval. An **entr' acte** is either an intermission or an entertainment during it.

irony. Irony is of several sorts. **Socratic irony,** named for Socrates, who commonly feigned more ignorance than he possessed, denotes understatement. The *eiron* (see °character) is the cunning fellow who plays the underdog. **Dramatic irony,** or **Sophoclean irony,** or **tragic irony** refers to a condition of affairs which is the tragic reverse of what the participants think. Thus, it is ironic that Macbeth kills Duncan, thinking he will achieve happiness; he later finds he loses all that makes life worth living. Oedipus accuses the blind prophet of corruption, but by the end of the play Oedipus learns (as the audience knew at the outset) that he himself is corrupt, that he has been mentally blind (ignorant) and that the prophet has had vision (knowledge). Oedipus meant what he said, but his words have proved to be ironic. (Aristotle's word for reversal is *peripeteia*.) We have dramatic irony, it can be said, when a speech or action is more fully understood by the spectators than by the characters. This sort of irony, based on misunderstanding, or partial knowledge, is common in tragedy, but comedy too has its misunderstandings; comic speeches or actions are ironic if they bring about the opposite of what is intended. More generally, the contrast implied in "irony" need be neither tragic nor comic; it is "ironic" that the strong man is overthrown by the weak man and that the liar unknowingly tells the truth.

Irony of fate (a phrase which H. W. Fowler's *Modern English Usage* aptly says is hackneyed), or **cosmic irony,** denotes the view that God, or fate, or some sort of supernatural figure, is amused to manipulate human beings as a puppeteer manipulates his puppets. Thus, by an irony of fate the messenger delivers the prisoner's pardon an instant too late. Consult Garnett G. Sedgewick, *Of Irony*; Alan R. Thompson, *The Dry Mock*.

Japanese drama. See °kabuki, °Nō.

jig. A short °farce, sung and danced at the end of some Elizabethan plays. Consult Charles R. Baskerville, *The Elizabethan Jig*.

kabuki drama. Although it developed out of ancient Oriental °rituals, kabuki drama is said to have begun in 1596 in the performances of a Japanese female ceremonial dancer. It soon became a popular all-male performance (actors who impersonate women are called *onnagata*) in which actors are richly costumed and heavily made-up. A run-way (*hanamichi,* or "flower-way"), by means of which the actors impressively enter and exit, passes through the audience, connecting the stage with the rear of the auditorium; the stage is equipped with a turntable (for shifts of scene) and trapdoors (for some entrances and exits), allowing for splendid effects.

The musicians and the stage assistants are visible on stage; the assistants change scenery in the view of the audience, adjust the actors' clothes, and °prompt. A kabuki play (usually melancholy romantic °melodrama, but sometimes comic) is not so much a literary work as a °*scenario* of episodes which allows for a fusion of spectacle, singing, and lively dancing; its success is due more to the actor (better called a dancer who holds striking poses) than to the author. Though plays may run several hours, a program today usually consists not of a play but of parts from several plays. Consult Earle Ernst, *The Kabuki Theatre*; A. C. Scott, *The Kabuki Theatre of Japan*.

katharsis. See °tragedy.

kothurnus. See °sock.

lazzo (pl. *lazzi*). See °*commedia dell' arte*.

lead. A principal role. See °protagonist, °stock company.

legitimate drama. An eighteenth-century English term denoting the spoken plays of licensed theaters, in contrast to the "illegitimate" musical entertainments offered by unlicensed theaters. The unlicensed houses could perform only burlettas; in the late eighteenth century a **burletta** was an amusing musical drama without spoken dialogue and with considerable spectacle, but in the early nineteenth century it could have spoken dialogue if it had at least five songs per act. "Legitimate drama" connotes plays, in contrast to musical entertainments, °vaudeville, movies, etc. For the conflict between licensed and unlicensed houses, consult Ernest B. Watson, *Sheridan to Robertson*, Ch. 2.

Lenaea. See °Greek theater.

lighting. Illumination of the theater, especially of the stage. Illumination of the stage plays so large a role today in controlling the mood, in unifying the stage picture, in acting as a curtain (scenery can be shifted on a darkened part of the stage), and in giving information about time (sunset, night) that it is hard to recall that lighting is a relatively new development. Even the custom of darkening the auditorium is only a century and a half old. Greek, Roman, and most medieval and Elizabethan drama was performed outdoors, illuminated only by daylight. But Italians in the sixteenth and seventeenth centuries — notably Sebastiano Serlio and Nicola Sabbattini — experimented with lighting apparatus. **Footlights** (lights at the front of the stage, level with the actor's feet) were used in Italy in indoor theaters around 1600, probably to counteract the heavy shadows under the chin and nostrils caused by chandeliers above the stage. Indoor theaters from the sixteenth to the beginning of the nineteenth century relied on candlelight or oil lamps, but in the early nineteenth century gas was used on stage and in the auditorium. Gas could easily be controlled to produce effects of sunrise, moonlight, etc. The house could be instantly blacked out, and a moment later could be ablaze with light (and flame; safety devices were primitive). **Limelight** (a piece of lime glows if heated by an oxy-hydrogen flame, and the glow can be directed by a lens into a brilliant white beam) was much used in the middle of the nineteenth century to illuminate centers of interest, but the invention of the electric light later in the century displaced limelight as well as gas. Adolphe Appia (1862-1928) is perhaps the most important theorizer about the importance of light as a substitute for (and improvement on) painted scenery. He was, of course, anti-°naturalistic, stressing light as an expressive and evocative agent that does not merely illuminate but also sculpts and defines. Lighting that illuminates a large area is **general lighting**; lighting that defines an object or group of objects by producing shadows is **specific lighting**. Consult Appia's *The Work of Living Art*, trans. H. D. Albright; *Theatre Arts Monthly*, August 1932 is an Appia memorial issue.

The chief lights used today are: the **striplight** (a unit consisting of a row of lamps; if at the front of the stage, at ground level, they are **footlights**; if suspended on iron pipes overhead, they are **borderlights**); the **flood light** (a lensless lamp, giving broad illumination); the **spotlight** (a lamp with a lens, outside of the set — for example, in the balcony — giving a narrow sharp beam). It is commonly agreed that illumination from above and from in front (*i.e.*, "from the beams," the auditorium ceiling) is necessary. **Dimmers** are devices that control the brightness of the light, usually by controlling the amount of voltage in a circuit. A **light-plot** is a scene-by-scene description of the lighting. Consult Lee Simonson, *The Stage is Set*; Stanley R. McCandless, *A Method of Lighting the Stage*, 3rd ed.; essays by Abe Feder and by Kelly Yeaton in John Gassner, *Producing the Play*; Wayne Bowman, *Modern Theatre Lighting*.

light-plot. See °lighting.

limelight. See °lighting.

line. (1) A rope or wire used to hang °scenery. (2) In the plural, the °dialogue in a play.

liturgical drama. See °medieval drama.

living newspaper. A genre invented by the Federal Theatre Project. (The Federal Theatre Project, established by the United States Government in 1935, sought to provide employment for professional theater people during the Depression.) A "living newspaper" is a theatrical performance intended to inform an audience by dramatizing a social problem. It commonly uses, in addition to actors, an off-stage voice, motion picture films, demonstrations, etc., and thus resembles the °epic theater of Piscator and Brecht. The Living Newspaper unit of the Federal Theatre Project was created in 1935; its first production was to have been of the

Italian invasion of Ethiopia, but this got only as far as a dress rehearsal; the first public production was *Triple A Ploughed Under* (1936). Other titles are *Power* and *One-Third of a Nation*. Because the Federal Theatre antagonized private industries and politicians, it was abolished in June, 1939. Consult Hallie Flanagan, *Arena*, and her Introduction to *Federal Theatre Plays*.

lobby. See °theater.

loca. See °medieval drama.

logeion. See °Greek theater.

ludus. See °medieval drama.

machinery. Mechanical contrivances (other than lighting devices) to produce effects or to change scenery. The Greek theater had its *periaktoi*, its *mechane*, and its *eccyclema* (see °Greek theater). The medieval church, when it served as a theater, sometimes had a movable light, representing the star the Wise Men followed. Renaissance Italy developed elaborate contraptions to represent clouds in motion, waves, the rising moon, etc. In Shakespeare's *The Tempest* (c. 1611) a table set with food vanishes by an undescribed "quaint device." The term "machinery" includes tracks, ropes, elevators, turntables, °effect machines, etc. Consult Lily B. Campbell, *Scenes and Machines on the English Stage during the Renaissance;* Harold Burris-Meyer and Edward C. Cole, *Theatres & Auditoriums,* Chs. 10-11; A. S. Gillette, *Stage Scenery: Its Construction and Rigging.*

make-up. As a verb, to disguise one's face by cosmetics, false hair, nose putty, etc.; as a noun, the materials applied to disguise the face. In the Middle Ages some costumes apparently were supplemented by make-up — God's face seems to have been gilded, and the faces of damned souls were blacked. In the Elizabethan period, surely Othello's face was blacked, but Elizabethan actors seem to have made no use of the cosmetics that were much used by Elizabethan women. Not until the early eighteenth century did make-up seem to be regularly used by actors, and then it presumably was to enhance appearance rather than to disguise the performer. Make-up is especially important when artificial lighting produces unpleasant revelations and distortions. On an artificially illuminated stage, make-up is required if one is to look natural. **Grease paint** (coloring-matter mixed with grease, available in sticks or tubes) was introduced about the middle of the nineteenth century, and became thoroughly established late in the century. Consult Richard Corson, *Stage Makeup,* 2nd ed.

mansions. See °medieval drama.

marionette. See °puppet.

mask. (1) A face-covering, worn by actors in Greek drama, in some Roman drama (see °*fabula*), in the °*commedia dell' arte*, and in the °Nō play, to mention only a few. Thespis, a Greek of the sixth century B.C., is credited with introducing the mask so that an actor could °double, but most anthropologists believe that the mask goes back to ritual dancing in which the dancers wore the heads of animals in order to gain extraordinary powers. In the twentieth century, W. B. Yeats used masks in order to attain (he says, in "Certain Noble Plays of Japan") "the distance from life which can make credible strange events, elaborate words." Some of Bertolt Brecht's minor parts are masked, presumably to generalize them. Eugene O'Neill used masks in several plays, notably in *The Great God Brown* (1926) to represent the characters' public images; the characters remove the masks when they °soliloquize. Consult Joseph Gregor, *Masks of the World*; *World Theatre*, X (Spring 1961); Margarete Bieber, *The History of the Greek and Roman Theater*; Eugene O'Neill, in *Playwrights on Playwriting*, ed. Toby Cole. (2) As a verb, to conceal. Thus, a °backdrop masks the stage-wall from the audience. (3) A kind of dramatic performance, usually spelled °masque.

masque, mask, disguising. An entertainment (apparently derived from an ancient °ritual) in the Renaissance court, wherein noblemen performed a dignified playlet, usually °allegorical and °mythological. The masque was lavishly produced, but its basic structure was generally simple: the masquers (costumed and masked noble performers) enter, supposedly having come from afar, they dance with the ladies of the court, and then they depart. Because the masquers are of the same rank as the ladies, and because performers and audience join in a dance, the masque is very close to the masked ball. Shakespeare's *Henry VIII*, I.iv, dramatizes the masque at which in fact the king met his second wife, Anne Boleyn, but Renaissance England's greatest writer of masques was Ben Jonson, who collaborated with the architect Inigo Jones. Jonson popularized what he called the **antimasque** (a grotesque dance of monsters or clowns), performed by professionals representing chaos, who are dispelled by the courtly performers. ("Anti," from "antic," meaning "a grotesque caper" or "a fool," is sometimes written "ante" because the antimasque precedes the masque.) Consult Enid Welsford, *The Court Masque*; E. K. Chambers, *The Mediaeval Stage* and *The Elizabethan Stage*.

Master of the Revels. In the late fifteenth century, the supervisor of court entertainments in England; a century later, the censor of plays; a century still later, he had lost most of his power as censor to the Lord Chamberlain, who still has it. Consult E. K. Chambers, *The Elizabethan Stage*, I, 71-105.

matinee. An afternoon (or, rarely, a morning) performance. The term is derived from the French *matin:* morning.

mechane. See °Greek theater.

medieval drama. Though the Christian church strongly opposed the Roman theater and suppressed theatrical performances during the Dark Ages, in the tenth century the churchmen themselves put on a playlet of a few lines as part of the Easter liturgy. A tenth-century manuscript preserves the text, which is based on Mark 16: 1-7: clerics dressed as the Three Marys approach the "tomb" of Christ (the altar) and are asked by a cleric, disguised as an angel, whom they seek. When they reply that they seek Christ, he tells them that Christ has risen and shows them the empty "tomb." This playlet — it has impersonation, dialogue, and action — is part of the service or liturgy and therefore is a **liturgical drama;** it has been entitled *Quem Quaeritis* (Whom do you seek), from its opening line. The performers were all male, and the dialogue (in Latin) was chanted or sung; probably the gestures were stylized. The *Quem Quaeritis* was later amplified (*e.g.*, the Apostles Peter and John were added, hymns were added, etc.) and detached from the liturgy. As characters were added, calling for several locales, the performance spread out over the church; here might be the booth of a man who sells ointment to the Marys, there might be a tomb, further over there might be the garden in which Mary Magdalene met the risen Christ. These settings, called **mansions** or *loca* or *sedes* or *domus* or **houses,** were all on the floor at one time, and the performers moved from one to the other, as the plot demanded. The system is called °**multiple setting** or **simultaneous staging,** and it continued for centuries, even when the drama left the church. Neutral (*i.e.*, unlocalized) ground was the *platea* (playing-space). By the mid-twelfth century some plays were done outside of the church, perhaps because they took too much space. In many places, however, drama continued to be performed undisturbed within the church up to the Reformation. The notable Anglo-Norman *Adam* (twelfth century) seems to have been staged outside the cathedral because the play called for demons, who could not be admitted into sacred ground. Laymen now did the acting, in the vernacular (though *Adam* contains some passages in Latin). By the mid-fourteenth century there had grown up in various communities great cycles of playlets: a **cycle** normally showed the history of existence from Lucifer's fall, through the creation and fall of man, to the Judgment Day. At York, for example, the cycle had forty-eight plays, and probably took a full day to perform; in some places the plays took several days. Various guilds (associations of merchants and craftsmen) acted in these **craft cycles,** performing plays appropriate to their trade: in some places the bakers did the Last Supper, the shipwrights Noah's Ark, the plasterers the Creation of the World. These plays of Biblical episodes and of saints' lives are com-

226

monly called **miracle plays,** or **mystery plays,** but some historians reserve "miracle plays" exclusively for plays about saints. ("Mystery" is derived ultimately from Latin *ministerium,* "office," "occupation." More immediately it comes either from *misterium,* "liturgical office," because the plays derived from part of the liturgy, or from *mysterie,* "trade," "craft," because the plays were performed by craftsmen. Cf. the modern French word, *métier.*) A play might also be called a *ludus* (Latin), a *repraesentatio* (Latin), an *auto sacramental* (Spanish), a *sacra rappresentazione* (Italian), or even a play. The plays were popular throughout the Catholic world, but they were especially splendid in France. A witness of the performances at Valenciennes in 1547 reported that angels descended from impressive heights, Lucifer wonderfully arose from a depth, water was changed into wine, and five loaves and two fish were miraculously multiplied into an abundance that was distributed among more than a thousand spectators. The Spanish *auto* had a long life; in the seventeenth century Calderón wrote them, and he had successors in the eighteenth century.

Though *Quem Quaeritis* had been performed at Easter, after plays moved outdoors they attached themselves in the fourteenth century to Corpus Christi day in June (hence such a play can also be called a **Corpus Christi play**), partly because of the favorable weather and partly to give a visible representation of the story of man's fall and redemption. In some cities the plays were given in several places; a spectator went to a convenient playing place, and waited for the first wagon (called a **pageant**) to roll up and perform the first play. Then this pageant rolled on to the next playing-place, while a second pageant rolled up and performed the second play. And so on. But even on a single wagon there might be a multiple set of, say, a pasture, a house, and a stable. These plays were at their height in the late fourteenth century; by 1500 they had seriously declined in England, though they were immensely popular on the Continent. The causes of the decline are uncertain; some scholars suggest that the guilds found the plays burdensome, some suggest that Protestantism found the plays idolatrous and stifled them, and some suggest that the rise of professional drama offered severe competition. Consult E. K. Chambers, *The Mediaeval Stage;* Grace Frank, *The Medieval French Drama;* F. M. Salter, *Medieval Drama at Chester;* Harold Gardiner, *Mysteries' End;* for a good short discussion of the drama in the church, consult Mary H. Marshall, "Aesthetic Values of the Liturgical Drama," *English Institute Essays, 1950,* pp. 89-115; for a collection of plays see *Everyman and Medieval Miracle Plays,* ed. A. C. Cawley.

The **morality play,** a later medieval development that remained popular well into the sixteenth century, was an °allegorical drama on some aspect of the moral life, including such characters as Everyman, Good Deeds, and Avarice. It usually showed the conflict between good and evil, or the way in which the Christian faces death.

One of its characters is commonly the **Vice,** descended either from the jester or from a combination of the Seven Deadly Sins; in any case, he is a mischief-maker who, with considerable foolery, attempts to seduce the character who represents man. Consult E. K. Chambers, *The Mediaeval Stage;* Karl J. Holzknecht, *The Backgrounds of Shakespeare's Plays;* A. P. Rossiter, *English Drama from Early Times to the Elizabethans;* for the morality play and its influence, especially on *Othello,* consult Bernard Spivack, *Shakespeare's Allegory of Evil.* There were in the Middle Ages also plays of a less literate sort than those discussed above. Doubtless in England there were secular °farces, but only a few puzzling scraps remain, and in France there was the °*sottie.* For a study of medieval dramatic foolery, consult Allardyce Nicoll, *Masks, Mimes and Miracles.* See also °folk play. For a study of °*tableaux vivants* and pageants, consult George R. Kernodle, *From Art to Theatre.*

melodrama. Originally, in °Renaissance Italy, an °opera; later, a drama with occasional songs, or with music (*melos* is Greek for "song") expressing a character's thoughts, much as in films today. In the early nineteenth century plays with musical accompaniment became so stereotyped that the word acquired a second (and now dominant) meaning: a play wherein characters clearly virtuous or vicious are pitted against each other in sensational situations filled with °suspense, until justice triumphs. The situations, not the characters, are exciting. The exotic horror (castles with dungeons) dominant in early nineteenth-century melodramas was often replaced later in the century by local horror (the cruel landlord), but whether exotic or local, melodrama is improbable, and virtue — unsullied by any touch of guilt — triumphs over unlikely circumstances. Melodrama is sometimes said to be °tragedy with °character left out (*i.e.,* it contains serious happenings), but by virtue of its happy ending and its one-sided characters it can better be described as °comedy with good-nature left out. Some critics use "melodrama" without any pejorative connotation to describe such serious, often sensational, plays as Emlyn Williams' *Night Must Fall* (1935), Robert Ardrey's *Thunder Rock* (1939), and Arthur Miller's *All My Sons* (1947). **Boulevard drama** (though sometimes sophisticated comedy) is usually melodrama; in nineteenth-century Paris melodramas were popular on the Boulevard du Crime, a street so called because its theaters nightly dramatized murders and seductions. Consult M. Willson Disher, *Melodrama;* A. Nicholas Vardac, *Stage to Screen,* Chs. 2, 8.

The Method. See °Stanislavsky System.

mezzanine. See °theater.

Middle Comedy. See °comedy.

miles gloriosus. See °braggart soldier, °character.

mime. A kind of ancient dramatic performance, or the player in such a performance, or (as a verb) to mimic. In Greece, there seem to have been popular dramatic sketches of scenes in everyday life; by the fifth century B.C. these were imitated by literary men; a few of these literary pieces by Herodas (third century B.C.) survive. One is of women bargaining for shoes, another is of a truant schoolboy who is flogged. In Rome, the playlet called a mime was probably a °skit — usually indecent — performed by wandering players at market places and in homes. The performers — who were perhaps acrobats and jugglers as well as actors and actresses — danced and gesticulated. Apparently one of them performed most of the playlet, the other two being °foils. In the first century B.C. the Roman mime became literary as well as popular, but it kept its sexual theme and was more in favor than the °*fabula togata*. By the third century A.D., it is said, mimes included the performance of sexual acts. The Romans from the second to the fourth centuries A.D. also had an entertainment called **pantomime,** in which a single actor or actress performed all the parts, by changing costumes and masks (the role of Venus called for no costume). The performer gesticulated and danced while a chorus sang to musical accompaniment. Because the themes apparently were taken from history and mythology (*e.g.*, the love of Mars and Venus), the Roman pantomime was for a while the heir of tragedy. Consult Margarete Bieber, *The History of the Greek and Roman Theater*; Allardyce Nicoll, *Masks, Mimes and Miracles*. "Pantomime" meant "player of all parts," not "all silent"; a scene of action without words is a **dumb show.** The Elizabethans often incorporated dumb shows into their plays. For example, before a tragedy the performers might silently mime the action that was to follow. Hamlet alludes to dumb shows in III.ii.14; and one is performed later in the scene. Consult George R. Kernodle, *From Art to Theatre*, pp. 144-145. In England, a pantomime is an entertainment chiefly for children, a sort of dramatized fairy tale filled with spectacle (especially with magical transformations), music, and jokes. Plot is a peg on which to hang songs and lavishly costumed dances. Perhaps the most famous English pantomime is *Harlequin and Mother Goose*, performed by the great clown Grimaldi in the Christmas season of 1806. Consult A. Nicholas Vardac, *Stage to Screen*, Ch. 5.

mimesis. See °imitation.

minstrel show. An American form developed around 1840, at its height 1850-1870, in which white men, sitting in a semicircle, impersonated Negroes. An interlocutor (not in blackface) was the pompous straight man for Mr. Bones and Mr. Tambo, the end men of the semi-circle. The performance usually consisted of jokes, comic speeches, impersonations, music (bones, tambourines, banjos, etc.), sentimental songs, dances (including Irish reels and an "Ethiopian Fling, à la Polka"), and a short °farce. On the whole, slave life was depicted as idyllic. After the Civil War, Negroes themselves sometimes took part. Consult Arthur H. Quinn, A *History of the American Drama*, I; Dailey Paskman and Sigmund Spaeth, *"Gentlemen, be seated!"*; Carl Wittke, *Tambo and Bones*.

miracle play. See °medieval drama.

mise en scène. The staging, including the °setting, °lighting, and arrangement of actors.

monodrama. (1) A piece for one actor, sometimes assisted by a °chorus or by a mute. Example: Strindberg's *The Stronger* (1890), which contains Miss X and Miss Y, but only Miss X speaks. (2) A piece of the sort written by Nikolai Evreinov (1879-1953), whose *The Theater of the Soul* (1912), subtitled "A Monodrama," holds that each human personality consists of several parts. In this play, one personality is represented by several performers, each of whom is a part of the personality. The roles include the rational soul (wearing glasses), the emotional soul (wearing a red tie), and the eternal soul (wearing a black mask). Furthermore, the spectator must be made to feel that he is the one character. "Monodrama," Evreinov said, "forces every one of the spectators to enter the situation of the acting character, to live his life, that is to say, to feel as he does and through illusion to think as he does." Consult Evreinov's writings, and Oliver M. Sayler, *The Russian Theatre*, Ch. 14.

monologue. See °soliloquy.

morality play. See °medieval drama.

morris dance. A dance, usually by dancers wearing bells and with blackened faces. The name is from *morisco* (Spanish: Moor), but the blackened faces may be vestiges of a °ritual in which the ashes of a sacrificial fire were rubbed on the face; the jangling bells are probably a vestige of clashing swords. The dance seems related to the °folk plays of death and rebirth.

Moscow Art Theater. Founded in 1898 by Konstantin Stanislavsky and Vladimir Nemirovich-Danchenko, with the latter as director. The chief goal of the founders was to present a true image of Russian life. The basic principle of fidelity to nature (see °realism and °naturalism) led the management to invite peasants backstage so the actors could see what peasants were really like. It early found vipers in its bosom; Meyerhold, who had joined in 1898, in a few years favored a highly °stylized approach, turning for inspiration to such forms as the °*commedia dell' arte* and the °kabuki. His stress on the importance of the director ran contrary to the Moscow Art Theater's stress on the creativity of the actor (see °Stanislavsky System). After the Revolution the Moscow Art Theater was allowed to continue, and around 1925 it found the Soviet regime congenial. Consult Vladimir Nemirovich-Danchenko, *My Life in the Russian Theatre*; Konstantin Stanislavsky, *My Life in Art*; Norris Houghton, *Moscow Rehearsals*; Nikolai Gorchakov, *The Theater in Soviet Russia*.

motivation. Grounds in character and situation that make behavior plausible. Such grounds are not always present, even in great drama: when Othello asks why Iago "hath thus ensnared my soul," Iago replies, "Demand me nothing: what you know, you know." See °character. Consult J. I. M. Stewart, *Character and Motive in Shakespeare*.

mount. See °director.

multiple setting, or **simultaneous setting.** A stage displaying at one time several locales. The °medieval drama given within the church in the eleventh century commonly had several "mansions" or "houses," presumably distributed from the choir to the nave. These houses would be simple representations of, say, the Garden of Gethsemane, Pilate's palace, the cross, the Holy Spulcher, etc., and the performers would move from one house to the other as the action demanded, while the audience watched from the side aisles. In the late fifteenth century, when °Renaissance humanists put on productions of plays by Terence, they grouped the houses together into a single unit at the rear of the stage; in this structure each character had his own door, by means of which he entered and left the stage. Thus these first revivals of Roman comedy were staged in a basically medieval manner, each character having a "house" now reduced to a door. In France, the Théâtre de l'Hôtel de Bourgogne used the convention of simultaneous sets even in the seventeenth century. In Shakespeare's *Richard III*, one scene calls for the tents of Richard and Richmond, though the tents of these enemies are supposedly some miles apart. Consult George R. Kernodle, *From Art to Theatre*; Allardyce Nicoll, *The Development of the Theatre*. See °medieval drama.

mummers' play, mumming. See °folk play.

music. When a part of drama, music is sometimes classified as either incidental music or integral music. **Incidental music** is only occasional (*e.g.*, the songs in Shakespeare's *Othello*), or if it is continuous it is a mere background to heighten the emotion. **Integral music** is in the foreground, a major part of the performance.

Music was important in the earliest extant plays, Greek tragedies. The chorus sang and danced, and the actors apparently spoke or chanted to the accompaniment of a flute. Probably one can call the music integral, though the plays retain uncommon power without it. (Consult Margarete Bieber, *The History of the Greek and Roman Theater*.) Liturgical drama (see °medieval drama) was chanted, and one of the earliest extant medieval plays, on Christ's resurrection, calls for bells to ring joyously at the conclusion; here we are closer to incidental music. In what we usually think of as Elizabethan drama (e.g., Shakespeare) the music is incidental, but it was sometimes important and of a high order: Shakespeare's lyrics are major accomplishments, and his use of music (e.g., when Hercules deserts Antony, or when Lear awakens) is brilliant. Music plays a much larger role in the °jigs and °masques of the period. For dramas in which music is primary, see °musical comedy and °opera. See also °dance, °minstrel show, °revue, °vaudeville.

musical comedy. A piece with songs, dances, and comedy, integrated into a story. (Most histories conventionally say that the first musical comedy was C. M. Barrass' *The Black Crook* [1866], but this piece was basically a °melodrama to which elaborate ballets were attached.) It is difficult to say how a musical comedy differs from an **operetta,** such as any by Rudolph Friml or Victor Herbert. Perhaps one can say that the operetta has a weaker libretto (**book**) and less spoken dialogue, making the piece closer to a series of songs than to a play. It usually has less dance than musical comedy. Some notable musical comedies are Rodgers and Hart's *Pal Joey* (1940), which, in addition to a clever book, includes excellent dances in a striking nightclub scene; Kurt Weill and Ira Gershwin's *Lady in the Dark* (1941), which shifts from a straight play into a musical by showing the fantasies of a neurotic editor of a glamor magazine; Rodgers and Hammerstein's *Oklahoma!* (1943), whose inclusion of a dream-sequence ballet was much copied; and Rodgers and Hammerstein's *South Pacific* (1949), which has been called a musical play, presumably because of the seriousness of the themes — extramarital sexual relations, and race prejudice. See °dance, °minstrel show, °vaudeville. Consult Cecil Smith, *Musical Comedy in America*; S. Green, *The World of Musical Comedy*.

music hall. See °vaudeville.

mystery play. See °medieval drama.

myth. Defined by Mark Schorer (in his *William Blake*) as "a large, controlling image that gives philosophical meaning to the facts of ordinary life. . . . All real convictions involve a mythology. . . . Wars may be described as the clash of mythologies." A myth, then, in the broadest usage is any idea, true or false, to which people subscribe. Thus, one can speak of the "myth" of democracy or of totalitarianism. Because the myths that were sacred truths for pagans were falsehoods for Christians, "myth" sometimes means any imaginary person, place, thing, or idea, such as the myth that the majority is necessarily right. A myth has sometimes been defined as a narrative, usually anonymous, of the origins of life and/or of the deeds (present or future) of supramortal creatures, often explaining the whys and wherefores of natural phenomena. For example, a Zulu myth explains that rain is the tears of the rain-god weeping for a beloved slain bird. Myths in the sense of primitive legends about gods, heroes, external nature, etc., have often been regarded by modern men as mere fantasies and legends, or as primitive explanations of natural phenomena, inferior to the explanations supplied by reason and experiment. But in recent years myth has been increasingly dignified, partly because Freud and Jung regarded it as akin to dreams — that is, as a "language" which, properly understood, tells us things otherwise unrevealed. Eric Fromm (see below) says that myths and dreams are "a language in which inner experiences, feelings and thoughts are expressed as if they were sensory experiences, events in the outer world."

Because most Greek tragedies were based on the traditional legends of gods and godlike men, it is often said that the Greek audience knew the happenings in the play and concentrated on seeing how the dramatist would handle this familiar material. But Aristotle says that in fact the stories were not known to many. In the present century, French dramatists have displayed a marked tendency to re-interpret the Greek myths (*e.g.*, Cocteau's *The Infernal Machine*, on the Oedipus legend; Sartre's *The Flies*, on the Orestes legend; Gide's *Theseus*). In Germany, Hofmannsthal wrote a notable *Electra*, and in America O'Neill reused the Orestes legend in his *Mourning Becomes Electra*. Consult H. J. Rose, *A Handbook of Greek Mythology*; Eric Fromm, *The Forgotten Language*; Gilbert Highet, *The Classical Tradition*, Ch. 23; Francis Fergusson, *The Idea of a Theater*, Ch. 1.

mythos. See °plot.

naturalism. Sometimes defined, like °realism, as the portrayal of "a scientifically accurate, detached picture of life, including everything and selecting nothing." The spectator looking through the peephole of the °proscenium, as a scientist looks through the eyepiece of a microscope, is to feel he is witnessing life rather than a symbolic representation of life. More commonly, however, "naturalism" alludes neither to a panoramic view nor to the detailed presentation of a narrow **slice of life** (French: *tranche de vie*), but to a particular attitude held by some writers since the middle of the nineteenth century. Though claiming to be dispassionate observers, they were influenced by evolutionary thought, and regarded man not as possessed of a soul and of free will, but as a creature determined by his heredity and environment. The movement in drama can be said to begin with the Goncourt Brothers' unsuccessful *Henriette Maréchal* (1865), but it is usual to say that the opening gun in the battle for naturalism was fired in Émile Zola's dramatization (1873) of his novel, *Thérèse Raquin*. Thérèse and her lover drown her husband, but are then so guilt-ridden that they poison themselves. In his preface Zola urged that the theater be brought "into closer relation with the great movement toward truth and experimental science which has since the last century been on the increase. . . . I have chosen characters who were completely dominated by their nerves and blood." In Paris, André Antoine opened his Théâtre Libre in 1887, devoting it mostly to plays showing the power of instincts and the influence of heredity and environment. These plays were staged as untheatrically as possible; for example, the actors turned their backs to the audience. In Germany, Otto Brahm opened the Freie Bühne in 1889, and in England J. T. Grein opened the Independent Theatre in 1891, both with Ibsen's *Ghosts* (1881), a play showing the destruction of a young man by inherited syphilis. Ibsen's greatness does not allow him to be pinned down by the label "naturalist," but he can be said to be naturalistic (among other things) by virtue of his serious interest in the effects of heredity and environment. Other dramatists who wrote naturalistic plays include August Strindberg (*e.g.*, his *Miss Julie* [1888]) and Gerhart Hauptmann (early in his career, say, through *The Weavers* [1892]), and Eugene O'Neill (again, the early plays such as *The Rope* [1918] and *Diff'rent* [1920]). Note, however, that the major naturalistic writers usually are more than naturalistic; Strindberg's *Miss Julie*, for example, has a preface that talks about the influence of heredity and environment, and it deals with sordid aspects of reality, but it also has symbolic overtones, notably in Julie's and Jean's dreams. Consult Mordecai Gorelik, *New Theatres for Old*; and (for Strindberg, O'Neill, and the sources of their ideas) Oscar Cargill, *Intellectual America*. See p. 80.

neoclassicism and **romanticism.** The neoclassical writer usually regarded himself as one who had avoided the eccentricities and blemishes of his predecessor, the Renaissance writer, by carefully observing the dictates of reason and the practices of the ancient Greeks and Romans. Speaking roughly, French and English neoclassicism is of the later seventeenth and eighteenth centuries. Here are some of the chief qualities. (i) Veneration for the traditions of Greece and Rome. Medieval drama had developed without help from ancient drama; when, during the Renaissance, ancient drama was rediscovered, the aristocracy sometimes called for a refined drama based on these ancient precedents. As the Renaissance wore on, the aristocrats and critics came increasingly to have their way, and various rules were established, allegedly based on the treatises of Aristotle or of Horace, and on ancient practice. Among the rules devised, first in Italy and then especially in France: a tragedy cannot include comic episodes, cannot cover more than a day, cannot change its scene (see °Three Unities), cannot be in prose, cannot have more or less than five acts, cannot include horrible sights on the stage. **Les bienséances** (as these principles of decorum or rules were called in France) had, of course, often been violated by Shakespeare. For example, *Macbeth*

234

has a comic porter, covers an indeterminate period of perhaps a year or more, ranges not only over Scotland but even into England, includes prose, almost surely was not divided into acts by Shakespeare, and concludes with the exhibition of Macbeth's head impaled on a pike. Shakespeare had to be "improved" before he could be presented on the neoclassical stage. Nahum Tate (1652-1715), finding *King Lear* "a heap of jewels, unstrung and unpolished," deleted the Fool, added a love affair between Edgar and Cordelia, and made some other changes that brought the play into line with the ideas of the age. The finest neoclassical writers, however, sometimes treated *les bienséances* casually. Pierre Corneille (1606-1684) was roundly attacked by the critics for improbabilities in *Le Cid*; Racine (1639-1699) said that "the principal rule is to please and to stir; all others are simply means to arrive at that end"; Molière (1622-1673) said "the only rule is to please the public," and he is reported to have said "Regularity must always be sacrificed to expressive truth." Under this heading it may be mentioned that many heroes of neoclassical plays are ancient Greeks and Romans. Shakespeare, of course, has Caesar, Brutus, etc., but he also has many plays with heroes of later societies. Nor could he speak of "the great dramatists of antiquity from whom I have taken my models," as Racine did. (ii) Respect for the rules of society. Neoclassicism was aristocratic; it assumed that the existing social order was good, and that a man must yield to it. In comedy, Molière shows the absurdity of deviations from a reasonable society; in tragedy, Racine (in *Bérénice*) shows that even an emperor and a queen must sacrifice their love to the inflexible Roman law that forbids the emperor from marrying a foreigner. Because the neoclassical heroes are dignified aristocrats, they avoid saying or doing anything ignoble. This means that their vocabulary is amazingly limited: Racine's vocabulary in all his plays has been estimated at about 2000 words; Shakespeare's at about 24,000. A neoclassical king could not say, as Macbeth said: "The Devil damn thee black, thou cream-faced loon;/ Where got'st thou that goose-look?" He would say (in the words of William D'Avenant's mid-seventeenth-century alteration): "Now, Friend, what means thy change of countenance?" Furthermore, to free the °protagonist from uttering ignoble ideas, he or she was provided with a °confidant, who could suggest a course of action that he could take but not propose. For example, Phèdre has incestuous feelings for her stepson; when news comes that her husband has died, the confidante suggests that now her love is no longer guilty. (iii) The setting is commonly within a sophisticated society. In tragedy, we are often in a dwelling of a noble Greek or Roman; in comedy, we are in the city, and we are never in doubt of the reasonable code by which intelligent men should live. (iv) The acting was restrained. Perhaps the best words are "statuesque" and "decorous." The actor apparently gave a dignified representation; he often kept his left hand on his hip while he gracefully extended his right hand, his acting thereby earning the name **teapot style** (illustrated in Bertram Joseph, *The Tragic Actor*, p. 177).

The romantic movement, which occurred in the late eighteenth century and ran into the middle of the nineteenth, can be more briefly described, partly because its characteristics are pretty much the opposite of those just set forth, and partly because it produced no writers of the rank of Corneille, Molière, and Racine. Its most important beginnings are in Germany, notably with Goethe's *Götz von Berlichingen* (1773), Schiller's *The Robbers* (*Die Räuber* [1781]), Goethe's *Torquato Tasso* (1780-1790), and Goethe's *Faust* (1808, 1831). The early phase of this German romanticism is called **Sturm und Drang** (storm and stress); a *Sturm und Drang* piece, such as *Götz*, stresses the feelings of a man who revolts against social injustice. In France, romanticism is most easily seen in the preface to Victor Hugo's *Cromwell* (1827), and in his *Hernani* (1830) and its preface. In England, though Wordsworth, Coleridge, Byron, and Shelley, among others, wrote plays, romanticism's most permanent contribution was in lyric poetry. (Note that this discussion is of a particular movement; a work written during this period, and with some of the characteristics listed below, is "romantic." But "romantic" is also commonly used to describe a work — regardless of its date of composition — that is improbable, fanciful, escapist, concerned with adventure and love.)

The following four headings, discussing drama of the romantic movement, relate to the previous treatment of neoclassicism. (i) Freedom from Greek and Roman traditions, and from neoclassical interpretations of them. Gotthold Lessing, for example, in *Hamburg Dramaturgy* (1769), insisted that although Aristotle said much that was valuable, he did not legislate for all times. Lessing also pointed out that the "rules" were not so much Aristotle's as later commentators', and that Shakespeare diverges from these rules. (ii) Rebellious heroes. Romanticism, a revolt against neoclassicism, is politically revolutionary. The idealized portrait of the robber baron who fights tyranny in *Götz* was followed by a similarly idealized robber in Schiller's *The Robbers*. Hugo's Hernani, too, is a highminded outlaw. Alfred de Vigny's *Chatterton* (1835) is about a poet surrounded by a hostile society. And the heroes, usually being men of the people, as well as heroes, have larger vocabularies than neoclassical heroes; their language can be commonplace, as the language of neoclassical heroes cannot. A French neoclassical adaptation (1792) of *Othello* had substituted a diamond-studded ribbon for Desdemona's handkerchief; Vigny's version (1829) restored the handkerchief — but the audience, not ready for so untragic an item, hissed when Othello demanded the *mouchoir*. (iii) The setting is commonly outside of sophisticated society, often in a forest or a medieval castle. Noble outlaws live in woods;

instead of being Greeks or Romans, they are, say, athletic Germans who fight tyranny. (This romantic interest in the medieval is perhaps best known through Scott's novels and Keats's poetry; not surprisingly, Keats's play *Otho the Great* [1819] is set in the tenth century. Equally unsurprising, Shakespeare's historical plays, which served as a model for *Götz* and which a century later were still serving as models, notably for Tennyson, were highly popular during the romantic period. Put it this way: one aspect of romanticism is nationalism.) The basically architectural set of neoclassical drama yielded to the romantic painted set that commonly showed — with as much historical accuracy as possible — medieval castles nestled in the landscape. The costuming is more accurate, too. Consult James Laver, *Drama*; Ernest B. Watson, *Sheridan to Robertson*, Ch. 12. (iv) The acting was less decorous than before. Talma (1763-1826) is said to have played Orestes like a madman. "To see Kean," said Coleridge, "was to read Shakespeare by flashes of lightning." "Kean is all effort, all violence, all extreme passion; he is possessed with a fury," wrote Hazlitt. A less impressed critic said of Kean, "He raves, he croaks, he storms." Finally, at the risk of oversimplifying, it can be suggested that neoclassicism stresses reason, romanticism stresses imagination. These biases come out, for example, in their critical theories: the neoclassical critic commonly examines the construction of the plot, but the romantic critic tends to neglect plot and focuses on individual speeches (*e.g.*, Shakespeare's soliloquies) which he finds highly imaginative and subtle revelations of character.

Consult Martin Turnell, *The Classical Moment*; Clarence C. Green, *The Neo-Classic Theory of Tragedy in England*; Hazelton Spencer, *Shakespeare Improved*; Gilbert Highet, *The Classical Tradition*; Emery Neff, *A Revolution in European Poetry*; Eric Auerbach, *Mimesis*, Chs. 15, 17. See °bourgeois drama, °melodrama.

New Comedy. See °comedy.

Nō or **Noh drama.** A Japanese aristocratic entertainment, which seems to go back to the fourteenth century and was mature in the fifteenth. Essentially a Nō play is a one-man performance: after some dialogue and song, the First Actor dances. The commonest theme is the salvation of the soul of a dead person: the ghost (played by the First Actor, who is usually masked) meets a wandering Buddhist monk, confesses timidly, and then (often after a change of costume) confesses openly and relives and expiates his sin in a dance, while the chorus sings his part. Nō plays are traditionally divided into six types: "god plays" (*i.e.*, the First Actor is a god who, at first in disguise, converses with a priest or official, and then reveals himself as a god and dances); "battle plays" (*i.e.*, the ghost of a warrior tells of a great battle); "woman plays" or "wig plays" (the First Actor impersonates a woman); "mad plays" or "revenge plays" (*e.g.*, a ghost of a man who hates an unfaithful woman); "earthly plays" or "melodramas" (unlike most Nō plays, these deal with human beings rather than with ghosts or deities); and "last plays" or "demon plays" or "supernatural plays" (e.g., the dance of a demon or monster). °Costumes are rich and bulky, grand rather than realistic, but °stage properties are simple. The stage, a square platform jutting into the audience, has four pillars supporting a roof; at one side of the stage is an extension for the chorus, at the rear is a platform for the musicians (flautist and drummers), and at the other side is an extension leading to a curtain or sliding door through which actors enter and exit. Consult Arthur Waley, *The Nō Plays of Japan*; A. C. Scott, *The Kabuki Theatre of Japan*, Ch. III; Makoto Ueda, "The Implications of the Noh Drama," *The Sewanee Review*, LXIX (1961), 367-374; for what Nō meant to W. B. Yeats, consult "Certain Noble Plays of Japan," in his *Essays and Introductions*.

nuntius. A messenger who recounts an off-stage happening. See °Senecan tragedy.

obligatory scene. See °*scène à faire*.

off stage, on stage. See °stage direction.

one-act play. A short play with no intermission and often no change of scene. A one-act play performed before a longer play is a **curtain-raiser;** a short °farce performed after a longer play (common in the eighteenth century) is an **after-piece.** Bennett Cerf and Van H. Cartmell have edited two collections, *24 Favorite One-Act Plays,* and *Thirty Famous One-Act Plays.* Consult Percival Wilde, *The Craftsmanship of the One-Act Play. The One-Act Play Today* is an anthology of essays on the genre, edited in 1938 by William Kozlenko.

onnagata. See °kabuki drama.

open stage. A performing area, usually a platform, at one end of a room, with the audience in front and sometimes at the sides. Unlike a °proscenium stage, the open stage is entirely within the auditorium. Consult Richard Southern, *The Open Stage;* Walter Kerr, "The Theater Breaks Out of Belasco's Box," *Horizon,* I (July 1959), 41-48.

opening. See °rehearsal.

opera. A form originated during the Italian °Renaissance, in an attempt to revive the musical declamation of Greek tragedy. The first such piece whose music is extant is Peri's *Eurydice* (1600), but the first important composer is Monteverdi, whose *Orpheus* (1607) survives complete. Though the word "opera" was used in the seventeenth century and much used in eighteenth-century England, until about 1800 the commonest terms for the genre in Italy were *melodramma* (*i.e.*, music-drama) and *dramma per musica* (drama through music). Sometimes the music in opera is continuous, sometimes not: speaking very roughly, the music is continuous in tragic pieces, interrupted in comic. Unhappy with works that consisted of a number of songs (airs, or arias, duets, trios, etc.) linked by musically unimportant narrative lines declaimed in a manner between singing and speaking (recitative), Richard Wagner (1813-1883) sought to write what he called *Musikdrama* or *Gesamtkunstwerk* (composite work of art) or opera. He maintained the primacy of the music, but (influenced by Gluck) he insisted that the libretto be substantial and that the whole work — including costumes and scenery, which he specified in detail — be not simply a musical performance but a fusion of the arts. For a criticism of Wagner's desire to be a combination of Beethoven and Shakespeare, consult Eric Bentley, *The Playwright as Thinker*, Chs. 3 and 4. For opera in general, consult Edward J. Dent, *Opera*; Joseph Kerman, *Opera as Drama*; Donald J. Grout, *A Short History of Opera*; and see p. 128.

operetta. See °musical comedy.

optique du théâtre. See °dramatic illusion.

orchestra. See °Greek theater, °theater.

pace, pacing, or **tempo.** The speed at which the scene, act, or play moves, including the speaking of dialogue and the execution of °stage business. Consult J. L. Styan, *The Elements of Drama*, Ch. 7; Harley Granville-Barker, *Prefaces to Shakespeare*.

pageant. See °medieval drama.

painted scenery. See °scenery, °neoclassicism.

panorama, panoramic cloth. See °cyclorama.

pantomime. See °mime.

parabasis. See °comedy.

paraskenia. See °Greek theater.

parodos. See °comedy, °tragedy, °Greek theater.

parquet. See °theater.

part, or **role.** (1) A character in a play. (2) The lines and actions of a character. When he was congratulated for writing "magnificent parts," Ibsen retorted: "Parts! I do not write parts. I create men and women."

parterre. See °theater.

passion play. A dramatization of the Suffering of Christ.

pastoral drama. Drama of idyllic shepherd life. The form, which owes much to those poems by Vergil in which shepherds speak, was popular in Italy in the second half of the sixteenth century, and soon spread to France and England. The chief activity of the shepherds and shepherdesses in these plays is wooing, often with song. There are difficulties: the shepherdess beloved by the first shepherd often loves the second shepherd, but things finally work out. Among the most notable pastoral plays are Tasso's *Aminta* (1573), Guarini's *The Faithful Shepherd* (pub. 1590), and Shakespeare's *As You Like It* (c. 1599). In this last, a duke banished to the greenwood finds "this life more sweet than that of painted pomp" (thus there is criticism of court-life) but he returns to the court when he gets the chance (thus pastoral life too is judged). Consult W. W. Greg, *Pastoral Poetry and Pastoral Drama*.

pathos. The quality that evokes pity. The pathetic is often distinguished from the °tragic; in the former, the suffering is experienced by the passive and the innocent (especially women and children), while in the latter it is experienced by persons who act, struggle, and are in some measure responsible for their sufferings. Discussing Aeschylus' *The Suppliants*, H. D. F. Kitto says in *Greek Tragedy* (2nd ed.): "The Suppliants are not only pathetic, as the victims of outrage, but also tragic, as the victims of their own misconceptions." °She-tragedy is especially likely to evoke pathos. See also °bourgeois drama.

periaktos. See °Greek theater.

period piece. (1) A play that is very much of its time. *Hamlet* is contemporary in every age, but a Victorian °melodrama is likely to be dated, and when performed now is presented as such. (2) A play that requires historic costumes and settings.

peripeteia, **peripety.** See °plot, °tragedy.

phlyax. See °*fabula.*

picture-frame stage. See °proscenium stage.

pièce à thèse. A play with a thesis, a play in which the dramatist argues a point. Commonly the thesis is not about, say, the benevolence of God, but about the merits or defects of some social institution; a play dealing with a social institution may also be called a **problem play** or a **drama of ideas.** Some critics distinguish between the terms, saying that a problem play merely poses a social problem, as Galsworthy does in *Strife* (1909), while a thesis play propounds a solution. Shaw says that "The material of the dramatist is always some conflict of human feeling with circumstances"; when the circumstances are "human institutions" (*e.g.,* divorce laws, penal codes) rather than unchanging facts of life (*e.g.,* death), and the audience is forced to meditate on the value of the institutions, we have a problem play. Shaw's essay, "The Play of Ideas," is in

Shaw on Theatre, ed. E. J. West. Consult also Walter Kerr, *How Not to Write a Play*, Ch. 5.

pièce bien faite, or **well-made play.** A play, with much °suspense and with little depth of characterization, that relies on a cleverly constructed plot, first developing a situation, then building the crisis to a climax, and then resolving the business. The type, perhaps it can be described as °melodrama with the fisticuffs left out, is chiefly associated with Victorien Sardou (1831-1908), but Sardou was indebted to Eugène Scribe (1791-1861). Shaw called their plays clockwork mice, and Sardoodledom, but the influence of Sardou on Shaw's hero, Ibsen, is undeniable. See °plot, and consult Walter Kerr, *How Not to Write a Play*, Ch. 10; Eric Bentley, "Homage to Scribe," *What is Theatre?*; C. E. Montague, *Dramatic Values*, pp. 63-74; *Camille and Other Plays*, ed. Stephen S. Stanton.

pinakes. See °Greek theater.

pit. See °theater.

platea. See °medieval drama.

platform stage. See °Elizabethan playhouse, °open stage.

play. As a noun, a story communicated by impersonators. As a verb, to act. See °drama.

play doctor. One called in to patch up a play's weaknesses by rewriting and adding bits of °stage business.

playhouse. A theater (which is literally a "seeing-place"), a building in which dramatic entertainments are presented. See °Elizabethan playhouse, °proscenium stage, °Restoration playhouse, °tennis court theater, °theater.

play-within-a-play. The representation of a drama within a drama itself. Example: the performance given in *Hamlet*, III.ii, by actors who have come to Elsinore. For the rich possibilities afforded by this device, consult Robert J. Nelson, *Play within a Play*.

playwright. See °drama.

plot and **character.** The plot is sometimes the "story," the "narrative," but usually it is the happenings *as the author arranges them.* In *Hamlet*, for example, the story involves the poisoning of the king, but Shakespeare omits this scene from his plot. Aristotle, in Chapter 6 of the *Poetics*, calls plot (*mythos*, in the present version translated as **fable**) "the whole structure of the incidents," and he speaks of plot as the "soul of tragedy," thus making it more important than character. By character he means the personalities of the figures in the story. For Aristotle, the aspects of

241

personality (whether a warrior is brave or cowardly, gentle or harsh, etc.) arise out of the action the writer has in mind. Menander (a Greek comic dramatist) is said to have told a friend that he had finished a comedy, though he had not yet written a line of dialogue; the anecdote implies that Menander had completed his idea of *what happens* (action) and in *what order* (plot), and he would find it easy then to write the lines of the characters necessary to this plot. The separation, however, between plot and character is misleading, for the two usually interplay. Although it is true that there may be much plot and little character (as in a thriller), in most great plays there is such a fusion between what is done and the personality of the doer that we feel the truth of Henry James's questions: "What is character but the determination of incident? What is incident but the illustration of character?" (See also °character.)

Most plots entail a **conflict,** wherein the °protagonist is somehow opposed. If he is opposed chiefly by another person rather than by a force such as Fate or God or by an aspect of himself, the opposing figure is the °antagonist. The German critic, Gustav Freytag, in *Technique of the Drama* (1863), held that a play dramatizes "the rushing forth of will power from the depths of man's soul toward the external world," and "the coming into being of a deed and its consequences on the human soul." The five-act play, he said, commonly arranged such an action into a **pyramidal structure,** consisting of a **rising action,** a **climax,** and a **falling action.** The rising action begins with the **exposition,** in which is given essential information, especially about the **antecedent action** (what has occurred before this piece of action begins). The two gossiping servants who tell each other that after a year away in Paris the young master is coming home today with his new wife are giving the audience the exposition. The exposition in Shakespeare's *The Tempest* is almost ruthlessly direct: Prospero tells his naïve daughter "I should inform thee farther," and for about one hundred and fifty lines he proceeds to tell her why she is on an almost uninhabited island. The action rises through a **complication** (the protagonist is opposed) to a high point or **crisis** or **climax** (a moment at which tension is high, and which is a decisive turning point). The falling action goes through a **reversal** (if a °tragedy, the protagonist loses power), and then into a **catastrophe,** also called a **denouement** (unknotting) or resolution. (Aristotle's word for the reversal is *peripeteia,* anglicized to **peripety,** and translated as "irony of events," would in a °comedy be a change from bad fortune to good, and the catastrophe would thus be happy.) The denouement frequently involves what Aristotle called an *anagnorisis* (**recognition, disclosure, discovery**). This recognition may be as simple as the identification of a long-lost brother by a birth mark, or it may involve a character's recognition of his own true condition. Shakespeare sometimes used a pyramidal structure, placing his climax neatly in the middle of what seems to us to be the third of five acts. In *Julius Caesar,* Brutus rises in the first half of the play, reaching his height in III. i, with the death of Caesar; but later in this scene he gives Marc Antony permission to speak at Caesar's funeral and thus sets in motion his own fall, which occupies the second half of the play. In *Macbeth*, the protagonist attains his height in III. i. ("Thou hast it now: King"), but he soon perceives that he is going downhill:

> I am in blood
> Stepped in so far that, should I wade no more,
> Returning were as tedious as go o'er.

Some works have a **double plot,** that is, two plots, usually with some sort of relation. For example, the **subplot** or **underplot** (the secondary narrative) might be a grotesque version of the serious main plot. In Shakespeare's *The Tempest,* the main plot and subplot both deal with usurpation. In *King Lear,* the main plot concerns Lear's relation to his daughters, while the parallel subplot concerns Gloucester's relation to his sons. For another aspect of the subplot, see °comic relief; consult William Empson, *Some Versions of Pastoral,* Ch. 2. On plotting see °*pièce bien faite* and °*scène à faire;* consult John H. Lawson, *Theory and Technique of Playwriting.* For the Elizabethans, a "plot" was a °prompter's outline of the happenings, specifying entrances and exits.

poetic drama. A play whose language is metrical. With the exception of some comedies by Molière and by a few seventeenth-century English writers, the great Western drama of all but the last one hundred years has been entirely or largely in verse. But the prose dramas of such men as Ibsen, Chekhov, Synge, and Shaw, in the last hundred years, make suspect the old idea that great drama must be in verse. Certainly prose has seemed an appropriate medium for the °problem play (see *pièce à thèse*), which commonly examines a social institution by means of much discussion. Consult Moody Prior, *The Language of Tragedy;* Ronald Peacock, *The Poet in the Theatre;* Dennis Donoghue, *The Third Voice;* Richmond Lattimore's introduction to his translation of Aeschylus' *Oresteia.* See °symbolism.

poetic justice. A term coined by Thomas Rymer in 1678, denoting the reward of the virtuous and the punishment of the vicious. Aristotle had said or implied that the tragic hero is undone partly by some sort of personal flaw — *i.e.,* he is at least partly responsible for the suffering he later encounters. (See °*hamartia,* under °tragedy, and p. 26.) "Poetic justice," with its idea that all characters reap the harvest of their just deserts, is a hardening of Aristotle's suggestion. Consult Alfred Harbage, "Justice in Comic Fable," in his *As They Liked It;* M. A. Quinlan, *Poetic Justice in the Drama.*

première. The first public performance of a work.

presentational staging. See °dramatic illusion.

preview. See °rehearsal.

problem play. See °*pièce à thèse*.

producer. See °director.

production. (1) A dramatic entertainment on the stage. (2) The process of getting the work on the stage, *i.e.*, financing, selecting actors, rehearsing, etc. For "producer," see °director. (3) The technical aspects of a play, *i.e.*, the °settings, °lighting, °costumes, and °properties.

prologos. See °prologue, °comedy, °tragedy.

prologue. (1) A preface or introduction. For the Greeks the *prologos* was the first scene, which gave the °exposition. Elizabethan prologues commonly summarize the plot, as the °Chorus does in this prologue to *Romeo and Juliet*:

> Two households, both alike in dignity,
>   In fair Verona, where we lay our scene,
> From ancient grudge break to new mutiny,
>   Where civil blood makes civil hands unclean.
> From forth the fatal loins of these two foes
>   A pair of star-crossed lovers take their life. . . .

But in the °Restoration theater, the prologue was almost an independent verse essay spoken before the play began. Consult Autrey N. Wiley, *Rare Prologues and Epilogues 1642-1700*. (2) The actor who speaks a piece of the sort described above.

prompter. One who reminds forgetful actors of their lines. Often he is the assistant °stage manager. He holds a **prompt book** or **prompt copy** — a copy with the director's annotation of stage business, cuts, etc. A published version of such a book is an **acting edition.**

property, prop. An object (other than scenery, costumes, and lights) required by the °script, including even machinery for °sound effects. Properties are commonly divided into two classes, hand props and set props. A **hand prop** is any item that a character handles (a pipe, a Chinese newspaper, a hat if it is not part of his costume). A **set prop** remains standing untouched on the floor (a cuspidor). Sometimes a third class, **trim props,** is established for draperies, pictures, and any other items hanging on the walls of the set. Properties are obtained by the **property man.** The **property plot** is a scene-by-scene list of required properties.

proscenium stage, or **picture-frame stage.** A playing-area framed in the front, and thus separated from the audience. This frame is the **proscenium arch** or the **proscenium;** the empty space it contains, sometimes filled with a curtain, is the **proscenium opening.** Commonly this opening is reduced by a **false proscenium,** consisting of a valance (the **teaser**) hanging from behind the top of the arch, and by a screen (**tormentor**) projecting from each side. Basically a **proscenium theater** has two rooms, one for the audience and another (with a hole in the mutual wall) for the performers. Such a theater is at least as old as the early seventeenth century, when the Farnese Theater was built in Parma. "Proscenium" has had several meanings: in the Greek theater, the *proskenion* seems to have been whatever was in front of the *skene* (scene-building), *i.e.,* the *skene's* façade, or the stage. (See °Greek theater.) "Proscenium" has also referred to the °apron, or forestage, that part of the stage that projects beyond the frame. Almost half of the stage in a °Restoration theater projected beyond the proscenium arch; doors were built into the arch, and actors entered through them onto this "apron." But in succeeding years the apron diminished, and now it is commonly only a few feet. In the last few decades the proscenium theater has been damned as a museum theater and a peepshow theater, chiefly on the grounds that it separates the performers and audience. See °arena stage. Consult Allardyce Nicoll, *The Development of the Theatre.*

proskenion. See °Greek theater, °proscenium stage.

protagonist. The chief figure in a play. In Greek the word means literally the "first contender," *i.e.,* the chief actor (*protos:* first). The second role was given to the **deuteragonist,** the third to the **tritagonist.** The protagonist is commonly opposed by the **antagonist,** played by the deuteragonist. For the relationship between the protagonist and the antagonist, see °plot.

Punch and Judy. See °puppet.

puppet. Broadly, a doll that can be manipulated. Narrowly, a doll whose body is basically a glove, into which the operator thrusts his hand and by moving his fingers causes the arms and head to move. A **marionette** is a doll controlled from above or below by (most primitively) a rod or wire attached to the head, or by wires or strings attached to the head, hands, elbows, etc. The usual marionette today is operated by nine strings, but the cruder marionettes with only one or two wires can still be found. (Consult the chapter, "South of Eboli," in Eric Bentley's *In Search of Theater.*) Doll plays have been fads in sophisticated European society, but chiefly they have appealed to children and simple adults who live in areas unvisited by actors. **Punch and Judy** is the most renowned puppet show. Punch, a hunchback who doubtless is descended from a comic servant (Pulcinella) in the °*commedia dell' arte,* and probably has an ancestor further back in the °*fabula Atellana,* is left to mind the baby when Judy goes shopping. The baby cries, and, when

Punch's attempts to soothe it are unsuccessful, he throws it out the window. Judy returns, fights with Punch, and is killed. Visitors are beaten up as they come, but Punch is finally subdued and taken to the gallows. He tricks the hangman into trying on the noose, and hangs him, and sometimes goes on to kill the devil. Consult Paul McPharlin, *A Repertory of Marionette Plays* (including, among other pieces, one by Goethe and one by Maeterlinck); McPharlin's *The Puppet Theatre in America*.

In the Orient, doll theaters of various sorts have attracted talented playwrights, especially in seventeenth- and eighteenth-century Japan. One of the most important species of doll theater is the **shadow play:** the audience faces a translucent screen behind which flat figures (operated by rods or strings) are moved in front of a light. Shadow plays are still popular in Java, Malaya, and Bali. Consult Earle Ernst, *The Kabuki Theatre;* Faubion Bowers, *Theatre in the East*.

Puritan Period. See °Commonwealth Period.

pyramidal structure. See °plot.

quarto. See °folio.

rail. See °flies.

raisonneur. See °chorus.

raked stage. A playing area that slopes upward toward the rear wall. It was widely used in conjunction with perspective scenery (see °scenery), and it is sometimes said to project the action into the audience, but it is rarely used today. Today the **rake** (slope) is likely to be under the spectators rather than the actors.

realism. The reproduction of life, especially as it appears to the eye and ear; the illusion of nature. Usually it deals with ordinary men in ordinary situations, moving in °scenery that closely imitates reality. In England, T. W. Robertson (1829-1871) insisted, for example, that doorknobs not be painted on the doors but be three-dimensional. Wings and a backcloth (*i.e.*, projecting flats at the sides and a painted cloth at the rear) were increasingly replaced by the °box set for interior scenes. (See °scenery.) Gas °lighting, introduced to the stage about 1820, soon became capable of producing effects of sunlight, moonlight, etc. The dialogue, as well as the sets, came closer to what the senses perceive. Realistic plays (in prose, of course) avoided °soliloquies, °asides, and declamation. (See °cup-and-saucer drama.) The great playwrights of the movement are Ibsen and Chekhov, but W. Somerset Maugham has somewhat impatiently described the little world in which Ibsen's figures move: "It is not a gross exaggeration to say that his only gambit is the sudden arrival of a stranger who comes into a stuffy room and opens the windows; whereupon the people who were sitting there catch their death of cold and everything ends unhappily." That realism shades into °naturalism is clear; that in Ibsen it shades into °symbolism is less obvious but is well demonstrated by John Northam, *Ibsen's Dramatic Method*, and by Mary McCarthy, p. 80. A simple example of Ibsen's symbolism: in *Hedda Gabler*, Hedda's hair is "not particularly abundant," but Thea's is "unusually abundant," suggesting Hedda's barrenness and Thea's fertility. Consult Mordecai Gorelik, *New Theatres for Old*; A. Nicholas Vardac, *Stage to Screen*, Chs. 4, 9; Ernest B. Watson, *Sheridan to Robertson*. In **selective realism,** some of the scenery (*e.g.*, a window and a door) closely reproduces reality, but some (*e.g.*, a framework *suggesting* a roof) does not.

recognition. See °tragedy.

régisseur. See °director.

rehearsal. A practice performance of a dramatic work, or of part of it. The first rehearsals are usually **reading rehearsals:** the °cast or the °director reads the play aloud; the director usually explains the °set for each scene before it is read. Some directors then go into a **line rehearsal,** in which the performers get familiar with their speeches, and next into a **blocking rehearsal,** in which the actors' movements are practiced, but many directors prefer to have blocking rehearsals before line rehearsals. A **technical rehearsal** is devoted to matters of adjusting °scenery and °lighting; the performers go through their parts casually while the technicians (*e.g.*, electricians, stagehands, etc.) practice. A **run-through** is a rehearsal of the entire play uninterrupted by director or stage manager. A **dress rehearsal** is a rehearsal in costume. A **try-out** or a **preview** is a public performance for which admission is normally charged but which occurs previous to the performance that, reviewed by critics, is considered the **opening.** In the professional theater the try-out is usually given in a city other than the one where the piece officially opens. See Shaw, p. 100.

Renaissance (from French, for "rebirth"). The alleged rebirth of learning and art in the fourteenth and fifteenth centuries in Italy and France, and in the sixteenth century in England. The learning that was reborn was supposedly that of the Greeks and Romans, and if rebirth is not quite the right word, it is nevertheless true that some ancient writings (especially Greek) unknown to the Middle Ages were discovered, and that the development in Europe (c. 1450) of printing on paper by movable type allowed learning to be widely disseminated. In Italy in the late fourteenth century °comedies were composed in Latin based on Roman models; early in the fifteenth century a dozen of Plautus' plays, unknown for centuries, were found, giving an impetus to the study of Roman comedy. In the middle and late fifteenth centuries Plautus and Terence were performed, and from about 1500 these authors provided models for Italian comedies, such as Niccolò Machiavelli's *Mandragola* (c. 1515). In England, Plautus and Terence were read in schools by 1520, and were acted by 1530. Among the earliest notable imitations is Nicholas Udall's *Ralph Roister Doister* (c. 1552), heavily based both in plot and in some characters on Plautus' *Braggart Soldier*, but *Ralph Roister Doister* is thoroughly Englished; the heroine, for example, is a virtuous English widow. Roman comedy continued to exert an influence on English Renaissance comedy, most obviously in one of Shakespeare's earliest plays, *The Comedy of Errors* (c. 1590), and in Ben Jonson's conception that comedy is a mirror of life and a castigator of follies. (Consult Jonson's Dedication preceding *Volpone*, and his *Every Man Out of His Humor*, III.vi. 195-209. Consult, too, George E. Duckworth, *The Nature of Roman Comedy*; Marvin T. Herrick, *Italian Comedy in the Renaissance*.) Greek °tragedy was little known, but Roman tragedy attracted much interest; as early as 1314 Seneca was imitated by Albertino Mussato, who wrote a tragedy on Ezzelino, an Italian tyrant. (For further comments on the influence of Seneca, see °Senecan tragedy, and consult John W. Cunliffe, *Early English Classical Tragedies*.) In addition to reviving or reshaping comedy and tragedy, the Renaissance rediscovery of the past caused Italian Renaissance scholars to invent °opera (an effort to reproduce Greek tragedy, which was known to have used music) and the °pastoral. Shakespeare, through the mouth of Polonius, in *Hamlet* II.ii, satirized the enthusiastic creation of genres: "The best actors in the world, either for tragedy, comedy, history, pastoral, pastoral-comical, historical-pastoral, tragical-historical, tragical-comical-historical-pastoral; scene individable, or poem unlimited. Seneca cannot be too heavy, nor Plautus too light." Finally, it must be mentioned that whereas the Middle Ages customarily staged its plays on the ground or on wagons or on temporary platforms, in streets or halls, the Renaissance built permanent theaters. Consult °Elizabethan playhouse.

repartee. See °comedy.

repertory, repertoire. The body of dramatic works that a °company is trained to do, and (usually) does in turn or often. A **repertory company** is one that performs a number of plays in daily, weekly, or at least monthly succession, rather than a single play for months on end.

repraesentatio. See °medieval drama.

representational staging. See °dramatic illusion.

resolution. See °plot.

Restoration playhouse. The Restoration (1660) of King Charles II to the throne of England reopened the theaters. Basically, the Restoration playhouse was a small roofed building with a stage that protruded about one half its depth through the °proscenium arch. Doors in front of the sides of the arch gave access to this half-oval (the °apron) in front of the arch, and doubtless much of the action took place on it. In short, the stage was halfway between the °Elizabethan platform stage and the proscenium stage that had established itself in Europe. The scenery consisted of painted flats (see °scenery) that slid in grooves, and borders (*i.e.*, horizontal bands of cloth across the top of the stage, decorated with tree-branches or clouds for exterior scenes and with some sort of suggestion of a ceiling for interior scenes). The curtain was drawn at the start of the play, scenery was changed in view of the audience, and the curtain was closed at the conclusion. The most elegant members of the audience sat in °boxes (see °theater) extending around three sides of the auditorium; commoner people sat on benches in the °pit, in front of the stage; the commonest sat in °galleries that ran over the boxes. Servants filled the highest gallery. The taste that dominated the stage was that of the courtiers in the boxes. See °heroic drama and (under °comedy) °Restoration comedy. Consult Allardyce Nicoll, *A History of English Drama 1660-1900*, I.

revenge play. See °Senecan tragedy.

reversal. See °plot, °tragedy.

revival. A production of a work long undone.

revue. A loose collection of musical numbers, °skits, comic bits, etc., sometimes united by a central theme or by the star performer. Unlike °vaudeville, which consists of separate performers, a revue employs a company, and a member may appear in several or all of the numbers. During the ten or twelve years after World War I, revues in America were usually coarse and brassy, reflecting the period of bootlegging and prosperity. Shortly before the Depression, however, these revues seem to have lost favor, and shortly after the Depression their place on °Broadway was largely taken by °musical comedies.

rising action. See °plot.

ritual. A ceremonial act, an observance or customary procedure, especially by worshipers. Primitive people perform ritual dances to induce rain, to drive out sickness, etc. Rituals, that is, often attempt to order seemingly chaotic experiences. We have rituals at most critical moments — birth, commencement, marriage, death — marking the importance of these moments and sometimes (as in some prayers for the dead) to induce a desired effect. Much literature seems to have originated in ritual — Greek °tragedy, for example. The precise ritual behind it is uncertain, but it is almost surely descended from some ritual imitating growth and death, or mutability. A common theory holds that it imitates the decline of a vegetation god from spring to winter; the potent tragic hero moves

249

from power to weakness, allegedly a remote descendant of rituals imitating the Year-Spirit who annually died. A ritual inducing the rebirth of the Year-Spirit (spring comes again) is often said to be behind the ancient comic pattern, which moves from threats to joyous feasts and marriages (*i.e.*, to fertility). Consult Jane E. Harrison, *Ancient Art and Ritual*; Herbert Weisinger, *Tragedy and the Paradox of the Fortunate Fall*; Francis Fergusson, *The Idea of a Theater*.

Roman drama. See °Roman theater, °comedy, °*fabula*, °Senecan tragedy.

Roman theater. A permanent theater was not built at Rome until the first century B.C. The plays of Plautus (254?-184 B.C.) and Terence (190?-159? B.C.) were performed on temporary stages erected in the Circus Maximus and the Forum during holidays. In the permanent Roman theater, the enormous audience (40,000 or more) sat in a semicircle around a level space that was a vestige of what had been called the "orchestra" ("dancing place") of the Greek theater. Behind this vestige was the stage, running through what would have been the diameter of the circle. The long, slightly elevated stage was backed by a façade (painted to resemble two or three houses) with several doors through which actors made some of their exits and entrances, the others being made at the ends of the stage. Behind the façade was the dressing-room. The Roman theater, unlike the °Greek and Hellenistic theaters, was a self-enclosed structure, built on level ground, not against a hillside. Consult Margarete Bieber, *The History of the Greek and Roman Theater*. See °costume, °curtain, °*fabula*, °Senecan tragedy.

role. See °part.

romanticism. See °neoclassicism.

rules. See °neoclassicism, °Three Unities (under °unity).

run. (1) The period during which a °company performs a dramatic entertainment. The long run, of months and even of years, is a relatively new phenomenon. Greek plays, written for a particular festival, normally had a run of one day, though after the great age (the fifth century B.C.), older plays occasionally were revived. Roman plays, too, seem usually to have been given only once. A new Elizabethan play seems to have been given about once a week for a dozen or so performances, and then occasionally revived if there was a demand. In the °Restoration a play might run only one day; if the author was lucky, his play ran three days and he collected the net profit from the third day. A few plays ran as many as a dozen nights, but John Gay's *The Beggar's Opera* (1728), which ran for thirty-two consecutive performances, had no precedent in Western theatrical history. (2) As a verb, to run (or to run through) a °scene or °act is to rehearse it without interruption from the °director.

sacra rappresentazione. See °medieval drama.

satire. A work ridiculing aspects of human behavior and seeking to arouse in the audience contempt for its object. Satirists almost always justify their attacks by claiming that satire is therapeutic, and because they assume that there are fixed norms to which men should adhere, they tend to be °neoclassical rather than romantic. Shaw says, in the preface to his *Complete Plays*, "If I make you laugh at yourself, remember that my business as a classic writer of comedies is to 'chasten morals with ridicule'; and if I sometimes make you feel like a fool, remember that I have by the same action cured your folly." Satire, however, is sometimes distinguished from °comedy on the grounds that satire aims to correct by ridiculing, while comedy aims simply to evoke amusement. Among notable satires (in addition to those discussed under °burlesque) are Aristophanes' *The Clouds* (423 B.C.), *The Frogs* (405 B.C.) — in fact, all of Aristophanes; Gay's *The Beggar's Opera* (1728); Brecht's *The Three-Penny Opera* (1928); Kaufman, Ryskind, and Gershwin's *Of Thee I Sing* (1931) — though Kaufman himself has defined satire as "that which closes on Saturday night." See °burlesque, °comedy. Consult Dane F. Smith, *Plays about the Theatre in England from "The Rehearsal" in 1671 to the Licensing Act in 1737;* Northrop Frye, *Anatomy of Criticism.*

satyr-play. A piece in which there is a chorus of lewd satyrs (creatures half-man, the other half either horse or goat). The Greek tragic playwright of the fifth century B.C. presented three °tragedies and a satyr-play for the dramatic festival. Apparently the satyr-play often °burlesqued a hero, showing him in a ludicrous situation. Only one complete satyr-play (Euripides' *The Cyclops*) is extant; it travesties the legend of Odysseus' encounter with Polyphemus. Consult Philip W. Harsh, *A Handbook of Classical Drama.*

scenario. A detailed outline of a dramatic entertainment. See °*commedia dell' arte.*

scene. See °act.

scenery. The carpentry and painted cloths (and projected images) used on a stage. Scenery may be used to conceal parts of the stage, to decorate, to imitate or suggest locales, to establish time or to evoke mood. For comments on early scenery, see °Greek theater, °medieval drama, and °Elizabethan playhouse. The Elizabethan public theater did not use much scenery. In *Twelfth Night,* when Viola asks "What country, friends, is this?" she is told "This is Illyria, lady," and the audience knows all that carpenters and painters can tell them. But even before Shakespeare's birth, Renaissance Italians had placed buildings, probably of lath and cloth, at the right and left of the stage. Behind the buildings, which were three-dimensional and were embellished with moldings, projected flat pieces cut and painted to look like other buildings at a distance, and behind these flat pieces were yet other flats, still smaller. By means of such a **perspective set,** the spectator seemed to be looking into a street or a square. A performer might enter a door in either of the houses at the front, but he could not, of course, go toward the rear of the stage lest he suddenly appear gigantic. (On the perspective sets designed by Sebastiano Serlio [1475-1554], consult E. K. Chambers, *The Elizabethan Stage*, III, 10-11, IV, 353-365; Allardyce Nicoll, *The Development of the Theatre*, Ch. 4; George R. Kernodle, *From Art to Theatre*, Ch. 6.

Scenery is sometimes divided into two classes, painted scenery and built scenery. **Painted scenery** is two dimensional; it includes **backdrops** (cloths — usually with a painting — hanging at the rear), **flats** (wooden frames covered with painted cloth), and **borders** (strips of cloth stretched across the top of the °proscenium opening, sometimes called **sky borders, arch borders, tree borders,** etc., depending on their decoration). A flat that projects onto the stage from the °proscenium arch is a **wing.** On the seventeenth- and eighteenth-century English stage, the scenery generally consisted of wings or flats (commonly called **shutters**) that slid in grooves; the scene was changed in view of the audience by drawing the flats offstage into the wings, revealing another set of flats behind them, or by thrusting flats from the wings onto the playing-area. Sometimes, apparently, a °backcloth was rolled up, revealing another behind it. Consult Allardyce Nicoll, *A History of English Drama, 1660-1900*, I. A group of flats, stacked against a stage wall or in a **scene dock** (storage room for scenery) is a **pack;** if the pack is to be used, it is a **live pack,** but if it has been used and is not needed again in the play, it is a **dead pack.** The second class of scenery, **built scenery,** consists of three-dimensional constructions such as stairways and mountains that an actor can climb. A **ground row** is as much a flat as a built piece; basically it is a flat with an irregular profile and a support at the rear that allows it to stand; it is cut and painted to look like a hedge, a mountain, etc. A **set scene** originally was one prepared in advance and revealed to the audience by withdrawing the scene in front of it, but because a set scene usually employed much built scenery, the term "set scene" has come to be contrasted with **flat scene,** which simply consists of flats that slide on and off the stage. For **box set,** basically a room without a front wall, see °set. A scene requiring a fair amount of built scenery is sometimes fully assembled on a **wagon** (a low platform on wheels or casters) and then rolled on to the stage. (For changes effected by a revolving stage and a wagon stage, see °stage.) Flat scenery is usually disposed of either by being carried off to the wings (here **wings** means not projecting flats but the space they conceal at the sides of the stage) or by being hoisted into the °flies.

Finally, it should be mentioned that **projected scenery** is cast onto the stage by lighting equipment, that in the twentieth century light has in considerable measure replaced painted scenery as an instrument for establishing a mood and for conveying a sense of place, and that scenery (such as the tilted arches, suggestive of instability, that Robert Edmond Jones designed for *Macbeth*) can be highly suggestive and evocative, *i.e.*, °symbolic. See °multiple setting, °scrim, °set, °stage. Consult Harold Burris-Meyer and Edward Cole, *Scenery for the Theatre*; Hubert C. Heffner, *et al.*, *Modern Theatre Practice*, 4th ed.; Arnold S. Gillette, *Stage Scenery: Its Construction and Rigging*; Robert Edmond Jones, *The Dramatic Imagination*; Lee Simonson, *The Stage is Set*; James Laver, *Drama*; *Stage Design Throughout the World since 1935*, ed. René Hainaux; Agne Beijer, *Court Theatres of Drottningholm and Gripsholm*, trans. G. L. Frölich.

scène à faire, or (in William Archer's translation of Francisque Sarcey's term) **obligatory scene.** "An obligatory scene [Archer says] is one which the audience (more or less clearly and consciously) foresees and desires, and the absence of which it may with reason resent." For example, a familiar legend may make a scene obligatory, or a dramatist may cause the audience to expect a certain scene. In *Hamlet* the play-within-the-play (III.ii) has been called such a scene: Hamlet has doubted the ghost, and we must see the ghost's words verified. Consult William Archer, *Play-making*.

scene dock. See °scenery, °theater.

scrim, or **scrim cloth.** A loosely woven gauze-like fabric. A **transparency** is such a cloth with a scene painted on it. The scene is visible when lighted from the front, but it disappears when the °set behind it is lighted.

script. The text of a dramatic work (written, typed, or printed), from which the actors learn their °roles.

sedes. See °medieval drama.

selective realism. See °realism.

Senecan tragedy. Any of the serious plays by the Roman author Seneca (4 B.C.-65 A.D.), or imitations of them. Of the ten extant Roman °tragedies, nine are attributed to Seneca, and these were probably written not for the stage but for private readings. The heroes seem to us to be almost madmen, but perhaps they are to be regarded sympathetically as people overwhelmed by passion. Seneca's influence on the Elizabethan dramatists was considerable; the **revenge play,** with its ghosts and its deranged hero who seeks vengeance, doubtless would have been different had Seneca not existed. Among the signs of Seneca's influence are: ghosts, revenge, deeds of horror (*e.g.*, children stewed and served to their parents), occasional stoical speeches but a predominance of passionate speeches, use of stichomythia (see °dialogue), a *nuntius* (messenger) who recites in a heightened style an off-stage happening (*e.g.*, the wounded soldier in *Macbeth*, I.i.). But, of course, not every use of any of these characteristics is necessarily attributable to Seneca's influence. And there are differences: *e.g.*, the horrors in Seneca are narrated, but in *King Lear* Gloucester is blinded on the stage. Consult F. L. Lucas, *Seneca and Elizabethan Tragedy*; Madeleine Doran, *Endeavors of Art*; Willard Farnham, *The Medieval Heritage of Elizabethan Tragedy*; Fredson Bowers, *Elizabethan Revenge Tragedy 1587-1642*. Howard Baker, *Induction to Tragedy*, minimizes Seneca's influence.

sensibility. See °sentimental.

sentimental. Generally a pejorative word in literary criticism, indicating a superabundance of tender emotion, a disproportionate amount of sentiment (feeling). It is sentimental to be intensely distressed because one has stepped on a flower. A character, say Hamlet, may display deep emotions, but they are sentimental only if they are in excess of what the situation warrants. More specifically, "sentimental" writing refers to writing wherein evil is facilely conquered, denied, overlooked, or bathed in a glow of forgiving tenderness. In the eighteenth century the ability to respond emotionally (usually tearfully) to acts of benevolence or malevolence was called **sensibility.** In its **sentimental drama** there is at the expense of reason an emphasis on tearful situations; man's benevolent emotions are overestimated, for he is assumed to be innately good, and villains reform, usually in bursts of repenting tears. There is little °wit (see °comedy), the characters are usually of the middle class, and they demonstrate their virtue by weeping at the sight of distress. In his "Comparison between Sentimental and Laughing Comedy" (1772), Oliver Goldsmith attacked sentimental comedy, saying that in it:

> "the virtues of private life are exhibited, rather than the vices exposed; and the distresses rather than the faults of mankind make our interest in the piece. . . . Almost all the characters are good, . . . and though they want humor, have abundance of sentiment and feeling. If they happen to have faults or foibles, the spectator is taught, not only to pardon, but to applaud them, in consideration of the goodness of their hearts; so that folly, instead of being ridiculed, is commended, and the comedy aims at touching our passions, without the power of being truly pathetic."

See °bourgeois drama. Consult Ernest Bernbaum, *The Drama of Sensibility*; Arthur Sherbo, *English Sentimental Drama*.

set, setting, décor. The stage, with °scenery and °properties (and, in some usage, °lights), prepared to receive the actors. A **curtain set** contains draperies, usually at the rear and sides. A **formal setting** is °stylized and usually simple. The décor is commonly semi-permanent; platforms and stairs may be added occasionally, but on the whole the actors move in the same architectural surrounding that in the previous production their predecessors moved in. Jacques Copeau's Théâtre du Vieux Colombier was of this sort, and so are most outdoor shells. A **wing and backcloth set** has a painted cloth at the rear, °wings (flats: wooden frames covered with painted cloth) at the sides, and a °border (strips of curtain at the top). A **box set** represents an interior; it is made of flats that form the rear, sides, and ceiling. In short, it is a room with the front wall missing, containing real furniture, and, usually, doors and windows that open and shut. It was introduced early in the nineteenth century, and by the end of the century the desire for realism was so strong that the box set dominated the stage. Consult John H. McDowell, "Historical Development of the Box Set," *The Theatre Annual, 1945*, pp. 65-83; and the references given under °scenery. See also °act, and p. 89.

       set scene. See °scenery.

       shadow. See °Elizabethan playhouse.

       shadow play. See °puppet.

       she-tragedy. A play in which the protagonist is a female whose lot is unhappy. The plays of Nicholas Rowe (1674-1718) are especially associated with the term. Consult Allardyce Nicoll, *A History of English Drama 1660-1900*, II, 99-102; T. R. Henn, *The Harvest of Tragedy*, Ch. 10.

       show. A theatrical entertainment.

       shutter. See °scenery.

       side. A sheet (usually 8 x 5½ inches) containing an actor's lines, °cues, °stage directions, etc. An actor usually has a packet of sides.

       sight line. The line of vision from any seat to the stage. In sixteenth-century Italian theaters, which employed scenery giving the illusion of a perspective view on the stage, the duke or prince who sat in the center enjoyed the illusion; the rest of the audience had poorer sight lines.

       simultaneous setting. See °multiple setting.

       skene. See °Greek theater.

       sketch, skit. A short comic dramatic entertainment, usually of one scene, especially in a °revue.

       sky-dome. See °cyclorama.

       slice of life. See °naturalism.

       sock and **buskin.** Performers of Latin comedy wore a

light slipper or sandal called the *soccus*. The sock is either this piece of footwear or comedy itself. In "L'Allegro" Milton says:

> Then to the well-trod stage anon,
> If Jonson's learned sock be on.

The high boot worn by Greek tragic actors was the **cothurnus** or ***kothurnus***. In Hellenistic times it acquired a very thick sole, giving the performer the height appropriate to a great man. In English this footgear (or tragic drama in general) is called the **buskin**, apparently from Old French *broissequin*, from Middle Dutch *brosekin*, a small leather boot. Consult Margarete Bieber, *The History of the Greek and Roman Theater*.

soliloquy. A speech wherein a character utters his thoughts aloud while alone. An **aside** is a speech wherein a character expresses his thoughts in words audible to the spectators but supposedly unheard by the other stage characters present. Both were important °conventions in Elizabethan drama and, later, in °melodrama, but the late nineteenth century sought so vigorously to present on the stage the illusion of real life that both techniques were banished. They have, however, been revived in the twentieth century, *e.g.*, in Eugene O'Neill's *Strange Interlude*, where the asides represent the characters' thoughts and unspoken desires. In **direct address,** a character turns from the world on the stage and speaks directly to the audience, telling it, for instance, to watch closely. Because the character thus seems to leave the play, direct address is sometimes (unfortunately) called **extra-dramatic speech.** Consult Una Ellis-Fermor, *The Frontiers of Drama*, Ch. 6; George E. Duckworth, *The Nature of Roman Comedy*; Max Beerbohm, "Soliloquies in Drama," *Around Theatres*. The soliloquy, the aside, and direct address are all monologues, but more often a **monologue** is either a long speech delivered by one character, which may be heard but not interrupted by others in his presence, or a performance by a single actor.

sottie. A short satiric piece popular in France during the Middle Ages. It seems to have been acted not only by amateurs but also by semi-professionals who wore the traditional fool's costume: dunce's cap, tights, and bells. Consult Grace Frank, *The Medieval French Drama*.

soubrette. (1) The minor °role of a young woman, especially of a flirtatious maid-servant involved in intrigues. (2) The actress who plays such a role.

sound effect. An imitative noise, usually produced by simple °machinery. Though a sound effect may be a mere imitation of nature, it may also be a richly symbolic suggestion. Chekhov's *The Cherry Orchard* (1904) concludes: "A sound is heard that seems to come from the sky, like a breaking harp-string, dying away mournfully. All is still again, and there is heard nothing but the strokes of the axe far away in the orchard." Consult Frank Napier, *Noises Off*.

spectacle. The last of Aristotle's six elements of drama (see p. 21), spectacle denotes what appeals to the eye, *e.g.*, °costume and °scenery. Greek drama was splendidly costumed and made some use of scenery. Aeschylus especially seems to have contrived moments that caught the eye, such as Agamemnon's entrance in a chariot. The °Elizabethan stage, though sparse in scenery, apparently was architecturally impressive, and doubtless military scenes were embellished with waving banners. In the °Restoration, spectacle sometimes got the upper hand. Alexander Pope complained:

> The play stands still; damn action and discourse,
> Back fly the scenes, and enter foot and horse;
> Pageants on pageants, in long order drawn,
> Peers, heralds, bishops, ermine, gold, and lawn.

In the nineteenth century the development of gas light and then electric light (see °lighting) made possible elaborate sunrises and twilights, and at the end of the century (especially in Russia) there was an emphasis on °ensemble acting which gave a °tableau-effect. Pictorial effects in late-nineteenth-century productions of Shakespeare were often achieved at the cost of Shakespeare's lines. At the very end of the century William Poel rejected spectacle and helped establish a trend to stage Shakespeare in what was thought to be an Elizabethan manner: an uncluttered stage, allowing the action to proceed rapidly. Consult James Laver, *Drama*; A. Nicholas Vardac, *Stage to Screen*, Chs. 3-4.

spotlight. See °lighting.

stage. A playing space, commonly elevated. The acting area or playing area is the part on which the actors act; it is customarily imagined as having six parts: **down left, down center, down right** (and, behind these) **up left, up center, up right.** Left and right are from the actor's view, *i.e.*, the reverse of the spectator's. **Upstage** is toward the rear, **downstage** toward the front, perhaps because in the Renaissance a stage sometimes had a °rake, that is, was pitched upward toward the rear in order to complement the perspective °scenery. ("Upstage" can also denote the area between the back of the set and the stage wall, sometimes called °backstage.) To upstage an actor is to go upstage of him, forcing him to face toward the rear; by extension, it is to treat him as an inferior. The spaces at the sides of the playing area of a °proscenium stage, invisible to the audience, are the **wings** (though the wings are also the °flats that project onto the stage). The stage may be equipped with various **traps,** doors through which it may be entered from the **cellar.** A **revolving stage** is a playing area that can rotate on an axis. In 1608 Ben Jonson's °*Masque of Beauty* used such a stage, and in the next century the Japanese °kabuki theater used one. But permanent revolving stages were not found in Western theaters until the late nineteenth century. An elaborate scene that has been set up at the rear of a revolving stage can be quickly brought into view simply by rotating the stage. Sometimes the stage is divided into three segments with sets instead of two. A **wagon stage** is basically a low platform on wheels or casters; it is prepared off-stage and then pushed on. Far above the stage there is commonly a grid or gridiron, to which scenery is flown, *i.e.*, hoisted up (see °flies). See °arena stage, °Elizabethan playhouse, °Greek theater, °open stage, °proscenium stage, °Restoration playhouse. To **stage a play** is to put it on a stage. Consult Harold Burris-Meyer and Edward C. Cole, *Theatres & Auditoriums*, Chs. 7-11.

stage business. Minor physical action — including posture and facial expression — by a performer. Business ranges from head-scratching to an addition Henry Irving made to *The Merchant of Venice*, II.vi: in Shakespeare's scene, Jessica and Lorenzo elope and the scene ends quietly; Irving added business in which Shylock entered, and knocked on the door of his empty house while the curtain fell. His successors amplified this business; Shylock entered the house, cried out, and reappeared, etc. Consult Arthur C. Sprague, *Shakespeare and the Actors*.

stagecraft. The ability to manufacture for the stage. It includes the construction of scenery (getting the scenery off the designer's drawing board) and onto the stage itself, and (somewhat metaphorically) the construction of a play itself. When Ibsen was asked if he were interested in architecture, he replied, "Yes, it is my trade."

stage crew. The carpenters, painters, shifters of °scenery, electricians, etc. A **stagehand** is one who moves scenery or places °properties in position on the stage.

stage direction. An instruction pertaining to actions, positions, lighting, etc. on the stage. Most simply, stage directions include "enter," "exit," etc. More elaborately, such a direction may specify one of the six parts into which the stage is mentally divided, down left, down center, down right, up left, up center, up right, customarily abbreviated DL, DC, etc. (see °stage). **On stage** indicates the acting area, **off stage** any part of the stage out of the acting area and invisible to the audience. Elizabethan stage directions are usually thin, and probably some of the most interesting ones (*e.g.*, "Enter Juliet somewhat fast, and embraceth Romeo") are interpolations. Consult W. W. Greg, *The Shakespeare First Folio*. Since Ibsen, there has been a tendency for playwrights to give elaborate stage directions. In O'Neill's *Desire Under the Elms,* for example, about four hundred words (describing the set and the gestures of some of the characters) precede the first speech, which consists of two words, "God! Purty!" Bernard Shaw outdid O'Neill in writing for the reader: many of his plays have enormous prefaces, and some (like *Candida*) have unactable stage directions: "They embrace. But they do not know the secret in the poet's heart."

stage door. See °theater.

stagehand. See °stage crew.

stage house. See °theater.

stage manager. Chiefly the co-ordinator between °producer, °director, °playwright, °actors, °stage technicians, etc. For example, he arranges for auditions, and when the director has chosen his actors, it is usually the stage manager who gets the chosen ones into the business manager's office to talk money. At rehearsals he (or the assistant stage manager) holds the °script and incorporates the director's suggestions. During performances, the stage manager is in charge °backstage; the assistant stage manager may be the °prompter. Consult Bert Gruver, *The Stage Manager's Handbook.*

stage picture. The playing-area as the audience views it, including the lighting and the actors.

stage technician. One engaged in any of the arts or crafts (other than acting) of °production, *e.g.*, a designer of scenery, an electrician, a carpenter.

stagy. See °dramatic illusion.

stall. See °theater.

Stanislavsky System. Because Konstantin Stanislavsky (1865-1938) modified and enlarged his theory of acting over a long lifetime in the theater, it cannot easily be summarized. Early he stressed historical accuracy in °costumes and °properties not as an end in itself but to help the actor experience the emotion of the character whom he impersonates. Later he moved away from this reliance on external truth but continued to adhere to truth of internal life, *i.e.*, of feelings and ideas. Rejecting the clichés of acting, he insisted that an actor doesn't pose or perform but gives himself up to feeling, absorbed not with the effect he is making on an audience but with the character's thoughts and experiences. By the recollection of some details and situations that have deeply moved him (**affective memory**) an actor achieves an **inner justification** that lets him enter into the character's experiences. Stanislavsky required his actors to create the past and future of their roles; in *Stanislavski Produces Othello* we get a hypothetical ancestry for Roderigo and we learn that perhaps he first saw Desdemona stepping into a gondola. His actors were required to practice by performing an **improvisation,** in which they invented lines and °stage business for a scene not in the script, *e.g.*, Hamlet's reaction on first hearing of his father's death. An actor must grasp the "through-action" or "trunkline of action" of a play (*e.g.*, in *Hamlet*, the revelation and punishment of the murderer of Hamlet's father), then get to learn the feelings or experience of his role. Though Stanislavsky's critics often charged that he ignored the distinction between art and life, and claimed that he required his actors to believe they were their roles, he protested that he required his actor to say not "I am Hamlet," but "*if* I were Hamlet how would I react?" In America, the Group Theater made much use of the system; the Group Theater version is commonly called **the Method.** Harold Clurman, in *The Fervent Years,* says the Group Theater especially used not only improvisations but also exercises of inner justification, in which "the actor was asked to recall the details of an event from his own past. . . . These 'exercises' were used to set the mechanism of the actor's emotions rolling, so to speak. When the actor was in the grip of this mood, . . . the actor was better prepared to do the scene calling for the particular mood that the exercise had evoked." In addition to the primary works — Stanislavsky's *My Life in Art* (mostly on the actor's state of mind), his *Building a Character* (mostly on the actor's craft), and *Stanislavsky on the Art of the Stage* (trans. David Magarshack) — consult Nikolai M. Gorchakov, *Stanislavsky Directs* and David Magarshack, *Stanislavsky*. See p. 110.

star. A leading performer, whose appeal is so great that he is given **star billing,** *i.e.*, his name precedes the title of the play in advertising. A player whose name (preceded by "with") immediately follows the title has **feature billing.** The remaining players are the **supporting cast.** On film stars, consult Edgar Morin, *The Stars*, trans. Richard Howard.

stasimon. See °tragedy.

static play. A drama, especially one such as Maeterlinck's *The Blind* (1890), with little or no development of °character, or with very little physical action.

stock company. A °repertory group of players attached to a theater. (In the summer such a company commonly changes its play weekly, performing with a visiting °star who the next week goes elsewhere with the same play. Such fare is **summer stock;** the theaters that offer it form the **straw-hat circuit.**) Because certain characters seem to recur from play to play, stock companies often consist of actors accustomed to playing a certain kind of character. Thus, there is the Tragedian (he plays Hamlet), the Old Man (Polonius), the Old Woman, the Heavy Father or Heavy Lead (Claudius), the Juvenile Lead (Laertes), the Juvenile Tragedian (Horatio), the °Ingenue (Ophelia), the Low Comedian (Grave-digger), the Walking Lady, Gentlemen, and Utility (various minor roles). For Shaw on stock companies, see p. 106. For °stock character, see character.

straw-hat circuit. See °stock company.

strophe. See °tragedy.

structure. See °pyramidal structure (under °plot).

Sturm und Drang. See °neoclassicism.

style. The mode of expression. Newman, talking of the writer's style, called it "a thinking out into language." This idea of "a thinking out" (but not into language) is applicable also to the style of the scene designer, the costume designer, etc. Kenneth Tynan in *Curtains* defines good style as "a happy consonance of manner with matter, of means with end, of tools with job." To **stylize** a play commonly means to present it with a noticeable artful manner rather than to present it realistically, though in fact °realism itself is a style. A **stylized production** usually is presentational or anti-illusionistic rather than representational (see °dramatic illusion). Consult George R. Kernodle, "Style, Stylization, and Styles of Acting," *Educational Theatre Journal,* XII (1960), 251-261. See °actor.

supernumerary, super. See °actor.

supporting cast. See °star.

surprise. See °suspense.

surrealism. A literary movement, especially vigorous in France in the 1920's and 1930's, that insisted that reality is grasped by the unconscious, the irrational, rather than by the conscious. The best art, it is held, is the dream. Among the forerunners were Alfred Jarry, whose *Ubu Roi* (1896) combined grotesque farce with anti-bourgeois satire, August Strindberg, whose *To Damascus* (three parts, 1898-1904) and *The Dream Play* (1902) had presented dream-like worlds, and Guillaume Apollinaire, whose *Breasts of Ti-resias* (1917) was called a *"drame surréaliste"* (the first use of the word) by the author. Perhaps the chief surrealist dramatist is Jean Cocteau, notably in his *Orpheus* (1926), in which a glazier is an angel and a horse dictates prophetic words. Consult Georges E. Lemaître, *From Cubism to Surrealism in French Literature.*

suspense. Uncertainty, often characterized by anxiety. Suspense is usually a curious mixture of pain and pleasure, as Gwendolen, in Oscar Wilde's *The Importance of Being Earnest,* implies: "This suspense is terrible. I hope it will last." Most great art relies more heavily on suspense than on **surprise** (the unexpected). One can rarely sit twice through a play depending on surprise; the surprise gone, the interest is gone. Suspense is usually achieved in part by **foreshadowing** — hints of what is to come. Dumas *fils* put it this way: "The art of the theater is the art of preparations." Coleridge, who held that Shakespeare gives us not surprise but expectation and then the satisfaction of perfect knowledge, once wrote: "As the feeling with which we startle at a shooting star, compared with that of watching the sunrise at the pre-established moment, such and so low is surprise compared with expectation." Thus, in *Hamlet*, the ghost does not pop up surprisingly, but satisfies the eager expectations that have been aroused by references to "this thing," "this dreaded sight," and "this apparition." Often, in fact, Shakespeare — like the Greek dramatists — used traditional stories; the audience presumably was not surprised by the deaths of Caesar and Brutus, and it enjoyed the suspense of anticipating them. Suspense is thus related to tragic °irony. The tragic character moves closer and closer to his doom, and though he may be surprised by it, we are not; we are held by suspense. If, in fact, he is suddenly and unexpectedly saved (as is a hero of a °melodrama), we may feel cheated. On surprise, consult David L. Grossvogel, *The Self-Conscious Stage in Modern French Drama* (reprinted in paperback as *Twentieth-Century French Drama*).

symbolism. Derived from Greek *symballein,* "to throw together," which thus suggests the essential quality of symbolism, the drawing together of two worlds; it presents the concrete material world of roses, toads, caves, stars, etc., and through them reveals an otherwise invisible world. As a noun, the original Greek word denoted half of something broken in two, and thus the word suggests not something that stands for something else, but something that is part of a larger unit.

Symbolism is often distinguished from °allegory. Where the allegorist commonly invents a world (the author of *Everyman* [c. 1500] invents a figure called Everyman, who seeks aid from figures called Goods, Kindred, etc.) in order to talk about the real world, the symbolist commonly presents the phenomena of what we usually call the real world in order to reveal a "higher," eternal world of which the symbol is a part. The allegorist is free to invent any number of imaginary worlds to talk about the real world, but the symbolist feels that there is only one way by which he can present the "higher" real world he envisions. The everyday world is often considered by symbolists as a concrete but transient version of a more important realm, and the symbolist who presents, say, a rose, is (he might hold) speaking about a rose and also about the eternal beauty of womanhood in the only possible way. The allegorist, who can invent half a dozen ways of embodying his idea, does not insist on the reality of his invented world. An allegory can with relative ease be paraphrased, but a symbol, because it not only stands for something else which cannot otherwise be expressed, but also is *part of something else and is itself too,* cannot be clearly explained. As Carlyle says in

Sartor Resartus, in a symbol "the Infinite is made to blend itself with the Finite, to stand visible, and as it were, attainable there." The symbol (which may be a situation, character, setting — *e.g.*, birth, an infant, a manger) is given unusual stress, perhaps by repetition within the play, or from one of the author's plays to another, and so it is highly potent, richly suggestive.

In the second half of the nineteenth century there arose in France the so-called **Symbolist Movement,** but it must be emphasized that symbolism of a sort is probably as old as literature. An author's insistence on some object may cause us to regard it as more than its apparent nature. For example, the storm in *King Lear* (c. 1606) suggests both the disorder in the kingdom and the disorder in Lear's mind. The flutes made by Willy Loman's father in Miller's *Death of a Salesman* (1949), are not just flutes but tokens of another way of life; in contrast to the unspecified product Willy sells, the flutes were made by the seller himself, and they produce beauty. Equally symbolic in the play is Willy's belated assertion that he must plant his seeds; the seeds, literally granules in an envelope, suggest a new life. But on the whole Shakespeare's plays, and Miller's *Death of a Salesman* (except in the scenes with Ben), do not leave the world of sensible reality. The plays of the Symbolists do. The Symbolic writer presents a world that seems to be a dream world, a world that is not the usual world enriched, but a new world. In his preface to *The Dream Play* (1902), Strindberg says he "has tried to imitate the disconnected but seemingly logical form of the dream. Anything may happen. . . . The characters split, double, multiply, vanish, solidify, blur, clarify." See °surrealism.

The best naturalists (Ibsen, Chekhov, Strindberg, and Hauptmann) at times wrote symbolic works, but the chief Symbolic dramatists are the French (if we include the Belgian Maurice Maeterlinck) and William Butler Yeats. In Maeterlinck's *The Intruder* (1890) a blind old man sees with his soul the approach of Death. In *The Blind* (1890) a group of blind men are lost in a forest; their leader was a priest, but he has died. Maeterlinck occasionally said some of his plays were for marionettes, and though his statement is sometimes held to be a mildly self-deprecating joke, in fact there is much in the plays that belongs to the realm of impassive, otherworldly dolls, not surprising in the work of a writer who said he wished to study "man . . . in the presence of eternity and mystery." Paul Claudel's *Tidings Brought to Mary* (written in 1892, revised in 1899 and 1912) was acted in 1912. Claudel, who said he had gained from Arthur Rimbaud (one of the leading Symbolists) "an almost physical impression of the supernatural," in this play envelops his medieval characters in a divine world, and dramatizes salvation. In Ireland, Yeats, who compared an artistic work to a magic talisman ("it entangles . . . a part of the Divine essence") wrote verse plays of Irish supernatural creatures and heroes. In *On Baile's Strand* (1903), for instance, Cuchulain, the protagonist, is said to have been sired by a hawk. The bird imagery is insisted on; Cuchulain's associates are chicks and nestlings, and the Fool (who represents Cuchulain on another level) is delighted with feathers. Near the conclusion of the play, Cuchulain rushes out to fight the waves, literally doing what Hamlet spoke metaphorically of doing.

In Russia, Meyerhold in 1906 staged Ibsen's *Hedda Gabler* (1890) as symbolically as possible, turning what had been a naturalistic play into a vision suggestive of another world, something (in the words of a hostile critic) "halfway between metaphysics and ballet." (Consult Nikolai Gorchakov, *The Theater in Soviet Russia*.) For symbolism in the sense of richly suggestive images, consult Alan S. Downer, "The Life of Our Design: the Function of Imagery in the Poetic Drama," *The Hudson Review*, II (Summer 1949), 242-260. On the Symbolist Movement, consult William Butler Yeats, *Essays and Introductions*; Arthur Symons, *The Symbolist Movement in Literature*; *Yale French Studies*, No. 9; Eric Bentley, *The Playwright as Thinker*; John Gassner, *Form and Idea in the Modern Theatre*.

sympathy. See °empathy.

tableau, *tableau vivant.* A tableau is the picture presented by motionless actors, especially at the end of an act. A *tableau vivant*, or "living picture," is a striking arrangement of costumed impersonators, especially popular as a Renaissance entertainment. Consult George R. Kernodle, *From Art to Theatre*.

teapot style. See °neoclassicism.

teaser. See °proscenium stage.

technical rehearsal. See °rehearsal.

technician. See °stage technician.

tempo. See °pace.

tennis court theater. Late in the sixteenth century some roofed tennis courts in France were converted into theaters by erecting a stage at one end. Spectators stood in front of the stage, or sat on benches at the end opposite the stage, or sat in the galleries that ran along the sides. Such a theater held about one thousand spectators. Consult W. L. Wiley, *The Early Public Theatre in France*, Ch. 7.

theater. (1) Etymologically a "seeing place," but also a hearing place, *i.e.*, a playhouse. Separate entries describe the °Greek and Hellenistic theaters, the °Roman theater, the °Elizabethan playhouse, the °Restoration theater, and the °tennis court theater. See also entries for °apron stage, °arena stage, °open stage, °platform stage, and °proscenium stage. What follows is a brief description of the usual theater standing today but built some decades ago. At the front is the **box office,** where tickets are sold. (Hence a play, author, etc. that attracts customers is "good box office"; one that doesn't is "box office poison.") Behind the box office is the **lobby,** where spectators lounge; then the **auditorium,** where spectators sit to witness the performance. The auditorium commonly has a **pit** (a trench) for the musicians at the front, but most of the auditorium's floor is the **orchestra,** more or less at ground level but sloping upward toward the rear (in the British theater, the orchestra is called **"the pit,"** and its front seats are the **stalls,** so called because they were separated by arms or rails). The rows of the orchestra not under the balcony form the **parquet;** the rear rows form the **parquet circle,** or **orchestra circle,** or **parterre.** At the sides of the theater, above the level of the orchestra, are **boxes,** compartments commonly with four or six movable chairs in them. Above the orchestra, at the rear, are **balconies** (British: **galleries**). The front of the first balcony is the **mezzanine;** the uppermost balcony — or its citizenry — is called **"the gods."** In front of the auditorium is the **stage house,** *i.e.,* the stage and the area above it (the °**flies**) into which scenery is commonly hoisted. Beneath the stage (playing-area) is the **cellar,** and behind the stage (*i.e.,* **backstage**) are dressing rooms and perhaps a **scene dock** (storage room for scenery), and perhaps a **green room** (lounge for actors and their guests). The **stage door** connects the backstage area with the street. There has been a great deal of building since the days when Lope de Vega (1562-1635) said that a theater required "Four trestles, four boards, two actors, and a passion." Consult Allardyce Nicoll, *The Development of the Theatre;* Harold Burris-Meyer and Edward C. Cole, *Theatres & Auditoriums.* (2) "Theater" can also denote a body of plays. "The theater of Racine" is equivalent to "Racine's plays."

theater-in-the-round. See °arena stage.

theater arts. The arts or crafts — such as writing, acting, stage designing, costuming — employed in the drama.

theater party. See °benefit.

theatrical staging, theatricalism. See °dramatic illusion.

theatron. See °Greek theater.

thespian. A journalistic word for actor, from Thespis, a Greek said to have introduced the first actor into Greek choral performances of the sixth century B.C. On Thespis consult Margarete Bieber, *The History of the Greek and Roman Theater.*

Three Unities. See °unity.

thunder-sheet. See °effect machine.

timing. The art of delivering words or performing movements at the effective instant, involving (most noticeably in comedy) phrasing, building, and waiting. Consult J. L. Styan, *The Elements of Drama*, Ch. 5.

tirade. A long declamatory speech, especially one in a French °neoclassical tragedy.

tiring house. See °Elizabethan playhouse.

top. See °Elizabethan playhouse.

tormentor. See °proscenium stage.

tragedy. For Aristotle, tragedy was a dramatic imitation (representation) of an "action of high importance." A Greek tragedy was serious, but it did not necessarily end unhappily. Aeschylus' *Eumenides*, for example, ends on a note of solemn joy. For us a tragedy is generally a play that faces evil, depicts suffering, and ends with death or (especially in the °naturalistic tragedies since the latter part of the nineteenth century) ends with the hero alive but spiritually crushed. Tragedy's essence, Alfred North Whitehead says (*Science and the Modern World*, Ch. 1), resides not in unhappiness but "in the solemnity of the remorseless working of things." H. D. F. Kitto says (*The Greeks*, Ch. 4) that Greek tragedy — and perhaps one might add the great tragedy of other countries — was in part the product of intellectualism and humanism. Intellectualism let the Greeks see that human life must be lived within a great framework of what might be called the will of the gods, or Necessity: "Actions must have their consequences; ill-judged actions must have uncomfortable results." Humanism denied the Greeks an easy view of a heavenly life, and gave them an "almost fierce joy in life, the exultation in human achievement and in human personality." The tragic note, Kitto suggests, is produced by a tension between this unalterable framework and this passionate delight in life.

Aristotle attributes *hamartia* to the tragic hero. This Greek word is variously translated as "tragic flaw" or "error" or "shortcoming" or "weakness," and in many plays it *is* a flaw or even a vice such as *hubris* (also *hybris*) — Greek for overweening pride, arrogance, excessive confidence. But in other plays it is merely a misstep, such as a choice that turns out badly. Indeed, the tragic hero may be undone by his virtue — his courage, for example, when others are not merely prudent but cowardly. It is a serious misconception to insist that a tragic hero necessarily has a moral fault (*e.g.*, to attribute lust or rashness to Romeo and Juliet).

Three other words ought to be mentioned here: Aristotle's *peripeteia* (anglicized to **peripety,** meaning **reversal**), *anagnorisis* (meaning **disclosure, discovery,** or **recognition**), and *katharsis* (**catharsis,** purgation). The reversal occurs when an action produces the opposite of what was intended or expected, and it is therefore a kind of °irony. In *Oedipus the King*, the messenger from Corinth tries to cheer up Oedipus, but the words have the reverse effect, and terrify Oedipus. In *Macbeth*, Macbeth kills Duncan to gain happiness, but his deed brings the reverse, unhappiness. (See, in addition to °irony, °plot.) For Aristotle the "recognition" or "disclosure" seems to be merely a recognition of who is who, by such tokens as birthmarks, clothes, etc. (see p. 30), but the term has been extended to include the tragic hero's recognition of himself and/or the essence of life. Thus Othello, having murdered his faithful wife, learns he was beguiled into thinking her dishonest, and finally recognizes himself as "one not easily jealous, but being wrought/ Perplexed in the extreme"; and he exacts justice from himself by suicide. Aristotle (p. 28), and countless followers, said that tragedy evokes pity and fear, and that it produces in the spectator a catharsis (purgation, or, some scholars hold, purification) of these emotions: it drains or perhaps refines these emotions, and thus tragedy is socially useful. (Aristotle's *Poetics* is the subject of much controversy; one cannot with security assert that Aristotle said anything, without a counter-argument being offered. For various views of catharsis, consult Lucas, cited below, and Gerald F. Else's monumental *Aristotle's Poetics*.)

Little or nothing is known for certain of the origin of Greek tragedy. The most common hypothesis holds that it developed from improvised speeches during the choral dance (the **dithyramb**) honoring Dionysus, a Greek nature god associated with spring, fertility, and wine. Thespis is said to have introduced an actor into these choral performances in the sixth century B.C. Aeschylus (525-456 B.C.), Greece's first great writer of tragedies, added the second actor, and Sophocles (496-406 B.C.) added the third actor and fixed the size of the °chorus at fifteen. For details, see °actor, °chorus, °Dionysus, °Greek theater.

All extant ancient Greek tragedy is of the fifth century B.C. A Greek tragedy commonly begins with a **prologos** (°prologue), during which the °exposition is given; next comes the **parodos,** the chorus' ode of entrance, sung while the chorus marches into the theater by two side entrances, and onto the °orchestra (see °Greek theater). The **epeisodion** (episode) is the ensuing scene; it is followed by a **stasimon** (choral song, ode). Usually there are four or five *epeisodia,* alternating with *stasima.* Each of these choral odes has a **strophe** (lines presumably sung while the chorus dances in one direction) and an **antistrophe** (lines presumably sung while the chorus retraces its steps). Sometimes a third part, an **epode,** concludes an ode. (In addition to odes that are *stasima,* there can be odes within episodes; the fourth episode of *Antigone* contains an ode complete with *epode.*) After the last part of the last ode comes the **exodos,** the °epilogue or final scene. The actors (all male) wore masks, and seem to have chanted much of the play. Perhaps the total result of combining speech with music and dancing was a sort of music-drama roughly akin to °opera with some spoken dialogue, such as Mozart's *The Magic Flute.*

Consult T. R. Henn, *The Harvest of Tragedy*; F. L. Lucas, *Tragedy* (2nd ed.); Herbert J. Muller, *The Spirit of Tragedy*; George Steiner, *The Death of Tragedy*; Richard B. Sewall, *The Vision of Tragedy.* For essays by numerous playwrights and critics consult Barrett H. Clark, *European Theories of the Drama.* See °bourgeois drama, °comic relief, °heroic drama, °irony, °pathos, °plot, °suspense, °tragicomedy, and the essays beginning on p. 15.

tragicomedy. °Renaissance critical theorists, embroidering on Aristotle's *Poetics,* assumed that °tragedies dealt with noble (important) figures and ended with a death; °comedies dealt with trivial (laughable) figures and ended with a celebration. A tragicomedy was some sort of mixture: high characters in a play ending happily, or a mingling of deaths and feasts, or, most often (as in many American films) threats of death which are happily — and unconvincingly — evaded. John Fletcher (1579-1625), who with his collaborator Francis Beaumont, wrote graceful dramas relying heavily on passionate outbursts and surprising turns of °plot, defined a tragicomedy as a play that lacks deaths (and thus is no tragedy) but "brings some near it, which is enough to make it no comedy." One of the speakers in John Dryden's *Essay of Dramatick Poesie* (1668) says: "There is no theater in the world has anything so absurd as the English tragi-comedy; . . . here a course of mirth, there another of sadness and passion, and a third of honor and a duel: thus, in two hours and a half, we run through all the fits of Bedlam." Consult Eugene Waith, *The Pattern of Tragi-Comedy.*

tranche de vie. See °naturalism.

transparency. See °scrim.

trap. See °stage.

trilogy. A unit of three works. Though Greek tragic dramatists submitted three tragedies at a time, the plays are only a trilogy if they have an internal unity. Aeschylus' *Oresteia* (458 B.C.) is the only extant complete Greek trilogy; Sophocles' three plays on the Oedipus legend — *Antigone* (c. 442 B.C.), *Oedipus the King* (c. 425), and *Oedipus at Colonus* (c. 406) are not properly a trilogy because they were written at widely separated times and do not cohere into a consistent, unified whole. A modern trilogy: O'Neill's *Mourning Becomes Electra* (1931).

tritagonist. See °protagonist.

troupe. See °company.

try-out. See °rehearsal.

type-cast. See °cast.

      understudy. One who prepares a °role normally performed by another in order to substitute when necessary. As a verb, to prepare another's role.

      unity. Generally means something like "coherence," "congruence"; in a unified piece the parts work together and jointly contribute to the whole. The subplot of a play may parallel the main °plot, or one character may be a °foil to another. In any case, unity suggests "completeness" or "pattern" resulting from a controlling intelligence. A current metaphor, **organic unity,** likens an artistic creation to an organism (*i.e.*, a living thing) rather than to a mechanism. A watch consists of parts stuck together; its total is the sum of its separable parts, and it can be analyzed by being dissected. A living organism, however, allegedly consists of parts so inseparable that none can without fundamental damage be separated from the others, for, as Henry James says, "in each of the parts there is something of each of the other parts." The whole (some critics say) must be grasped as a totality, rather than as a collection of mechanically joined parts. In the *Poetics*, Aristotle had said that a tragedy should have a unified action (see p. 22), and he had mentioned that most tragedies cover a period of twenty-four hours (see p. 19). Italian critics, making his comments rigid, in the late sixteenth century established the **Three Unities** of Time, Place, and Action: a play (1) must not cover more than twenty-four hours, (2) must be set in one locale only, or, at worst, in various parts of a single city, and (3) must be either entirely tragic or entirely comic, rather than a mixture of (as Sir Philip Sidney said) "hornpipes and funerals." (Consult H. B. Charlton, *Castelvetro's Theory of Poetry*.) Actually, the time covered by Greek tragedies is vague; characters come from distant places in the space of relatively few lines. For example, in *Oedipus the King*, a shepherd, who lives in the "farthest" fields from Corinth, is sent for in line 863 and arrives in line 1108. Nor is unity of place invariable in Greek tragedy; there are violations of it in, for example, Aeschylus' *The Eumenides* and Sophocles' *Ajax*. See °neoclassicism.

      upper stage. See °Elizabethan playhouse.

      upstage. See °stage.

      vaudeville. (1) A stage entertainment of several independent parts, *e.g.*, song, conjuring, acrobatics, °skits, trained poodles, etc. A performer does a "turn," *i.e.*, performs his specialty or act, and is followed by another. A **music hall** is the British term for a vaudeville theater. Vaudeville was popular in the late nineteenth century and the first quarter or so of the twentieth. Speaking broadly, the audience was lower- and middle-class, and the entertainment was unsophisticated and (when not comic) sentimental and patriotic. But vaudeville had great performers, including Will Rogers, Jimmy Durante, and Fred Allen. Marie Lloyd, a renowned English singer in vaudeville, is the subject of a piece by T. S. Eliot in his *Selected Essays*. During World War II many an ancient juggler took his Indian clubs out of the trunk and entertained American troops throughout the world, but today such performers are largely confined to television variety shows. The word "vaudeville" probably comes from Vau (or Val) du Vire, the Valley of the Vire, a place in Normandy noted in the fifteenth century for its singing. See °revue, and consult Abel Green and Joe Laurie, Jr., *Show Biz from Vaude to Video*. (2) A short comic play, a °skit.

vehicle. A play especially suited to exhibit the acting skills of a performer or °company.

Verfremdungseffekt. See °epic drama.

vice. See °medieval drama.

wagon. See °medieval drama, °scenery, °stage.

wardrobe mistress. See °costume.

well-made play. See °*pièce bien faite.*

wing and backcloth set. See °set.

wing(s). See °scenery, °stage.

yard. See °Elizabethan playhouse.

zanni. Comic servant (so-called from the Bergomask pronunciation of *Gianni*, "Johnny") in the °*commedia dell' arte*; sometimes anglicized to **zany,** especially to denote a clown who apes a principal actor.